Run Away

One Woman's Story of Resilience

Run Away

is

dedicated to the

50 million American Women and the

billions of Women around the world

who live with similar hardships.

Run Away

One Woman's Story Of Resilience

Jeanhee Kang

♦

"My thoughts ran rampant. What if I really did run away? What if I went away from Korea forever? No one here would miss me, they would be glad to have one less bad girl to pollute their perfect world. I would leave and go to a place where no one would question my past. What if I went to America? I would find a way to get there, and I would finish high school in English in America. I would put the worlds together like a puzzle to make sentences, and sentences into paragraphs, and paragraphs into a new life."

♦

Dear Joni,

"Dreams Do Come True!"

Jeanhee Kang

Run Away: One Woman's Story of Resilience
Copyright © 2009 Jeanhee Kang

ISBN 978-0-9853269-5-1

Front/Second Cover Graphics/Art Copyright © Thinkstock Imagesages/ Comstock Images/Getty Images"
Front/Second/Rear Cover Design/Formatting by Lasting Impressions e-Book Creations. & Tim Mask

Printed in United States Of America

The Library of Congress
Control # 1-727666621
WGA West Registry for Film Rights # 800882933

This is a work of nonfiction, a true story about Jeanhee Kang, Author.

Please note: *English not being her first language means that in some instances English is broken but kept in place during the editing process to allow readers a greater understanding and feel for a woman that has come so far and made America her home.*

Dedication

Women all over the world, who are facing same hardships
and challenges in life as I have in the past.

And

My three sons

Jason, Ahmad, and in Memory of Josh

Table Of Contents

Chapter One

Run Away Plan

As a five-years-old, I understood what it meant, even at that young age, to get an *education* and live like the dam keeper in the village where I was born. He got to live in a beautiful house, wear clean clothes, and eat steamy white rice every day, a meal none of the villagers could afford. As I stood with at least six blood-sucking leaches attached to my skinny legs in muddy rice paddy, I said, "I want an *education* like the dam keeper has." I was determined to get out of there as soon as I could find a way.

The mountain outcroppings looming beyond the village of Sinheung Dong are shaped like a man's face. I was certain that profile belonged to God. No man had a hand large enough to shape such a tall, unyielding rocky mountain into his likeness.

As a child, catching shrimp in the river beyond the rice paddies, I used to pray, "God, I'm hungry. Bring me something to eat. Just this once, let me catch enough to fill my belly." Sinheung Dong was poor—the kind of poor that causes eyes to sink and bellies to ache. As a child, I often daydreamed of my next meal, a mixture of barley, beans, small clumps of white rice, and watered-down soybean paste soup—on better days. On unlucky days, my siblings and I ate nothing but flour dumplings with kimchi, a fermented vegetable dish. We almost never had meat, and we never had enough food to go around, especially for me, the eldest. My mama always managed to cook exactly enough to barely feed everyone. I see now what a terrible skill that must have been for her to learn.

Only on our birthdays did my siblings and I get to eat a bowl filled with steamy white rice and watered-down meat soup laced with seaweed and chicken. With the exception of my mother, who never told us when she was born, everyone's birthday was celebrated in the same way, and this treat was sometimes the only reason to look forward to being alive for another year. Mama would catch the slowest chicken and wring its neck. Its legs would still thrash, even after she chopped its head off. She'd dunk the kicking bird into boiling water and pull it back out, dunking it once more before plucking the feathers from its pocked skin. Her fingers were so callused the water didn't burn her. With a butcher knife sharpened on a river rock, she'd slice the dead bird wide open, splitting the breast in half and lifting out the gallbladder before it burst. She'd find the liver and kidney, still pumping inside the limp bird, slice them off, rinse off the blood, and dip the organs in rocky sea salt before popping them into my mouth. First the liver and then the kidney as a reward for helping her while my siblings played.

While my mother cooked, my siblings and I rubbed our stomachs and paced, asking when the food would be ready. If she was having a bad day, my mama shooed us outside. On good days, she gave us a pinch of rice to quiet us down. After what felt like days, she would garnish the chicken soup with seaweed and we'd devour it in seconds, the whole time wishing our birthdays came more than once a year. We ate the feet, the gizzard, the intestines, and the fat, and even chewed the bones for their juices, spitting the sharp edges back into the bowl. As the oldest, I ate the quickest and pounced first on the leftover scraps at the bottom of the pan.

When fruits were in season, I was the first out of bed to check to see if any had fallen off the trees. I'd trek to the river to find wild berries, immature peanuts, and raw potatoes. I ate everything and spent many hours doubled over in pain as my stomach cramped. If my mother caught me like this, she'd grind special leaves for me to drink. I tried not to let her see my discomfort. Most of the time the aches were better than the gloppy green goo she made to cure them. If she'd known the cause of my belly aches, she would've yelled at me for not having the patience to wait until the corn or peanuts were mature, but I couldn't bear to tell her about my hunger when she herself ate only after we were fed.

One afternoon, I went fishing for shrimp with my grandmother and offered up my usual prayer, asking God in the mountain for hills of rice, chicken stacked as high as my house, kimchi and seaweed, ripe fruit, and thick meaty soups. The swaying young rice shoots rippled sea green across the horizon, and the seven matchbox houses that made up our village shrank beneath God's stern brow. With the blue sky wide overhead, our tiny village had a quiet beauty, but to me it felt like a prison. As far back as I could remember, I longed to see what lay beyond the mountain that marked our village boundary. I longed to venture into the world beyond God's face.

We hadn't been fishing long when Mama called out, "Jeanhee Ya!" The time of day had come to return home to scrub the floor before sunset. I never minded the other chores—tending the rice paddy, hauling water from my neighbor's well, feeding the pigs, chickens, and my sweet yellow dog—but I hated scrubbing that floor with a deep and consuming passion. Every day my mother called me in with her stern voice to mop the floor of our two room house with filthy, torn-up old rags. Our floor was dirt, and even as a little girl, I knew dirt couldn't be cleaned, no matter how hard I scrubbed. Besides, I wanted to spend this afternoon with my grandmother. Her stories transported me beyond my small horizons and into the adventures of her youth. The hours I spent by her side passed quickly.

I was an obedient child, however, and did what my mother asked, gritting my teeth angrily while fierce tears rolled down my nose, plopping into the swirling mud and those disgusting rags. I scoured around the large cast iron cooking pot and the small black pans that surrounded it, silently cursing my heavily pregnant mother for making me spend my time on such useless tasks. Though I could not see him from inside the small room, I pictured my rock God looking down upon me, taking note of my misery.

While I scrubbed the dirt floor with the torn up dirty rags, my father and cousin went out to the riverbank to chop wood in preparation for the coming cold. We used our mud stove for both heat and cooking, and in the winter, we closed the front of the stove off with rocks to disperse the warmth into the room. Unless we sat close to the floor and covered ourselves with a two-inch thick cotton blanket, the house was bone-numbingly cold. In the spring, summer, and fall, we could hear the rain, wind, and hail. But in winter, the treacherous snow was silent, and my siblings and I often got in trouble for poking our fingers through the rice paper to see if it was indeed drifting down. Without their careful preparation, we surely would've frozen to death during one of those cold winter nights.

Not long after I came home to scrub floor, my father and cousin returned, laden down, not with a bundle of logs, but with my dead grandmother. Her clothes were waterlogged and ripped; her wrinkled face, pruned and gray. They brought her through the sliding rice paper door into the house and laid her out on the floor. She had drowned after I came home to scrub the mud floor for my mama. As I looked at her helpless open mouth, anger surged through me. Had I been with my grandma, I could have saved her. Because of the stupid dirt floor, I'd been robbed of her gap-toothed smile and warm, scarred hands smoothing my tangled hair. My mother and her endless, backbreaking chores had pulled me away.

That was my first brush with death, but not my first contact with the unfairness of the world. I can't remember a time when I thought the world was a kind place. Even then, I didn't expect it to be.

As a young woman, my grandmother had been able to toil in the rice paddies as long and energetically as any man, but now, passed over to join her ancestors, she'd become a shell. As my dead grandmother lay on the floor, and later in her hand-hewn casket, my stomach roiled with regret. Korean funerals are not somber affairs, however, and mixed with my grief was a keen appreciation of life. We sent rice paper invitations with the date and time of the funeral to all my relatives and busied our hands with preparations for the day, thus distracting us from our mourning hearts. We set up tents outside of our house in case of rain. Neighbors brought envelopes of cash to help pay for the funeral, and so our usually empty kitchen was suddenly filled with delicacies I'd never heard of, much less tasted. Mountains of fluffy white rice and pig's-blood-stuffed sausages rose off lacquered plates, along with sculpted rice cakes, rows of colorful popped rice, pears, apples, persimmons, chestnuts, steamed spinach, bean sprouts, salted sesame seed leaves, sting ray salad, various grilled choggi, dried myungtae, ozingyu, chopche, ssangchae, kimchi, kkaktuggi, grilled pork chops, and bulggogi. My dad would move chopsticks from banchan to rice, on to another banchan, then back to rice to enable my dead grandmother to enjoy her last feast before she left us for the spirit world.

Jugs of Makuly, a poor man's wheat wine, filled the prayer table. The head of a pig, slaughtered in my grandmother's honor, looked down upon the feast, its mouth open as if it, too, were about to share some precious remembrance. The food had been prepared soft, without too much salt or spice, as the dead do not like hot pepper. We poured wine into a goblet for my dear grandmother in case she got thirsty, and we burned incense day and night in her honor.

My grandmother's funeral went on for two days and two nights. It was a celebration of the transformation of death, and cries of *Algo* filled the air as neighbors and family members bent over her still, shrunken form. The men gambled, and the women and children ate and gossiped. When the time came to lay my grandmother to rest, my mother washed her with a clean rag and dressed her in pristine white clothes. My father placed pennies in her mouth and upon both eyes to pay for her passage to the afterlife. She was his mother, and I could see from his shaking hands how her death had affected him. That day was the first time I ever saw any emotion in his face other than anger.

Eight pallbearers carried my grandmother in a Korean-style hearse decorated with delicate white paper flowers. They marched her solemnly from the house into the swaying paddies, all the way to the ancestors' mountain, located in another village. My siblings and I followed behind them, singing funeral songs in rhythm with the funeral director's ringing bells, and my mother and three aunts crying, "Napalzza ya! Our mothers are dead and gone! Umunni, Na Do dyutggo ga!"

Their voices wailed, shrill and somber. I never knew people could cry that much. "Nega mujuyjookyuya hanundae! Algo! Na Mottssalyu!"

Even my mother, who had never gotten along with my grandmother, cried all the way to Burial Mountain. Her hair, usually tightly bound, flowed down her shoulders and back as an expression of mourning. After they placed my grandmother in the ground, the men pressed damp earth over her coffin in the shape of a round moon. Then they seeded grass in the loose dirt and left behind burning incense, a sliced fruit, and a cup of white wine to hold my hungry grandma over until our next visit. As we left, our songs drifted up the mountain to the place where the ancestors lived. We prayed they'd love her as we did when she joined them in eternity.

Though I was devastated by my grandmother's passing, her funeral was the first time in as long as I could remember that I had worn fresh, clean clothes. Even if they were *Sangbok,* made for the family of the dead, the thin, off-white poplin fell softly against my arms and belly. Each woman and girl related to my grandmother pinned a tiny white bow to her head, to be worn for a year. The bow told others of our loss and reminded our neighbors to be glad they did not suffer as we did.

From the time of her death, my family prayed to my grandmother at each Thanksgiving and New Year's, setting up an elaborate display of fruits, rice cakes, wine, meat, and fish dishes we could not afford on any other day of the year. After she and my ancestors had their choice of the food, we bowed twice, circled a cup of wine twice over each stick of incense, and prayed for our ancestors to give us peace and prosperity. Then we would eat. I dreamt of those days all year long. The sweet, crisp crunch of fresh fruit and the flavor of warm, sinewy meat filled my dreams long after the delicacies had passed through my stomach.

Though I couldn't wait for each holiday, my mother dreaded them. Since my grandmother's death, my mama had been burdened with deep, inconsolable guilt that stemmed from her animosity toward my grandmother. My grandmother had blamed my mother for not satisfying my father enough to keep him at home with his family and my mother felt the sting of this judgment. My grandmother's sudden death had made it impossible for them to reconcile, and my mother grew increasingly certain that one day my grandmother would come back to haunt her, cursing her with illness, sudden death, a lost limb, or ungrateful children, punishment for taking me away that afternoon instead of letting me stay to catch shrimp.

Three years passed before my mother was able to save enough money to hire a *Mudang for the Goot Ritual*. The *Mudang* and her *assistant, Mudang in training,* came to our home with bamboo sticks, bundles of bamboo branches, two large swords, two sets of extra *ritual customs,* and a large metal *Jing* to drum, which she needed to chant for the dead to come back. The *Mudang* inspected both rooms of our house, asking my mother for my grandmother's clothes and a lock of her hair to more accurately reach her in the spirit world. For two days and two nights, the *Mudang* chanted as she changed into different outfits, drummed the *Jing,* and mumbled nonsense words to the spirit world, petitioning for the passage to open for my dead grandmother to come across. Nobody, including all the neighbors, could sleep with all the drum banging, but no one complained in fear of possible backlash from the spirit world.

My siblings and I were bleary with exhaustion when the witch finally stiffened, threw back her head, and stretched her claw-like fingers towards the ceiling.

"Be ready. She's coming," the *Mudang* warned.

We stepped back, our eyes wide. My brother Junghee, my parents' firstborn son and the carrier of the bloodline, turned pale; he was my grandmother's favorite, too young to fully understand what was happening. He was afraid, and so was I, though I never would've shown it.

"One of you must be the medium for her to speak through," The *Mudang* commanded in a firm, husky voice.

Our neighbor stepped forward and gripped the bamboo.

"Let her spirit enter your body," the witch crowed.

Within a few minutes, my neighbor started to shake. Her eyes rolled back, and her eyelids fluttered as she jerked about, nearly knocking the bowl off my grandmother's altar. Finally, her body calmed, and my grandmother's voice rang through our small house.

"*I am here.*"

My mama looked as if she wanted to run, but she stood her ground and let the *Mudang* speak.

"Your daughter did not mean to let you drown," the witch said in a soothing tone. "She was nine months pregnant and tired. She needed Jeanhee's help. Your daughter has given you two grandsons, and now she has called you back so you can make peace. Let her rest easy in her life here on earth. Let there be peace. Will you please forgive your son's wife?"

As the *Mudang* spoke, the neighbor, filled with my grandmother's spirit, stroked my mama with a sharp blade, running it over her arms and legs and around her stomach and neck. My mama remained stiff, and the knife never once nicked her skin.

"Please," the *Mudang* continued, "honored ancestor, it's

time to make peace. Drop the blade and your bitterness along with it. Give your daughter-in-law peace."

The *Mudang* continued her pleas, her face drawn with the effort. She'd gone two days and nights with no food or rest, and I worried she might faint. After nearly an hour, my grandmother dropped the knife.

"*Let us have peace,*" she agreed as she left the medium's body. Free from my grandmother's spirit, our neighbor crumpled to the floor, drained and confused.

"What happened?" she asked, wiping her brow. She didn't remember a thing.

The Mudang packed her tools and trudged out the door. Inside the house, the air felt fresh and clean. Still, my mother was unhappy. Though she rested easier knowing revenge was not around the corner, her shoulders remained slumped for the rest of her life, the invisible yoke of guilt bowing her head toward the ground.

"I should've hired the witch back when grandmother died," she mumbled often, forever regretful.

*****

I knew from a young age I was born to my mama as an extra laborer. From the time I could toddle along on my own, I walked behind her, planting black beans, soy beans, black-eyed peas, English peas, corn, garlic, sugar cane, sweet potatoes, regular potatoes, lettuce, cabbage, millets, barley, wheat grass, wheat, onions, scallions, green and red peppers, eggplant, cucumber, and Napa cabbage. I placed rice plants in the paddies as leeches sucked thirsty streams from my legs. None of our land was barren, and we cherished each tiny sprout and curling vine as promises of a future in which we'd have more to eat. And yet our family was better off than many of the other families in Sinheung Dong. We used every square inch of farmland to grow anything edible; my mama always reminded us how lucky we were to have land to grow food to eat after the Japanese lost the war to American GIs.

"The only reason the Japanese didn't take our land is that it was too heavy to carry back with them," she would say.

We had more rice paddies and farmland than our neighbors, but that didn't mean we had more to eat. They simply had less than we did.

Our village was an endless paddy of dead dreams, and the only news we received of the outside world came in on the thin dirt road that divided our village in two. Trucks and buses sped by, leaving behind clouds of dust that choked our lungs and blurred the mysterious world beyond our horizons. Like everything else hinting of modern life, the speeding vehicles left us behind. Only once or twice a week did a horse- or cow-drawn wagon roll through town to buy whatever harvest we'd managed to gather, taking our crops to market in the larger city far beyond. No one we knew could afford the bus fee, and so the bus never even stopped in our village. Our only visitors were bicycle vendors, pedaling through town pulling small carts filled with goods, stopping often to ask if anyone had any extra eggs or dogs. When we had eggs, we sold them, saving only one for my father.

Sometimes, when I was feeling brave, I would steal an egg and hide it for days until I got a chance to run away to the next village, where my father's sister lived. In her town was a small candy store where I'd trade my egg for a piece of candy, enjoying the exhilarating rush of sugar. I'd stay with my aunt until my cousin ran me off or my mama showed up, yelling at me all the way home for pulling her away from the farmland.

My workload grew as I got older. As the oldest of five kids, I toiled on the farm and scolded my siblings, including Junghee, the firstborn son who always got away with mischief when he was with my mom. He was more afraid of me than anybody, including my dad. I kept him and the others from drowning in the river, carried water from the neighbor's well to our own water tub, and fed the chickens, pigs, dogs, and rabbits we raised and sold for meat. By the time I was seven, my hands and feet were as calloused and cracked as any grown man's.

I knew early on that I did not want my mama's life of

hunger, patched, ill-fitting clothes, and endless farm work. I didn't want to have a posse of dirty kids tying me down. Afraid I'd wound my mama's already broken spirit, I didn't share these thoughts. Instead, I kept my dreams to myself, fantasizing about a future in which I'd be clad in sheer silk inside a big, beautiful house, with a maid to pick up after me and deliver big bowls of steaming white rice to the table in front of me three times a day. I didn't see why I had to do the same chores day in and day out, only to remain poor forever.

Worse than the pinching hunger, the filthy rags at sundown, and my grandmother's heavy absence was my father. He was rarely with us except during harvest season. The trip from the city was long and troublesome, and we all wished that one day he'd drive down that dirt road and never return. When the rough *thunk* of his bicycle hitting the side of the house echoed through the air, I would draw up against my brothers and sisters and shake. In only seconds, he'd burst into the house, his voice slurred and his face red.

"Get them out," he'd scold my mother, ordering her to drag us into the freezing winter air and line us up in our thin nightclothes and bare feet. Then with a branch stripped smooth from a nearby tree, he'd beat our backs, legs, and bottoms until welts rose on our tender young skin and blood beaded through the bruises. I always positioned my body so my drunken father would aim for the center of my buttocks, rather than my bony joints or hands where no fat cushioned his whip. The pain spread across my body until my mind dulled, and I dreamed only of killing the trees that produced my father's weapons. My little sisters and brother quaked in fear, and I pulled them back in line, holding them up so they wouldn't get a worse beating for stepping out. The easier it was for him to beat us, the more quickly he became tired and passed out. When he finally slumped to the ground, smelling of cheap alcohol and sweat, I pulled my little sisters and brother under my arms and tucked them underneath the blankets in our room.

"Put your hands over your ears," I whispered softly as I pulled the covers over their heads. I didn't want them to hear our mother cry when our father came to and decided to punish her, too.

Her shrill voice would reverberate through the house when she screamed for my father to hit her instead of us.

"I brought them into this miserable life. Hit me!" she'd yell. "Kill me dead. I never asked for this life! I don't want to live anymore!"

Spurred on by his fury, she couldn't stop. She'd rant for hours, unable to understand how she had ended up with such a harsh life.

"I never wanted a woman like you!" my father would retort. "Ugly and useless. Look at you! Why should I come home to dirty kids and a dirty wife? Why should I take care of you?"

"I must've done something terrible in my past life to deserve you, drinking your life away and giving our money to whores," my mother cried. "Algo ya! You can live without me, but not without them. One day you'll come home, and I'll be gone! Then who will raise your children? Your whores?"

Her pleas and accusations echoed across the rice paddies. My brothers and sisters, exhausted from fear, fell asleep easily, but not me. As the oldest child, I felt I had a duty to feel my mamma's pain as my own, and I worried helplessly until my eyes grew dry and heavy, unable to close. As a child, I didn't understand the devil that lived in my father's chest. I thought his anger, directed at my siblings and me, must be our fault. On those nights, when I felt guilty for being alive, the blissful release of sleep eluded me.

At breakfast, my father was sober and quiet. He'd nod without meeting our eyes, his neatly combed black hair bobbing on his head, acknowledging us as his children, not by speaking to us, but by sharing our table. My bruised mother served him our only egg on white rice. The rest of us ate barley, and no one, not even my youngest brother, asked for a bite of his egg. My father scanned the newspaper, written in Chinese characters, and drank hot rice water. When he finished, he puffed a cigarette and stared into the vegetable garden outside, his calmness only a shadow of the previous evening's terror.

I don't remember exactly when I began to hate my father. Those fearful nights following our beatings, when my mother's sobbing finally died down, only to be replaced by my father's drunken snores and dream chatter, have all run together, but while I listened to the sound of his slumber, I made myself two promises.

I will not get married.

I will not have children.

I repeated these promises to myself every time my father came home drunk and dragged us into the yard, and I never imagined they'd become promises I'd have trouble keeping. With all I'd seen so far between my own parents and other families in the village, I often wondered why people ever married. Why would they choose to fight and struggle and stay tied to someone they hated? I especially wondered why people had kids. Who needed extra mouths to feed and haunted eyes staring, asking for something you couldn't give? I thought all children were like my siblings and me, crawling with lice, arms and legs scratched and bruised, faces gaunt.

*****

Of course, my childhood wasn't all work and beatings and hunger. My siblings and I didn't have many places of refuge that allowed us to sneak away from farm work to play with the other kids in our neighborhood. The river became my playground during the warm season. From the shore, my siblings and I waded into the water once a day to bathe. When my brothers and sisters got too far from my reach, I'd dart after them, pulling them from the currents onto the shore. Afterwards, I'd pull the leeches off their bodies as gently as I could. They never complained; they learned early that those small black demons were the cost of swimming.

Afterwards, we girls hid ourselves in the bushes so the older boys wouldn't see us squeezing the murky water out of our underwear before putting it back on. In the winter, we only bathed once a month. We heated the water over the cook stove, even when snow was piled high in drifts against our house. We washed fast and rinsed even faster, drying ourselves with lightning speed before putting our dirty clothes back on. Our teeth chattered for hours afterwards. I hated each winter bath almost as much as I hated washing the floor.

The favorite summer game among the kids who could swim was hide and seek. We held onto dead branches to stay afloat in the fast stream, ducking under to hide ourselves from one another. Whenever my mother's cry of "Jeanhee Ya!" echoed impatiently over the paddies, I would sink as far as I could, holding my nose as snakes slid swiftly through the current above me. Only when the dam was open could I truly drown out my mother's call.

The dam keeper let the water out during the warm season, and when he did, it roared beneath the village bridge. One day in early spring, while my cousins and I were crossing it, I looked down as I always did to find the water way down in the main waterway. The marshy grassland sat a little higher than the lower bank where water usually ran beneath the bridge. I picked a landing spot and lowered myself a little below the column underneath where I stood to get closer to where I wanted to go. For a few seconds, I was a bird, the wind rushing past my arms and legs. Amazingly, I landed on my feet, but I reeled from the hard impact and curled into a fetal position. *It didn't look that far from the top of the bridge. Oh, boy, was I dead wrong.*

"Jeanhee's dead!" my cousins screamed as they rushed down the bank to retrieve me. For a moment, I thought I was, too, but I could hear them in the distance, and then one of my cousins said, "Not yet, she ain't."

They knew I didn't fall and figured I had jumped. I used to joke with them, telling them that one day I would jump off. They hadn't believed I would actually ever do it.

"Crazy, Jeanhee, *Ya! Michutshu*?"

"We are in so much trouble with *Emo* because of you!" they scolded as they picked up my limp body and carried me to my mama by taking turns hoisting me onto their backs. I didn't cry. I wanted to but could never bring myself to dare. My body pulsed with hurt, the pain way beyond that helped by teardrops. I feared my spine had been broken and that my brain might explode, if it hadn't already. I didn't break any bones; my mama reassured me, and yet my back seized up, forcing me to skip my chores and lie flat on my bed for a few days. Though I was in pain, the laziness felt delicious. Three times a day, I ate an apple my mother bought from passing vendors to lure me to drink cups of boiled, blackish, yucky Chinese dragon medicine while marveling at the joy of not working and enjoying rare attentive affection from my mother. No one ever asked why I jumped off the bridge, and I never explained. Perhaps I'd been possessed by my grandmother's spirit. If I had told them how I wanted to feel the freedom of empty air and the rush of falling, no one would've understood.

When my back healed, farm work and housework resumed. I hauled water from the neighbor's well, carrying it on a long wooden beam that crossed over my shoulders. I would overfill my two water buckets and, on the walk home, wish they weren't so heavy. Every step I took came with the same regret, but I never wanted to make more trips with a lighter load. In the winter, the ground was slippery with ice, and I crept down the frozen, uneven steps in my neighbor's yard, knowing that if I missed just one, I'd not only be soaked and freezing, but would also be forced to redo the arduous chore. In monsoon season, the steps grew slick with mud, and a misstep would send me sliding twenty feet into the stream below.

The burdens on my shoulders grew heavier as my father's absences grew longer. Even though I was a girl, because I was the eldest, I had to fill in his slot planting the muddy rice paddy. Villagers took turns planting each other's fields. We lined up across the field, holding poles attached by strings. One yell meant to pull up, while two yells meant plant. Leeches inched up my legs every time, but I never stopped to peel them off. Planting rice required perfectly synchronized teamwork, and one extra movement would throw off the entire row.

During breaks, I pried the baby leeches from my calves and dropped them onto the dry grass to shrivel and die. And finally, I took the time to deal with one big black leach that had been sucking my blood with its fat mouth all morning. The farmer next to me loaned me his machete to slice the leech carefully away from my skinny leg. The snakes in the paddy were less troublesome. Except for the poisonous one with the triangular head, which I took care to avoid, I jumped over their slithering bodies and worked around them. Some of the braver villagers captured the snakes for food or home remedies for some rich man in the city, but hungry as I was, snake meat held no appeal for me. I hated those sneaky, tangled creatures.

Our village contained seven households, including the dam keeper's home on the hill. No matter how hard we worked, the dam keeper never left his house to help out in the paddies. He had a paying job from the government, to guard our dam, and so he didn't have to work the land. He wore pressed Western style slacks and never fought with his wife. His house was built with wood, not mud, and had real windows. His home was also the only one with a telephone, and he used it to call the other dam keepers to coordinate when to open and close the irrigation gates for farmers to plant rice. The children and even the adults whispered about him—about his nice clothes, his government paycheck, and the rumor that he ate steamed white rice with toasted seaweed for every meal.

One day I asked my mama why he got to live in that big house with a telephone and didn't have to work.

Without pausing from planting corn, my mother told me he had gotten an *education* from a high school in the city to get that job.

From that day on, I knew an *education* would get me out of the life I hated. How hard could it be to finish high school, if you get to eat white, steamy rice with toasted seaweed every meal after that and live in a house without having to work in the fields?

I started scheming about how I could talk to the dam keeper and learn his secrets. His son was a baby and too small to play with me, and I couldn't spy because the dam keeper had a window in every corner of his house and would see me.

One day, I shook the dust from my clothes, smoothed my tangled hair, and walked to his house. I hadn't had a bath in months and hoped he wouldn't notice. I knocked on the door and waited for him to answer.

"Mister," I said, my heart pounding when he did, "I came to see what a telephone looks like, please." I'd chosen to visit him at lunchtime in hopes he would be generous enough to give me a bowl of steamy white rice.

He lifted his left eyebrow and pointed down the hallway. "There it is," he said, indicating a shiny black box that protruded from the wall. I'd never seen a telephone before and couldn't believe that small machine would allow him to communicate with people miles away. I waited for it to ring and stared in awe as he picked up the receiver and talked to an invisible colleague. I couldn't believe how quietly he spoke. I was sure he'd need to yell to be heard across such a distance. I knew he must've learned to use that strange machine in high school.

I sat while his family ate lunch, my eyes trained on their chopsticks piled high with white steamy rice and toasted seaweed, traveling from their bowls to their mouths. Eventually, the wife saw me staring and nudged her husband.

"Here, this is what you wanted, isn't it? Go on home now." He handed me a bite of seaweed-wrapped steamy white rice and shooed me out the door.

I bowed and ran off, cramming the wrap into my mouth the second I passed outside their gate. The seaweed and steamy rice was heaven, and I tried to chew slowly to make the sticky flavor last, knowing that while my mouth was satisfied, my stomach was still growling. After I'd finished, the taste of sea salt and toasted sesame oil lingered on my lips. That one bite was the dam keeper's way of getting rid of my stare, but its taste lasted my lifetime. Being wealthy, I learned, was something to desire, and the way to get there was to be like the dam keeper and graduate high school. I made a promise to myself then and there that I would somehow get an *education* and finish high school. If the dam keeper could pass, so could I.

On the way back home, my little brain worked overtime. As soon as I burst through the door of our little mud house, such a change from the clean fancy house of the dam keeper, I asked my mama to send me to school.

She looked at me with pity in her eyes. "You're only five-years-old. No one goes to school at five, especially girls. Wait until you're seven or even eight-years-old. They won't take you now. Besides, I need you here."

"Mama," I started to cry. "I want to go now. I know I can do it, Mama"

"No." My mother refused to hear me. "Hush. Get out there and finish your chores."

As I walked to the neighbor's well to draw water for our dinner, I thought about how I never wanted to plant rice or pry leeches from my legs or wash the dirt floor or eat unripe fruit to fill my empty belly ever again. I stared at the face in the mountain.

"Please," I begged. "Help me. I don't care how hard I have to work to get there. Give me an *education.*

Chapter Two

Smile

From the moment I saw the dam keeper's glorious telephone, I had something other than a birthday bowl of watery meat stew to crave. An *education*, I knew, was my ticket to a good life, far away from Sinhung Dong. My mama didn't encourage me to get an *education*, and whenever I begged, as I did every day, she'd mumble, "One less kid would be fine with me." Of course, she couldn't have meant that. I was her biggest help and closest companion on the farm.

Despite my mother's reluctance, on March 1, 1963, just six days after my sixth birthday, she agreed to take me away from feeding the animals, tending the rice shoots, and collecting eggs and walked me ten miles to my new school. My heart hummed with the excitement of getting out of farm work. She bathed me in the open air in a round clay tub with warm water she had created by mixing half cold and half hot water she had boiled, washing me before the water got cold. I hated to get my hair combed; she used a fine wooden comb to brush as many lice and strings of eggs as she could from my long, tangled locks. I put on clean underwear and brushed my teeth using rock salt and my index finger, being extra careful not to miss the red freckles of pepper flakes from Kimchi. I washed my face with cold water, and my mama dressed me in my newest sweater that had fewer holes, American GI family's hand-me-down my uncle had sent me from Kunsan City.

The morning we left, the air was chilly, but the sun shone down brightly, its vibrant rays full of promise. For the first time ever, I was getting out of our village. I gripped Mama's hand tightly. She took long, fast steps, and though I always lagged behind, she never slowed. I walked as quickly as I could without complaint. If she'd asked me to fly that day, I would have, a skinny Jeanhee bird in the sky.

She asked me, "Can you study like other kids?"

"I can do it, Mama," I told her, knowing she was worried because I was so young. "I will be a good student."

I had no idea what school would be like since I had never seen any kids going to school before, but I was going to school so that I could live like the dam keeper one day when I grew up.

The road we followed was unpaved and dusty, filled with small stones that skittered beneath my feet. Despite my excitement, I tried to remember every landmark we passed—the twisted tree in the chicken yard, the boulder shaped like a horse's hoof, the old barn with its thatched roof half caved in, tilled farmland waiting for warmer weather to plant, some patches still grassy and covered with early morning frost. I knew my mother wouldn't be waiting after school to walk me home.

The homes we passed looked better than the ones in our little village. The sun glinted off the brightly colored metal of their roofs, and some of the nicer houses even had glass windows. A few homes had tall metal gates unlike ours that was barely attached to its post, and these I knew belonged to the lucky rich families who did everything they could to keep poor visitors like my family from their doors.

The homes got nicer as we neared the Wonbulkyo area, and I noticed there were no rice paddies in sight. That was fine with me. I didn't have time to do battle with thoughts of leeches and snakes as I walked to school. To the right sat the Wonbulkyo temple and the small homes with cement roofs that housed its members, and to the left was Wonkwang University. Three story buildings with glass windows rose from behind thick stucco walls patrolled by uniformed security guards, and tall draping trees stretched across the campus. Even at six, I wanted to study there. The scholars inside had fair, beautiful skin, not tanned and swarthy like my own, and they read books on the benches outside the campus while they waited for the bus. They must've all had rich parents, I decided, to let them pursue such expensive *educations*.

Beyond Wonbulkyo was the town Sin Dong, which had general stores on every corner. Though none of the stores were open so early in the morning, the grocers were already out, arranging their wares, and a lone dog skulked along the side of a building. I passed a town registry office, a police station, a butcher shop with dark green walls, an empty beauty shop with black and white photos of the newest hairstyles, and a pharmacy. Compared to our Sinhung Dong, this was a thriving metropolis. As we passed ceramic barrels of fermenting rice, my mama told me the rice brewery was owned by distant cousins I'd never met. "They're very rich," she said. "And they never run out of delicious food."

At the edge of town, the red clay road wove between the general store and a candy store. Next to a small fruit farm was Bukil Elementary School, where I would start my *education*. No mansion would ever look as beautiful to me as that building on the first day I saw it.

When we reached the school, I glanced down at my thin chest, sure I could see my heart fluttering through the fabric. I clutched my new possessions tightly, marveling at the pristine blank notebooks and the sharp pencils Mama had managed to buy for me. So enamored was I with the new grounds, I barely noticed when she left my side to fill out papers in the teacher's office. The school was just one floor, shaped like an L, with a large dirt meeting ground in the center where the Korean flag waved proudly. At one end sat an office for the teachers, and at the other was a small room where they took turns sleeping at night to ward off potential robbers. The classrooms were identical—spare and austere, with windows on each side and a stove in the center. A shiny silver pipe rose from each stove and ran along the ceiling to release the smoke into the sky. Dark wooden desks with cubbyholes for books lined the classroom walls, and bells chimed to mark the hours, study breaks, lunch, and release. From the moment I set foot in the building, I was determined that unless it was the height of monsoon season or snowed more than waist high I would not miss a single day.

When my mother was done with her business in the office, she left me in front of my classroom. "Don't dawdle around after school is dismissed, Jeanhee ya," she said. "The chores on the farm won't wait for you, and I can't do them alone." Then she turned and strode away, her shoulders strong as she headed back to the life I wanted so desperately to escape.

I turned from the hallway and marched into my new classroom. Unlike in the upper levels, boys and girls attended elementary school together. I wasn't intimidated. I had cowed bigger boys back home than the ones here, and I knew no one could match me with words. While some of the other kids wore clean clothes without rips, others had shirts and dresses with more holes than fabric. I was most fascinated by the wealthy girls who had shiny, combed hair, immaculately braided, without a strand out of place.

I hugged my notebook and sat down at one of the desks. I was excited to be in that rough-hewn schoolhouse, ready to fill my head with whatever wisdom my teachers could give me. I felt shy. The other students scowled and complained. They weren't interested in studying numbers, picture books, or the Korean alphabet. These things would not help them produce a better harvest or keep up with the endless demands of village life. Still, their angry attitudes intimidated me. The only kids I'd ever seen, besides my own siblings, were the nine neighbor kids. Eighty kids filled my classroom alone, with six total rooms in the school and one teacher per grade. Not one of these strangers was a village kid I'd bossed around and run roughshod over with my words. That first day, I chose to say nothing.

When my teacher walked into the classroom, the boisterous chatter and chaos came to halt. All eyes followed her as she placed her books and her whipping stick on the large desk at the front of the classroom, next to the blackboard. Before she'd even called roll, Ms. Soomi lined us all against the wall, arranging us according to height in order to determine our designated seats for the year. As the youngest, shortest student in the class, I was seated by the teacher's desk, eye to eye with her whipping stick.

*****

Sadly, my home life interfered with my good intentions to be the best student. I managed the best I could, but it was hard to find time to do my lessons, and when I failed to complete my homework, Ms. Soomi tiredly took her whipping switch from her desk and ordered me to stand against the wall with the other children who also didn't do the assignment. The beatings hurt, but I had no time to keep up. In the afternoons, when I got home from school, I had to do chores and take care of my siblings. The village boys were always up to no good, stealing fruit from our trees and anything else they could get, and the time I spent yelling at them took me away from my studies.

One night a neighbor boy climbed our chestnut tree, not realizing that in the moonlight I could see him clearly.

"I see you!" I called from beneath the tree. At first he pretended he wasn't there, but I wasn't fooled. "Come down right now, or I'll get my mama!"

All the village kids had heard my mama yell at one time or another, and none of them were eager to be on the sharp side of her tongue. He scrambled down, making excuses.

"I was just seeing how high I could climb," he said. "This is the biggest tree in the village, so I wanted to try. I don't even like chestnuts. They're too hard to peel."

"That's not true. You were trying to steal our chestnuts," I said briskly. If he were smart, he would bargain with me for water privileges. His house had the only well we could draw fresh water from. But he had never gone to school and was too stupid to bargain.

One time, one of the village boys stole from my brother, Junghee. We never had store-bought toys, but the boys in each household knew how to make wooden guns, bows, and nets to catch fish. One winter, Junghee made a pair of ice skates, complete with metal blades on the bottom so he could glide across the frozen river. I'm not sure where he found those blades, but he was deeply proud of his invention and went out to try it as soon as he was finished. A little while later he came back, crying, "Sister! Sister! A big boy took my skates."

I took his hand. "Show me where he is."

We went toward the river, and he pointed out the tallest boy on ice.

"There he is," Junghee said. "He stole my skates."

I walked up to the boy, who was twice as tall as me. Stretching myself high toward the sky, I put my hands on my hips. "Hey, you, big boy! Give my brother his skates!"

"What?" He looked around, his eyes finally lighting on me. "Shorty, are you talking to me?"

"Give my brother his skates!" I insisted. "Otherwise, you'll be sorry."

The boy laughed. "These are my skates. I made them myself."

"You're lying. Why would you make them so small? Your big foot barely fits in them."

I could tell he was questioning himself. He looked around. All the other boys stared at him. He took off the skates and tossed them across the ice so I'd have to run after them. Then he turned and stalked off.

My brother ran after his skates and tucked them proudly under his arm. What a priceless moment. I won my young brother's heart in that instant. He didn't have a father to look up to, and so from then on, Junghee looked to me for guidance and protection.

Before we reached the house, I told my brother to stay on our side of the river. "Next time, that big boy might not want to give the skates back."

*****

At night, I studied under a small kerosene lamp that barely put out enough light for me to see my writing. I had to keep my papers directly under the flickering glow in order to read, and making progress required squinting. I often awoke bent over my work with a headache and watery eyes.

"Let's play ghost," my little sister Sunhee wisper, draping herself in Mama's big shirt. She'd dart in front of the kerosene lamp, laughing at the flickering, spectral shadow that chased her from the wall, moaning, "Woo... I'm coming to get you!"

The other kids whirled around too busy tracking the shadow with big, frightened eyes to focus on who was wearing the shirt. Since we didn't light the lamp often, it was their chance to play. The shadow ghosts inevitably morphed into shadow ducks and chickens quacking across the wall. Meehee cried because even the farm animals scared her, and Junghee yell because he couldn't contort his small fists into a rabbit shadow as well as Sunhee could. I'd lie on my belly and prop myself up on my elbows, tracing my finger below the characters in my textbook, trying my hardest to focus despite the play. Meehee set on my back and Sunhee tickled my ribs.

"Get off!" I yelled. "I'll get a whipping from the teacher if I don't finish! And if I do, I'm going to come home and share that whipping with you!" Getting me to stop studying was its own game, one they played nightly.

Finally, I'd agree to tell them a ghost story to buy a few minutes' peace.

"In the side of the mountain where we bury our dead, a tall tree has lived so long it grew twisted and wise from all it has seen," I told them. "The tree god noticed this and turned it into a man. Its bent limbs became arms, and the hard knob on top of its trunk where the vultures liked to roost became its head. The tree god had never turned a tree into a man before and though it remembered to turn little chips of bark into toenails and fingernails and a woodpecker's hole into a bellybutton, he forgot to give the tree man a set of teeth. The tree man's lips sunk into his face, and he grew hungrier each day.

"One day he was desperate to fill his tummy and went to the river to drink cold water. Some children were splashing by the shore. They'd run away from the rice paddies where they were supposed to help with the planting, and they giggled loudly at their mischief. The tree man watched the children from behind a rock. They looked so sweet and soft, and his hungry belly growled. When the children started skipping rocks, he couldn't help himself any longer. He snuck up behind them and bit off their hands."

I told the same story every night, and though they knew it well, the younger kids would sob in fear every time they heard it. Sunhee would grab Meehee's small hand, pretending to take a big bite.

"Yummy, yummy. Give me that other hand," she'd say, in a deep tree-voice. Meehee would cry frantically, and I'd bite my tongue to keep from laughing.

"Tomorrow night could be Junghee's hand," I'd say to Sunhee. "You better keep your hands under the cover so the tree man can't find them." Eventually, the kids would stop squealing and then would fall into quiet games for a bit before they forgot and started bothering me again. I learned to work fast in the sporadic minutes I had.

But I was still a child, too, and sometimes I gave in and played with them. We didn't have a closet, so all of our blankets and clothes were usually in a heap in the corner. In the winter, when we were trapped inside, we would wrap our summer clothes in a sheet to play on a make-believe stage. I had to blow the kerosene lamp out when I wasn't using it because, as mama said, anything we couldn't grow cost money, and she had trouble enough finding cash without my wasting oil. Then we played in the dark, telling each other silly stories until we all fell asleep. My mama never played with us. She was too tired at the end of the day to do anything except fall into her soft bed on the floor. I couldn't have woken her with anything less than a fire or an ancestor coming through the door, though sometimes, when I sat up late studying, she would stir and say sleepily, "You done your study, Jeanhee ya?"

"Yes, Mama," I'd reply. Some nights, I was too bone tired to concentrate, and I wouldn't fulfill my promise to myself to complete my studies. Other times, I didn't understand the homework. Math and science were difficult for me, and I couldn't ask my mama for help. She could barely read and would become frustrated and embarrassed by my questions. Despite my fear of a whipping, I often left those questions blank.

My favorite day of the year was field day. The teacher got to school early to hang a banner from the eaves and draw lines with white chalk on the red clay ground until she had turned the yard into a make-believe sports arena. Some of the kids brought lunch bags with goodies on this special day, and I begged for tastes of their food to mix with my white rice and kimchi. Class was canceled and all the kids put on special black shorts with tight elastic to keep us from revealing our bellies as we participated in rock throwing, hurdles, rope pulling, and foot races. The boys would compete against the girls, and then whole grades would compete against each other. We'd yell taunts, calling each other weak chickens and limp-wristed ducks as we screamed in pleasure.

When I was in third grade, I entered the hundred-meter race. I felt confident that, despite my bare feet and the soft red clay, I could outrun a few of the big girls. I knelt behind the white chalk line and took off when the whistle blew. The sun was high that day, the blue sky, crisp and bright. I made my short legs go as fast as I could, paying no attention to the other girls. When I reached the end of the race, I was surprised to see my father there, watching me. He'd never come to my school before, and I had no idea what prompted him to come that day, but he stood up straight when the teacher called my name as the winner. "Kang Jeanhee!"

My first photo with my Dad

I stood proudly to claim first prize—a notebook—in front of all the tall kids with longer legs than mine. I'd won the race! I ran up to my father to show him my brand new notebook. I couldn't believe he'd come all the way from the city to watch me race. My dad looked handsome in his black suit and gray tie and shiny leather shoes. His hair was nicely greased and combed, and I felt suddenly shy. Of course, my stylish father didn't want to stay at home with his dirty children who barely had enough to eat and a wife who was perpetually tired and wore ugly T-shirts every day. My father was proud of me, though, and asked a photographer to take a picture of us. I hugged my notebook to my chest and tried my best to look good standing next to my father. I wasn't sure what people were supposed to do in front of a camera. As I stood, my father lowered his arm around my shoulder. It was my first-ever photo, and the first time he had ever touched me gently.

School wasn't always so rosy, and like my father, my teacher was moody. My upper class teacher often gave me and the other children whippings, slashing at our legs between the knee and the ankle with a stripped- down branch. The welts lasted for days. Mr. Tak would always say to me each time, "I am whipping you to teach you lesson. You must do better."

I never understood his logic. My legs hurt too much to think about school work. When my mother saw the bruises, she would shake her head. "Jeanhee ya! You said you finished your work. You used enough kerosene to finish two weeks' worth of work! What happened?"

In winter, the snow was knee high, and I often shivered the whole walk to school. No matter how many layers I put on, I never had enough American hand-me-downs to keep me warm. With no snow boots, I had to pick my path carefully, avoiding deep drifts so that I didn't get my shoes and clothes wet. At school, it took an hour for my feet to thaw enough for me to feel my toes. My gloves had been patched so many times they barely held together. I often walked with my hands tucked into my armpits, holding my shivering body. At night my hands and feet would be swollen from frostbite, each digit barely able to bend. Before I went to sleep, my mama would fill my dad's socks with soybeans and tie them to my hands and feet. The remedy worked like magic. Each morning the swelling had gone down. The scars from the freezing remained for the rest of my life, though, reminding me of my hard childhood.

The cold wasn't the most frustrating enemy of my *education*. In the spring, I battled buses. Every day, they sped by, throwing dirty, melted snow onto my ironed school clothes and puffing exhaust into my face, making me cough hoarsely. Monsoon season was no better. The buses splashed filthy water and mud in a quantity no umbrella could block. If I did have an umbrella, the wind and the downpour would turn it inside out before I got home. I would've had more luck trying to walk between the raindrops than using my broken umbrella to protect my head. Since my book bag wasn't waterproof, I either had to leave it at school or try my best to keep it dry, standing forlornly under the eaves of neighbors' roofs until the rain slowed.

As I got closer to school, I'd join a group of kids in the woods near Wonkwang University. No one had a watch to know what time to meet or how far we were from school, but we knew the pace of our walking speed by heart and we always arrived on time. We chattered and sang, ducking off the road when we heard the familiar roar of the bus behind us. I often wondered what it would be like to ride that sardine-packed bus to school, traveling there in half an hour rather than the two it took me to walk. I never asked my mother if I could try the bus because I knew her answer. "Jeanhee ya! What are you thinking? Why would you pay to ride in a big lazy bus when you have two good legs to take you?"

One Sunday, a bicycle vendor stopped at our home, the last stop before a long stretch on the dirt road to the next village. My mama handed over eggs after counting twice, and then she walked over to my yellow dog, released his chain, and pulled him over as the vendor tried to get a grip on his collar. My heart burst and I cried silently, knowing my protest would not stop my mean mama from selling my dog. I called him Yellow Dog. Every day I fed him scraps we couldn't eat. He was always hungry like me and ate everything I gave him in his beat-up tin can food bowl. Unable to save him from going to the butcher shop for some rich man's remedy, I followed him as he was pulled to somewhere far away to meet his death. I hated my life. My beloved yellow dog, tied to back of the bicycle with string, turned back to see me. He didn't want to leave. He turned back to see if I was still standing there as the impatient bicycle vendor pulled away, and he did that until he could no longer see me.

I cried for him, and my heart has cried for me and my yellow dog for as long as I can remember. Even today, that loss still hurts. I can draw a picture of my yellow dog; he never left my heart. Losing him hurt more than losing my grandmother not too long before. I hated my mama; I hated my life, born to such a poor home. I hid from chores to get revenge on my mama and swam in the river as long as I could. I dipped down into the cold water near the bottom, my tangled hair floating in lazy circles around me. It was murky and quiet there, and I held my breath as long as possible, reveling in my private world beneath the river's surface. When I came up for air, I put my foot down on a jagged piece of broken glass. A hazy cloud of blood oozed from my foot. I hopped back to our house, my toe throbbing. The slash was too deep for my mama to patch with her usual home remedy. She washed the wound with clean water and wrapped it in the cleanest piece of cloth we had, hovering around me for hours and fretting until the bleeding stopped.

I hung my head. I had shirked my chores in my short-lived hatred of my mama who couldn't spare my yellow dog's life for me, and I had been punished for it. With the cut on my foot, I couldn't limp those ten miles to school and back. I would get behind, and when I returned, the teacher would whip me for my absence. That night I struggled to hold back my tears. I didn't want my siblings to see my cry.

Then, like a dream, the next day my mama shook me gently awake and pulled me from the pallet on the floor. I knew it was too late to make it to school on time, and I thought she was trying to make up for it when she fed me extra white rice for breakfast. After I had eaten, she told me it was time to go to school. I didn't question her, though I wondered how I could possibly limp that many miles when I had trouble walking to the end of the yard. To my surprise, she stopped at the nearby road where the buses roared by and stuck out her right arm, motioning for one to stop.

When the jouncing bus slowed, my mama squeezed my shoulder. "Run up the steps when he opens the door and sit down if you can. If you can't, hold on to a seat when he takes off again; otherwise, you might fall down and hurt yourself again."

"Yes, Mama!" I answered, my eyes shining. I'd never known that my mama's calloused hand had the power to bring that monstrous machine to a dead halt. And now that I knew the secret—raising my hand in the air and waving it up and down—I had the power, too.

The mean driver, who tried to splash me every rainy or snowy day, morning and afternoon, as I walked to school, opened the door to let me on. Before I darted up the steps, my mother tucked the return bus fare into my hand.

"Don't lose that," she yelled as I climbed the stairs, "or you'll have to limp home!"

Once in the bus aisle, I bent down and tucked the money into my sock, where I could feel it and know I hadn't lost it. I stood up, bumping into several men and then a pregnant lady. The bus was packed like shoots in a rice paddy, everyone crammed together in a sweaty hodgepodge. The air stunk of kimchi breath, and conversations filled my ears as each person talked louder than the next to be heard over the noise. Used to open spaces and country life, the controlled chaos panicked me. I was too short to find a bar to hold on to, and the other riders were tight around the poles, so I couldn't squeeze through. I was hesitant to shove anyone, not because I was afraid of being rude, but because I was afraid someone might step on my already throbbing toe.

When the bus started, I saw I wasn't going to fall. If the bus jerked, I would bounce off other people's hips and legs. The bus lurched and slowed, taking on even more passengers, and I barely had room to take a deep breath.

Outside the window, the wheels splashed muddy water on those unfortunate enough to have to walk wherever they were going. *I can get used to this*, I thought. If I rode the bus instead of walked, I'd have energy for school and chores. I tried to remember exactly where in the river I'd cut my toe. If this was the consequence of an injury, then I would go back and find that jagged glass. I needed to do more damage quickly, before my first cut healed.

My daydream got interrupted by a strong hand inching across the small of my back and snaking around my stomach, pushing down towards my bottom and private area. I sucked in my stomach and looked down. The hand was covered in curling black hairs. The nails were short and dirty. I didn't dare turn around to see who was touching me, but I was certain it was a monster man. I held my breath as the fingers inched downward, past my belly button, wrinkling my dress up past my knees. My heart raced as I wiggled through the jutting hips and bulky packages, limping away. I pushed and shook, squeaking quiet apologies as I squeezed through the crowd to a section of the aisle that contained more women than men.

My breath came heavily, and my small body trembled.

My mama had told me to never let anyone touch me there. I felt ashamed. For the rest of the bus ride, I felt nauseous; worried the monster man would find me and try again to touch me in that forbidden spot. At school, throughout my lessons, I plotted how I could avoid the monster man's hand. My ears rang as I tried to forget the slippery strong feeling of the snaking hand, and I didn't hear a word the teacher said.

The second my teacher dismissed us, my classmates zoomed off toward their villages. My wrapped toe throbbed as I limped on my barefoot heel, homework tucked into my armpit, my bus fare in my sock. I had to walk a mile to the bus stop in town, and as I teetered across the stepping stones over a small creek, I made up a plan to wait for a less crowded bus, one where no man could shove up against me and slip his hand, unseen, across my body. Buses passed by, one after another. Earlier that day, using my mama's magical bus power and raising my right hand to halt the lumbering vehicle would've given me a thrill, but when I finally saw a bus that looked relatively empty, waving my heavy hand made my stomach queasy. I would be late getting home and unable to give a good explanation as to why. My mama would need my help, and with my hurt toe, I'd be almost useless.

My heart raced as the bus pulled to a halt, and the door squealed open. I spotted an empty seat behind the driver and raced to it. I could see the bus driver in the rearview mirror, and I waited till he looked at me, his dark eyes inscrutable. I nodded hello. I wanted him to know I was there—I was sure he wouldn't let anything happen. I arrived home without incident, but from that day on, I walked to school no matter the freezing rain, knee-high snow, throbbing toes, or monsoon mud. I never told my mama what happened that day on the bus. I was ashamed, and she had enough to worry about.

Not long after the bus incident, walking to school got better. At one of the intersections near the school, the Red Cross started providing a hunk of hard-as-rock cornbread and a cup of warm milk to each child at lunchtime. Somehow, the teacher, who was in charge of handing out the meal, knew how to get just enough with no extra for us students. No one ever got a second serving. While it wasn't a feast, the food was better tasting and more nutritious than what I ate at home. Besides, my eating at school meant more food for my siblings and mother.

The girl who helped the teacher pass out the lunch was one of my classmates, and she was beautiful. Even her name was lovely, the syllables like sparkling mountain water: Woojung. She was one of the richest students in the school and the teacher's pet. She knew every answer and always did her homework. She was also courteous and friendly and never seemed to have a bad day. Everyone loved her, and I wanted to be just like her. I daydreamed in class about her clean, silky hair, wondering how she kept it so shiny and lice free. Her teeth were straight and white, not yellow and crooked like mine. She always wore clean, matching clothes, clothes that actually fit and had obviously not come as charity from a GI base. I was dying to know her secrets. I couldn't picture her bending down in a rice paddy or stuffing raw peanuts into her starving mouth only to endure painful heaves and stomach cramps later. She was too lovely for any of that.

For months, I watched her from afar. I couldn't imagine approaching her. I wasn't even sure she'd talk to someone like me, someone so obviously poor. One day, as she was passing by me, she stumbled and dropped her books. I bent down and scooped them up. She smiled at me, radiantly. Since I had her attention, I asked if she wanted me to carry them to her desk for her.

Her smile grew wide, showing every white tooth in her mouth.

"Okay," she said. "Thank you."

I later found out that she was often ill and even the smallest tasks tired her. My friendly offer touched her deeply.

I'm sure the teachers and other students alike wondered why a girl like Woojung hung around with me. She sat straight where I slouched, kept her hands folded neatly while mine fiddled with a pencil. When she laughed, she laughed gently, her mouth a small "O" of amusement, whereas my laugh was a hooting shriek of joy. We couldn't have been more different, but we quickly became best friends. She was the teacher's pet, and I became her pet. I helped her carry the cornbread and warm milk since the bucket was too heavy for her slim, weak arms, and she passed the meal out to the long line of ever-hungry students.

The day Woojung and I finally spoke, I raced home from school and tried futilely to comb my hair into a straight black curtain like hers. When that turned out to be impossible, I started using my dad's rock salt twice a day to whiten my teeth. I couldn't do anything about the gap between my two front teeth or the crooked zigzags that filled the rest of my mouth. Usually, when one of us had a loose tooth, my mother would either pull it out herself or tie a sewing thread around the tooth and the doorknob and close the door quickly to pull out the tooth. Both methods caused a mouthful of blood and brought on many tears. After the first few times I endured my mother's amateur dentistry, I learned not to tell her about any loose teeth. Instead, I'd play with the tooth with my tongue until it was ready to pluck out. I'd spit what little blood spilled from my mouth and then feel with my tongue for the new tooth already poking through my gums. My teeth grew in hopelessly crooked.

Because of Woojung, I paid more attention to my style. Her dresses, always made of soft pale fabrics, fit her body perfectly, and she seemed to have more of them to wear in one week than I'd owned throughout my entire life. Standing next to her made me feel filthy. I started shaking the dirt off my dresses before I went to school, taking care to wear clothes with no visible holes. I couldn't do anything about how my dresses looked. My mama made dresses for all three of us girls in the same style—A-line, with a hole cut in the center to put our heads through. We only got new dresses when the harvest season was good, meaning that sometimes one dress had to last us a few years, even if we grew.

Even during bountiful years, my mother could only afford the cheapest fabric at the market. She would then spend half a day measuring and cutting it. Since I was already shorter than my sisters, mine were always smaller. The dresses were all the same color because she couldn't afford to buy three different bolts of fabric. However, I didn't complain. I'd have worn anything that wasn't a hand-me-down, and the day I got to wear my homemade dress was always the best day of the week.

My dedicated care about my appearance and my devotion to my new best friend paid off. One day after school, Woojung told me her mother instructed her to make a poor friend to play with and to bring her assignments when she missed school.

"She wants me to have company so I'm not lonely," Woojung said. "She said you can come home with me sometimes." I had a feeling that Woojung's house would be nicer than the dam keeper's, and I was dying to see it.

The whole walk there I pictured a gleaming stone house, with shiny glass windows, crisp curtains, and a tidy *keewha* roof. I imagined an immaculate yard full of flowers, an imposing iron gate, and a yard without chickens running wild and clothes flapping in the wind. I wasn't disappointed. Her home was close to Wonkwang University. Unlike the shoddy wooden gate that led to my mud-walled house, her gate was built with ornate, scrolling metal and opened up to a drive edged by trimmed tall trees. At the end of the drive was a large courtyard, with a big house in the center and smaller identical houses on each side. As we walked up that path, I thought, *This is what I want. I want to live like this. This is why I need an education.*

A small garden filled with beautiful flowers and elegant plants surrounded a water pump. No one had to haul water to Woojung's house. In fact, no one even had to walk through the mud when it rained. Little round stones were scattered throughout the grass in crisscrossing walkways. The roof was made of cement, not woven rice leaves like the mats that covered my home. I was sure she didn't have to worry about leaks during the monsoon season or about replacing the roof every year. The place was magical and enchanting.

Several pairs of black shoes were lined up in perfect formation under the little deck beside the front door, none of them dirty or scuffed. They looked as if they'd never been worn. No dirty clothes were scattered about like in my house, either. Everything was folded neatly and tucked away in cabinets and closets. The wooden foyer leading into the main room was spotless. Dirt knew better than to enter that perfect house.

Before I'd seen the whole place, I had to stop my enthusiastic observations to go to the bathroom. I didn't see an outhouse in the yard, and I looked around, confused. Woojung took me to a little closet inside her house that held a sink with running water and a string hanging down from a porcelain water tank. Everything in the room looked completely alien to me. I had never seen anything like it.

I asked my friend, whispering, "Where is the real bathroom? This is not funny. I have to go right now, Woojung."

But it *was* the real bathroom, right inside her house. Woojung never had to go out in the cold snow or pelting rain to go to the bathroom. She showed me how to squat on the shiny white circle and pull the string. A roll of clean, white toilet paper was attached to the wall next to the hole, and she assured me I could use it to wipe myself.

I walked out of the bathroom with my mouth open. "This is how rich people live," I said with a gasp. I could've gushed for hours without running out of details to admire, but my friend had put on her serious face. So I shut up.

"Jeanhee ya," she said, "I'm sick. The doctors say I won't live much longer unless I follow their instructions exactly. Look at my medicines."

She pulled me over to a little cabinet and showed me the many different bottles of brightly colored pills. She took a few out and washed them down with a little cup of water.

"Yuck!" she said.

I had never seen medicine in a bottle before. Each pill was a perfect bright circle tailored to a specific ailment, almost like magic candy. My mama's remedies were mostly cure-alls made from ground grass and leaves, and when they didn't work, I had to endure whatever discomfort I was suffering until my body fought off the sickness itself.

"Can I have one?" I asked. I couldn't imagine those shiny

little tablets could taste bad. Woojung nodded. She was right. The pill did taste funny, but I decided to like it. It might be the last time I ever had real medicine, especially in such a beautiful, clean home.

I wondered if maybe Woojung's family could adopt me. I wanted to live in this big, beautiful home, wear pretty clothes, and have long shiny hair and straight teeth and a maid to clean up after me. I decided that you had to be pretty to deserve such wealth, and I was not pretty like her. But that didn't mean I could stop wishing for her life and wondering how I could get it. I decided I would just have to try harder to make myself pretty and maybe that, along with my *education,* would help me become rich.

After I swallowed the bright pill, Woojung took me into the main living room. Hanging in the middle of the wide back wall was a photo of a man Woojung told me was their living God.

"How'd you get his picture?" I asked. Besides the mountain that looked like God's face, I'd never seen a depiction of God before. I didn't know what *a living God* even meant.

"Our religion is called WonBulgyo," Woojung explained. "We're taught to be good to each other and kind to weak and poor people. Otherwise, in our next lives, we could come back as ugly dogs or stray cats. Really mean people come back as snakes."

I was quiet; perhaps, I had better start being nicer to my younger brothers and sisters and stop beating them up for not following my orders. I sure didn't want to come back as an ugly dog or cat. This life was bad enough. If I came back as a snake, some paddy farmer would catch me and turn me into a home remedy. I wanted to come back as someone like Woojung. I wanted to be beautiful. She must have been a saint in a past life. I bet she never so much as stole an egg to trade for candy.

"One more thing," Woojung continued. "You must smile more today than you did yesterday. People will like you and be nicer to you. You'll have more friends."

"Do I have to smile at people I don't like?" I asked, suspicious because that meant everybody. Everyone I knew fell into the category of *I don't like,* except maybe my youngest brother, who couldn't talk yet.

"Yes," she said with a nod, "at everyone. Smile all day, all the time."

I wasn't sure about this. First of all, what was there to smile about? It was easy for Woojung to say. She didn't go to sleep hungry each night on a dirt floor. But I would do anything for my beautiful friend. Maybe smiling was the secret to wealth. I stretched my teeth away from my lips, grimacing.

"No," she said, laughing. "You look like you just ate a piece of bad fish. Look happy. Try again."

I did, and she laughed even harder.

"That's worse than the first one. You're not trying, Jeanhee."

"Don't I need a reason to smile?" I asked. "Why would I smile when there's nothing to be happy about?"

"If you smile, you'll feel happy," she insisted. "Stretch your lips away to the left and the right at the same time. Then open them and show your teeth."

She smiled at me, a glamorous, glorious grin that made me want to smile back. I could count on one hand the number of times I had seen my mama look happy, and that was usually when relatives came to visit. She did her best to hide her unhappy life from them so that they could go home pleased with how well her life had turned out. My mama would wash her face, comb her hair, and wear her one decent dress, throwing my dad's worn out shirts that she wore to the rice paddies in the rag pile temporarily.

After many tries, my smile met Woojung's standards, and she let me stop practicing so my facial muscles didn't get sore. Later, she told me that making me smile more had been a task given to her by her mother as part of practicing their religion. "You're my enlightenment subject," she said.

As unhappy as my life was, smiling was hard. I tried to think of reasons to be happy, telling myself that I would add one reason a day until I did nothing but smile, but it wasn't easy. Planting fields and scrubbing the floor certainly didn't make me happy. Neither did my long walks to school or my obnoxious brothers and sisters. Smiling seemed like a lot of effort to stretch out my face and show off my crooked, yellow teeth. The smile trick worked for Woojung, but I wasn't sure it would perform the same magic for me. Until I met Woojung, I'd thought smiling was a way for rich people to show off their fancy straight teeth.

I remembered that I'd smiled when I used her clean, indoor bathroom, wiping her soft white toilet paper across my privates, watching water I didn't have to carry flush down a hole and disappear into the ground. Thinking about it, my lips curved up naturally. I peered into the broken piece of mirror in my house. I wasn't pretty, but my face was kind and inviting. I'd always seen myself as a loner, a dirty, unhappy girl from the country, and yet the girl in the mirror looked as if she had friends and a happy life, even if it was difficult. She looked like the kind of girl I'd want to be friends with.

The longer I peered in the mirror, the more Woojung's advice made sense. Of course, my cousins and classmates and neighbors didn't like me. I'd always looked mean and unhappy. I made it a goal to smile every day and be nice to everyone so I wouldn't come back as a dog or a snake in my next life. I even practiced smiling, learning to do it with my lips closed so no one could see my ugly teeth, and I brushed more frequently with sea salt. My mama must've thought I was crazy, standing so many hours in front of the mirror, but she didn't say anything.

The next time I saw my cousins, I tested my new philosophy on them. Instead of giving them an earful whenever they made me mad, I gave them compliments. At first, they were confused.

"Are you sick?" one of them asked. He put his hand on my forehead to see if I was running a fever. "What happened to Jeanhee?"

"I'm fine," I answered.

"No way," they laughed, when I told them about Woojung and her toilet with running water and soft paper. "Why would a rich girl be your friend and let you play in her beautiful house? You're making that up."

I started to lose my patience, but just in time blurted out a compliment and saved myself from a future life as a legless, armless snake. "She'd be friends with you too if she met you," I said. In my next life, I wanted to be as pretty as Woojung, living in beautiful home, eating fluffy white rice.

Soon, my smile became so natural that everyone, including my classmates, started calling me "Smiley." The lines on my brow from my constant scowl faded, and I found that I had more friends in my class. I thanked Woojung for her lesson, and she laughed and said, "I told you, Jeanhee. My mother will be so happy."

Woojung was often sick, and she missed a lot of school. On the days she was absent, I'd stop by her house after school to play. If she wasn't able to get up, I'd say hello from the door. Sometimes, Woojung was lively and in good spirits, and we would romp and run from glorious room to glorious room. Other days, she was wan and lethargic, and I would worry all night until I visited her again. I didn't understand why she couldn't get better with all her expensive doctors and beautiful round pills.

Whenever I came to visit, Woojung's mother would say, "Jeanhee Ya! I'm so glad you came over." She said it in such a welcoming, heartwarming tone that I always believed her and felt as if I were doing her and Woojung an honor, instead of the other way around.

Woojung's mother was elegant and kind and smelled faintly of flowers. Unlike my own mother, she didn't have a single line on her face, even when she smiled. She had attained the highest rank in the ladies' division of their religion and was well respected in the community. As I started coming over more, I recognized her religion in her body language and actions and in the sincere way she made me feel welcome in her house. I felt like a cave girl who crawled right out of the dirt when I entered their beautiful house, but every time I walked through the door, I was accepted and treated as an equal. Her kindness made an impression on me, and I learned to be good to others.

After I became friends with Woojung, I kept myself cleaner, brushing my hair no matter how much it hurt pulling out the tangles, and I took more frequent baths, even in the cold winter when I had to carry extra buckets of water across the icy path from the neighbor's well. I even asked my mama to help me pick the lice out of my hair and clothes although since we all slept under the same blanket there was no way to keep them from crawling back onto my body.

Woojung couldn't play too actively because she wasn't well enough to run around, so when we played hide and seek, I would stay close and stick out my hand or my foot so she could find me easily. I was her only friend, and her mother was glad to have me keep her company. Looking back, I see that I probably helped her as much as she helped me, but at the time I could only see their generosity, and I felt grateful.

Dinner at Woojung's house was the highlight of my week. Whenever she asked, I would excitedly say, "Yes, yes, yes!" Those were the only times, besides holidays, that I truly felt full. Many days she was too tired for me to stay, but when she had the energy to keep me, I smiled so big she laughed out loud.

"No one loves food like you, Jeanhee," she often said. "I never knew rice could make someone so happy."

I'd eat my steaming bowl so fast that Woojung would scoot hers over to see how much more I could hold.

"Jeanhee, where do you put all of that rice?" she asked. "How can you eat so much at once?" I couldn't explain to her what it was like to always be so hungry your stomach hurt. She'd never daydreamed about her next meal or wondered how many hours would pass before she could eat again.

Halfway through her bowl, I'd ask, "Are you sure you don't want any?"

"No, I'm on a diet," she'd say. "I can't eat anything else."

The first time she said that, I'd never heard the word before.

"Diet?" I asked. "What's that?"

She explained it meant she had to pick and choose her food by the doctor's order. Overeating was bad for her. What a shocking concept to a hungry country girl like me. At her house, where food was plentiful, I relished eating until my stomach was stretched tight as a drum.

"In my house, we only eat steamed rice on our birthdays," I said. "And we have to share it. Only on New Year's day do we get fruit and meat." Woojung had never been to my house, and I wasn't sure she could imagine what it was like to be me. I explained again that what we ate on New Year's was nothing like what I ate at Woojung's. Her whole family would watch me eat in wonder.

"May I have more dried fish?" I'd ask. "And some toasted seaweed?" I was never too shy to ask for seconds, and there was never a shortage on her table.

When I absolutely could not eat anymore, a maid would whisk my dish away. I was always sad when I had to walk home. My house looked smaller and shabbier after spending time with Woojung, and my mama was always furious when I was late. I didn't dare tell her how much fun I had in that beautiful, clean house because I knew it would hurt her feelings. The whole time I walked home, I knew my Mama was waiting in the yard, looking up from her chores to see if I had crossed the bridge to come help.

Instead of telling my siblings stories about Woojung, I listened with my siblings as my mother lamented her difficult life. "Why did I marry your no good father? When the matchmaker brought two men, your dad and another, the other one was very wealthy and sweet, but he was a one eyed ekku man. How could I have made such a terrible mistake? I should have chosen the one eyed ekku man instead of choosing your father's good looks."

She was very unhappy, and we all knew it. Koreans don't hide their true feelings.

"I'm stuck here with five kids," she groaned, "Algo, Nepalzza! Algo!"

We all were so used to hearing these stories that we often repeated them, lessening their blow by making fun of them. We knew she wouldn't leave us or run away, even when she became melancholy. She tried to scare my dad once by running away to her mother's house in Kyeyado Island, a one hour boat ride from Kunsan City, but she came back quickly. She hadn't been able to leave her five children. And when she found out my father had been feeding us toasted soybeans and bony sparrows he caught in a string trap, she promised never to run away again. We were skinnier and more haggard than when she'd left, and we'd supplemented our meals with swigs of soy sauce and slurps of bean paste when my father wasn't looking.

Though my mother vowed never to leave us again, staying made her sorrow return. I knew that if she hadn't had us, she would've left my shiftless father and never looked back. We were the reason she was stuck in a life with no hope.

One night, her ragged sobs pulled me out of a deep, restful sleep. When I sat up drowsily, I saw she wasn't in the room. I followed her voice to my grandmother's old bedroom. Her face was pale and contorted, and her stomach was severely swollen.

"Jeanhee!" she said. "You must run to the pharmacy as fast as you can. Tell the pharmacist I drank rat poison, and I need help. Go quickly. I'll die if you don't. Go, Jeanhee ya. Run!"

I bolted out the door and started towards the faraway town where I went to school. I'd never made the journey in the dark before, and the tall, dark trees kept the moon from lighting the road. Their swaying branches turned into the bony hands and toothless mouth of the monster man that filled the stories I told my brothers and sisters each night. Except for the staccato barks of distant dogs, the night was dead quiet. Not one person passed by. I focused on the moon behind the trees, too scared to look back, certain that something would jump out of the woods and carry me off.

I broke into a run when I could and walked fast when I got winded. When I reached town, no lamps burned in any of the windows. The shops were closed, their doors latched tight. I pounded on the pharmacy window, not caring who I woke. Finally, the pharmacist yanked open his door.

"Who is it?" he snapped. "How dare you come here this late?"

His angry tone faded when he saw me standing before him, small and shaking. "What do you need, child?" he asked, adjusting his glasses in order to see me better. "Who's sick?"

"My mama," I answered. "She drank rat poison. She said to tell you she'll bring money when she feels better. Please, sir, help me."

"Hush, child. Come inside," he said. "Tell me how she

looked."

He lit a lamp and moved over to the shelves behind the counter where he rummaged through various remedies while I talked. After some deliberation, he handed me a few pouches of medicine to take to my mama. His tight, drawn lips told me I needed to hurry, and that even then I might not make it.

I ran, no longer worried about the ghosts and monsters that might be following me. The moon god kept me safe. When I got to my grandmother's room, chest heaving with exertion and legs on fire, I could tell my mother had been crying in pain ever since I left. She choked the medicine down and lay back, exhausted.

I shook with worry. I'd already lost my grandmother, and I didn't know what I would do without my mama. She had sacrificed for me, and I loved her deeply.

She stayed sick for a few days, and during that time, neither of us worked. I skipped school and stayed by her side, making sure she took all of the medicine the pharmacist sent. I never told anyone about that terrible night with my mama. Not my dad, nor my brothers and sisters. Luckily, they all slept soundly and never even knew I'd left. I kept the secret of my mama's suicide attempt to myself.

My sympathy for her was short-lived, however. As soon as she was better, I returned to school, and when I came home, she screamed at me the very second I opened the gate.

"Jeanhee ya! Where have you been? Do you think the floor scrubs itself? Do you think the beans pick themselves? If they did, I wouldn't be so tired!"

I never told my mama where I'd been when I visited Woojung. The first time I was late, I said I'd walked slowly because my stomach wasn't feeling good. The trick worked. She put her energy into grinding leaves for me to choke down and stopped yelling. Other times, I simply endured her anger, putting my head down and going about my chores while she admonished me.

Though my lack of loyalty made me feel ashamed, I knew that eventually I'd run away to where my mama couldn't find me and make me work. I wondered how many rich people there were in the world and promised myself that one day, when I was bigger and stronger, I'd live in a mansion and eat heavenly steaming rice whenever I wanted. My ambition outpaced my guilt.

Though I spent time with Woojung, I never neglected my studies. In fact, seeing Woojung's life gave me renewed passion and dedication for my *education,* and I stayed up later and later to finish my homework. As the year wore on, the other children grew restless, ready for the harvest season break, but I dreaded the day when school let out. No school meant I wouldn't be able to walk to Woojung's to visit. I'd be stuck at home with my constant hunger, those never-ending chores, and my father's ruthless beatings. I knew my life wouldn't improve if I simply hung around. No one was going to bring the life I dreamed about. As I gathered eggs or planted seeds or hauled buckets of water, I reminded myself of my secret dream, my *runaway* dream.

Chapter Three

"Hershey Bar" Story

In early spring, a neighboring village farmer pulled his mule to our land. Just as she had said to him during the previous year, my mama told him she couldn't pay him in paper money. Instead, she gave him her *word of honor* that she would pay him with the newly harvested rice in the fall. The task of pushing a hoe behind his tired mule took a day and a half, but when he was finished, the rows were immaculate, long vertical lines with space between them for the monsoon waters to flow and mounds of soft soil to nestle the beans.

Ever since I was old enough to walk, my mama had enlisted me to help her plant. We each tied a half- full bag of beans to our left hip, leaving an opening just wide enough to pinch out four beans. We squatted and stepped forward in half-foot increments, staying even with the row without getting up. At eight, I was almost as fast as my mother. I followed behind her, covering the freshly planted beans with earth. We never talked as we worked, though sometimes, as the sweat rolled off her nose, my mama broke the silence with soft cries of "Algo! My bad decisions make my daughter suffer so."

Somehow, I interpreted her words as thanks. My mama appreciated my helping hand, and that lessened her suffering.

We didn't take breaks. Not finishing meant more work for us the next day. My mother looked at the sun's distance from the horizon to determine when to pause to cook lunch and nurse my youngest brother, who was almost a year old. She could also tell when rain was coming just by smelling the air. Turning her face and closing her eyes, she would say, "Big rain coming, Jeanhee Ya. I knew my legs were sore for a reason."

Often, while I knelt over the beans, I drifted into my most favorite daydream. How hard could it be to *run away?* Besides walking to school, I'd barely been outside my village, and I didn't know how people made a living other than by slaving all day farming, keeping a small store, or working for the government like the dam keeper. My dream was for a new life, but what that life would be I couldn't imagine.

One day, as I planted beans with my mama, a boom ending with a loud screech echoed through the village, as if something had exploded out in the road. Rather than ducking or running away, I dashed across the field for a clearer view. A hulking, dark-green GI truck had pulled over on the shoulder, and four Americans, two black and two white, piled out of its doors to see what had gone wrong. I wasn't afraid of these strangers. American GIs had saved us from the Communist North Koreans, and I couldn't believe they'd pulled over right in front of my eyes.

The other village kids came racing behind me, chattering excitedly. We'd seen GI trucks pass along our road before, but none of us had ever seen American GIs so close. The black GIs had tight, frizzed curls and dark brown eyes, while the white GIs had soft yellow hair and blue eyes. They were all so tall. Taller than any men we had ever seen. Their big eyes, noses, and lips were larger than our delicate Korean features, and they spoke a strange language that teased my ears, as though their tongues had been tied to coins inside their mouths and couldn't get free. I'd never imagined people such as them.

The other kids and I stuck out our sweaty, dirty hands and shoved each other with our elbows, trying to get close to the uniformed strangers. Their rear tire had blown out, and they were stuck until they fixed it.

"You're on our road!" we cried. "Pay up!"

How rude they must have thought us, ragamuffins with stinky kimchi breathe, ripped clothes, bare feet, and unkempt, lice-ridden hair, screaming for presents.

Seeing that we wouldn't leave, the GIs stomped in their shiny black boots to the side of the truck, where they began handing out square tins labeled with bold English letters and pictures of bright pink square meat. The other kids weren't sure what the odd presents were, but they knew the gifts were from America, and that was good enough. They clutched their new treasures and sprinted home to gloat to their brothers and sisters who hadn't been smart enough to catch the GI truck.

I wasn't so easily pleased. I shook my head when one of the blond GIs held out a can. Inside the truck, sitting on a crate, was a flat, hand-length package wrapped in dark brown paper with big dark block letters and shiny foil that stuck out from both ends. I'd been eyeing that treat for some time, and I pointed to it, sure the GIs were holding out.

The blond GI, whose boots looked as big as our rice pot, followed the line of my finger with his eyes and handed me the wrapped rectangle. I bowed to him, polite now that I'd gotten what I wanted, and ripped the slick paper and silver foil. Inside, a perfect block of dark brown candy squares shone in the afternoon sun, ready to be snapped apart easily. I placed a tiny morsel on my tongue and closed my eyes. Creamy sweetness, better than anything I'd ever tasted, filled my mouth. Even the candy I'd bought at my aunt's store with a stolen egg hadn't been this delicious. I broke another square off the bar and popped it into my mouth. I couldn't believe the flavor. When I was old enough, I vowed I would *run way* to *Meegook,* the beautiful country, America that had condensed such an enormous flavor into such a teeny brown square.

While the second sweet square melted on my tongue, I remembered my family. I didn't want to be a snake in my next life. My duty as a big sister and a good daughter required me to share my treasure with them.

The candy was already softening in the heat. I could see it seeping out the edges of the foil, smearing the paper. I yelled at my mama, who'd never missed a beat in her planting, "Be right back," and balanced the candy flat on my open palm, knowing that if I clutched it, it would surely melt faster. I burst through the broken wooden-gate of our house and called out, "Look what your big sister got for you from the Americans!"

My siblings, huddled around the open fire pit, barely looked up when I burst in. Any other time, they would have danced around me, clamoring to see what I'd brought, but instead they ignored me. I tiptoed behind them and peeked over their shoulders. My brother Junghee had a dead rat skewered on a stick and was holding it over the flame.

My siblings' eyes grew wide as the flames licked at the rat's body. Its hair singed crisp and fell to the floor, and its tail curled up toward its body. An acrid stench filled the house.

"Are you going to eat that, brother?" Sunhee asked.

"Don't you tell Mama," Junghee hissed.

"Try this instead," I said excitedly, holding out a square of chocolate. "It tastes like heaven." Without taking his eyes from his roasting prey, Junghee put the candy into his mouth.

"This won't fill me, *Nuna,*" he said.

Annoyed at Junghee's response, I dropped a square into my baby brother Younghee's mouth. His lips worked to catch my finger, thinking it was my mama's nipple. Tied with a sling to Sunhee's back, he puckered his lips, smearing the chocolate along her cheap dress. I gave Sunhee and Meehee a full square each, but they were too mesmerized by the rat to be impressed. Fire licked its singed fur, and its flesh shriveled and sucked toward the bones. Its teeth poked menacingly from its bumpy skull.

My heart hurt with disappointment. Who knew when I'd get such candy again? I gave up trying to talk Junghee out of eating the rat and ran back to my mama. I could already hear her calling "Jeanhee Ya!"

When I returned to the field, I was out of breath. "Close your eyes and open your mouth," I panted. "I have something yummy for you!"

She did as I said, and I dropped the last square of the Hershey bar onto her tongue.

"Is it good, Mama?" I asked.

My mama didn't even look up. She went right back to what she was doing without even grunting an acknowledgment.

"Mama," I said. "This candy came from America, and when I grow up, I'm going there to get lots of it."

"You crazy girl. First, you want an *education,* and now you want candy. How are you going to get to America? Do you even know where it is?"

I hung my head, unable to answer.

"*Michutsyu!*" she scoffed. "Get back to planting. The sun will go down soon, and we need to start on the soy beans tomorrow."

Defeated, I picked up my bag and knelt beside my mama. I knew I wasn't crazy even if no one believed me.

*****

I was ten years old when my father drunkenly gambled away our rice paddies and farmland, forcing my family to move into a town near the Makuly brewery. There, he found work making cheap wine. My mother had saved enough money to rent a small house with its own well a mile from Bukil Elementary. I was able to wash up with soap, and though the water was cold, I started to like bathing in the open air. I washed my hair often and brushed my teeth with a real tooth brush we all shared. I was ecstatic. Living in

Sin Dong town meant no more endless farm work and more time to devote to my studies.

During the three years we lived in town, my dad seemed truly repentant. He worked hard at his very first job ever in countless years and came home every evening to join my family for dinner. On Fridays, he turned his money over to my mother, keeping just enough to buy cigarettes. Occasionally, he'd even ask how school was, and when I got to seventh grade, he insisted I go to Namsung Middle School, the most expensive school in Iri City. I was excited that my father noticed my fierce desire to study. And when I first got my Namsung uniform, I was so proud. I washed it every day after school, hung it out to dry and ironed it for the next morning. From the moment I put it on, inspecting myself in the mirror attached to my mother's dresser, I was a new Jeanhee. This photo was the second picture ever of me. I was 12.

7th grade in Namsung Girl's Middle School Uniform.

My family was still poor. We didn't own land to grow food. Though we used a small lot that came with the house for vegetables, they weren't enough to feed all of us through the winter. My parents took what little money we had to buy groceries, and paying my middle school tuition on top of that was hard on the family budget.

Guests weren't ever allowed over for dinner. My mama was so ashamed of our meager portions and cheap food that she always made sure the gate was shut when we ate. She couldn't risk anyone stumbling upon our meals and judging us. What we ate was still never meat, although occasionally Mama managed to save enough to buy a can of Crisco from the black market. She would stretch the white grease as long as she could, giving us a spoonful each to mix in with our rice, soy sauce, and sprinkles of toasted sesame seed. At school, I unpacked my lunch box alone. My small portion of beans and barley, sparely supplemented with white rice and kimchi, broadcast my poverty. The other girls brought different treats and white rice every day of the week, and I felt sure they would laugh and gossip if they saw my meals.

Though I had friends I saw after school and on Sundays, I never felt close enough to them to share my secrets. They were all two or three years older than I was, and they knew stuff about boys that made me red in the face. The only girl at school from my town was a known teacher's pet named Jungsil. Her family owned a small candy store and a few rental rooms for out- of- state students near Wonkwang University. Jungsil and I talked on the walk to school, but once we arrived at school, she left me for her straight A friends and never acknowledged she knew me. Still, I felt lucky to be in Namsung middle school, and her snobbery didn't particularly bother me. Instead, I paid attention to my books, trying to be a good student to show my mother and father they weren't wasting their money sending me to this fancy school. I wished every day that Woojung was at Namsung with me, but she'd scored high enough on the placement test to go to the top school in the city. She rode the bus, and I walked, and we never saw each other again.

Unlike Woojung, I wasn't born school smart. I had to earn every grade point by studying twice as much as the other students. Even then, I only sometimes scored high enough to pass. I constantly looked up to those smart kids and wished I was more like them. While I planted beans, they studied. Sometimes, it felt as if I would never catch up. I liked most of my classes, and while math and science weren't my favorite subjects, the class I hated with an all-consuming passion was my seventh grade homeroom teacher's music class. The first day of school, Mrs. Lee marched into the room dressed in all white. Her suit jacket, miniskirt, sheer stockings, high heels, and gloves were all white. After she told us who she was, she patrolled the classroom, peering at each student from her teetering height. When she got to my desk, she told me to put out my hands, and she slapped both my palms with her thin wooden stick.

"Why don't you wash your hands?" she asked.

My dark tanned hands looked as if they belonged to an old man, covered as they were with scars from frostbite and farm work. I hid them under my desk and didn't answer. No matter how much I washed, my hands still looked weathered and dark, and I hated Ms. Lee for pointing this out to the entire class.

From that day on, I did my best to ignore music class. I knew I wasn't born a song bird and would never play the piano like her. I hated Maria Calais's soaring voice, and the sad Mozart sonatas Mrs. Lee played felt like punishment to me. I fell asleep while the other kids nodded appreciatively to *Fur Elise* and woke when the teacher slapped my dark skin with the thin stick she always carried. "Jeanhee, wake up!" she sneered.

But Ms. Lee's lessons were a small price to pay for being in Namsung, and I soon felt as if I had too much luck, no longer working in the fields and attending such a prestigious school. I felt certain that something would happen to drag me back down. And it did.

My father's reform was too good to last, and at the end of three years in Sin Dong town, he quit his job and fell back into drinking, gambling, and cheating on my mother. My mother's tearless years came to an end, and she had no income to pay our rent. Her lips soon grew tight and pinched. We had no money and nowhere to go.

Just before we were evicted, my mama gathered all five of us children together. We sat solemnly around her. She never stopped working in the middle of the day, and I worried she was sick or my father had left us for good. I studied my mother's face for symptoms. She wasn't pale or quivering, but I knew some sicknesses ate their victims from the inside out, only making themselves visible just before death.

"Children," she said. "We have to take a chance and make a better life for ourselves. Your aunt from the brewery has a small hotel in the city, and she's agreed to let me work with her. This is my chance to provide for you. We're moving."

This was Mama's desperate attempt to make better life for us, and she needed us to give her hope that she was making the right decision. She was scared of being on the street without a home for her five kids if she didn't make it.

My siblings protested. They didn't want to leave their friends and classmates, and neither did I, though I shushed them. My mama never spoke with emotion, and I could tell from her tone of voice that she finally had hope. Her eyes filled with tears, a sight that shocked us into silence.

"Your father can't support us," she said. "We have no land. So if we stay here, we'll be homeless. Okay?"

All of us, said, "Yes. Mama, we agree."

Sinheung Hotel is in Iri city, near the Iri train station, and my mother became its manager. The neighborhood was seedy, filled with bars and prostitutes, and not at all a safe place for children. When my father had abruptly quit working at the brewery for my aunt, bad blood spilled between them. I can't imagine how much my mama cried and begged to get her position.

My mama's do or die decision to move into the city turned out to be one of the best she ever made. She learned the fourteen room hotel business quickly, adapting well to overseeing four employees, two maids, a room service boy, and a cook, and welcoming customers in a good old-fashioned way, bowing to everyone as they checked in and checked out, always saying to them, "Please, come back and spend another night with us. I will have hot barley tea ready in your room just for you."

Her employees worked hard for her because she treated them with kindness, and my aunt was pleased with the subsequent increase in business. For the first time in my life, I wasn't constantly obsessed with finding more food. Since the hotel kitchen made quality meals for the paying guests, the leftovers often ended up on our table, and they were dishes we never could have afforded on our own: grilled chogi, myulchi bokoom, kimchi soup with pork meat, odeng bokoom, and sometimes even toasted seaweed. We didn't care at all that they were leftovers. Good food was finally ours.

In addition, we no longer had to make outhouse visits on cold, wintery nights; our bathroom was like the one I had used in Woojung's home. And as Mama made more money, our life style became even more polished. We took better care of our teeth by using actual toothbrushes and toothpaste instead of rock salt, and we had plenty of facial soap to wash our faces. She even bought us shampoo for our hair. Soon, all traces of lice had disappeared from our hair and underwear.

The move to Iri city was my second relocation in three years, but I didn't miss life in Sin Dong any more than I missed the farm in Sinnheung Dong. The city was a blessing for my *education.* The Sinheung Hotel was just a ten-minute walk from school, one block from a movie theatre, and three blocks from an open grocery market. Now, my mother had money to spare. She shopped daily for groceries to cook for the hotel guests, her purchases trickling down to us to fatten our bellies.

Despite these improvements, my grades were still mediocre. No matter how hard I tried to be in the elite group, I was only an average student. Only in English class did I excel. Though we weren't learning much more than simple grammar and basic words, I threw myself into my English studies with passion. In math, I could never score above a seventy-five, but I didn't care. My high English score cancelled out my low math marks, keeping my class rank high. I ruled English class. If anyone had questions, they knew to ask me. I could pass a written English test better than the smartest student in our class. I was so proud that I'd finally found a subject where no one could outdo me. This was the first time in my life where I shone the brightest, and my confidence grew. No longer was I just poor and dark. I was also admired. My

English scores stood unmatched by my peers, and I glowed with the knowledge that I had a special talent.

No one understood why I was so passionate about the subject. I didn't share my *run away* dream with a soul, not even my best friend, Oksoon. When my English teacher talked about his experiences in America as a young scholar, I propped my head on my hands and leaned in, listening to tales of the Beautiful Nation, *MeeGook*. Mr. Kim told me that America was the most polite society in the world. Before people passed each other on the street, they said "Excuse me," apologizing if their clothes so much as brushed one another. Everyone had a car and a room with beds, and they showered each morning with hot water. Each house had a kitchen and a dining room, and the bathrooms had toilets like chairs. Children slept in beds in their own private rooms, never on the floor.

"Schools there," Mr. Kim said, "are easy. No one has to test into middle school, and attendance is free." And they say, "Thank you!" about ten times a day.

I absorbed every phrase I could and, during other classes, daydreamed of eating Hershey bars while strange English cadences rolled fluently off my tongue. Mr. Kim was impressed with how fast I learned, and I soon became his pet. He taught me words with R, F, Z, PH, and TH, sounds that most Koreans have trouble with, and I felt proud to be liked for my intelligence.

"Listen to how Jeanhee says these words," he would say in class when other kids had trouble. "Copy her."

I did it exactly as he taught me, mimicking his accent and inflection. I even asked him how to write my name in English. The letters were alternately curved and stiff, different from the curved characters in Korean. "J-E-A-N-H-E-E."

My American name looked beautiful. I wrote those clumsy letters all over my notebook cover. "Kang Jeanhee. Kang Jeanhee."

"No," Mr. Kim said, when he noticed my doodles. "Americans write the family name second. In America, you are Jeanhee Kang."

I didn't care how he changed my name—backwards,

forwards, or upside down—as long as I got to use it in America.

As I progressed through each grade, I no longer received just average grades. Because of my high English marks, I was proud to see my name on the school's main bulletin board one day. It read, *Best test scores: Third place in the 10th grade, Kang Jeanhee.*

I couldn't wait to share my progress with my mama.

"That's very nice, Jeanhee Ya," she said, when I told her about my high ranking. "Are you sure you didn't see it wrong?"

"Mama," I said, rolling my eyes. "I can read. That's what I'm best at."

My high marks pushed me to spend even more time at school, earning higher scores to beat out the other girls who were smarter than I. I often stayed at school until ten o'clock at night, a privilege I was allowed as a top student. Every so often, I'd look up from my books and see my mother through the window. She had walked all the way from home to make sure I hadn't lied to her about staying late. Her growing distrust toward my devotion to my studies was a stone in our relationship.

I didn't understand her apprehension. I was studying to score better on the next test in hopes of one day scoring high on a college entrance exam. In those days, few girls actually cared about finishing high school, much less going on in their scholarly pursuits. Most couldn't wait to submit their name to a matchmaker to see if they could land a wealthy husband who would take care of them. I had no interest in marriage. My father's tempestuous relationship with my mother had scared me off. Still, I understood why other girls weren't interested in higher *education*. The only jobs open to women after college were in schools and banks, and I found neither one appealing.

"You might be able to go to America if you're a reporter," Mr. Kim said. "Your pronunciation is better than any student I've taught. You'll pick up the language fast once you get there. Times are changing. I see no reason why you couldn't make it as a female reporter." I liked envisioning myself as a reporter, traveling in airplanes and cruise ships, having the chance to go to America and bring back news from abroad.

Few Koreans visited America. Since nobody returned home, tourist visas weren't issued to many Koreans, especially poor ones. If someone did score a visa, their family was routinely denied. The government wanted to make sure the departing family member had a reason to return to the country. Their loved ones became a sort of ransom, hostages held against the traveler's return. The only people besides students who got to go to America were those lucky enough to marry an American or diplomats in the country on official government business. Only a handful of Korean *Chebyuls* were allowed to travel freely; since they were so rich, there was no danger of them not wanting to return home. When I asked my teacher how he'd gotten to America, he told me a missionary had sent him to study there and that he had been sent back once he completed his *education*.

I focused harder as I advanced through the grades, envisioning myself the winner of a scholarship to study abroad. Though I had little spare time, I read all of Shakespeare's plays, Ernest Hemingway, Mark Twain, Leo Tolstoy, Boris Pasternak, and O'Henry. To say I had read famous Western novels marked me as an intellectual, whether I'd understood them or not. And I truly loved reading. Once, when I ran out of novels from school, I read a series of illicit books by Kum Byung Mae, sneaking them out of my dad's hidden collection. I knew he would kill me if he found out, but I couldn't put them down—those Chinese men and the dirty things they did with their concubines enthralled me.

Trying to fit in with other girls who had primarily grown up in the city and were much more privileged than I was difficult, but my beautiful friend Woojung's lesson to "smile each day more than the day before" proved invaluable. Despite all those years of working under the sun that had marked my skin dark and permanently lower class, my creamy-skinned classmates called me "Smiley" and treated me kindly. I even made fun of myself when my friends asked why my skin was so dark. Instead of wasting my time telling them about my hardworking childhood, I said, "I was adopted right after birth because I was so dark; my real mama didn't want me." One of my good friends, Jumsook, actually believed me. One day, she met my brothers and sisters, who were taller than I and all had fair skin.

She said, "I got it; you truly are adopted. I thought you were kidding! Does that mean you're the black sheep of the family?"

For some reason I liked that term.

"Yeah," I answered. "That's me. I am the black sheep, Jeanhee. Baa..."

Attending an all-girls school was a coveted honor and in order to stay enrolled, we had to follow strict rules set forth by the school's rulebook. Each school had its own style of uniform, and as I walked around the city, I could instantly recognize where a girl went and how much respect her intelligence deserved. However, despite the different uniforms, the school rulebooks were pretty much the same. Every girl had to wear her school uniform in school and outside the home. Our hair had to be parted from the right to the left and hang one inch below the ears. Everyone entered the same entrance gate to the classroom, walking in a solemn line with student guards who were the top students. Disciplinary teachers stood on either side to inspect us. If a girl's hair looked too long, the teacher would measure it with a ruler and pull out her scissors and cut it into an embarrassing zigzag as a statement to the rest of the school. Colored hair pins, make-up, nail polish, and headbands were strictly forbidden. We were also required to wear white tennis shoes with four—not six—grommets, laced so the shoe strings overlapped rather than crisscrossed. If they could've standardized our height and complexions, I'm sure they would have done that, too.

The school's strict disciplinary policies extended beyond our appearance and dictated our social lives as well. We were forbidden to go to movies the school didn't pre-approve. We could socialize only in family-oriented restaurants and only with girls. No public radio stations played hard rock and roll songs, so I grew up listening only to pop songs by singers like Olivia Newton-John, the Carpenters, Simon and Garfunkel, Tom Jones, and Neil Diamond. Pool rooms, adult coffee shops, and dance clubs were off limits. Getting caught with a boy, regardless of the circumstances, guaranteed automatic suspension by the school's disciplinary board. For those of us who dreamed of going to college, such a punishment was unthinkable.

Though corporal punishment was practiced by all of our teachers, each punishment was unique. Once, somebody ate lunch too soon, filling the room with the thick, pungent smell of kimchi, and the teacher whipped all eighty-three of us for the offense to his nose. Another time, a girl in the back called a teacher *baldy,* and, again, he whipped the whole class. He didn't care who had said it. He refused to accept any disrespect. One girl, whose crime the teachers refused to tell us, was forced to kneel on ice in the center of campus and be whipped while the entire school looked on. The whole school watched her cry in the snow that day. The fear tactic worked. I never wanted to experience such humiliation. I vowed to always be a good student and to make my parents proud.

But no matter how hard we tried, we couldn't make all of our teachers happy. The P.E. teacher especially liked to pinch the skin on our rib bones when we didn't behave, leaving bruises that lasted for days. Our impeccably dressed tenth grade English teacher, Mr. Bae, who always wore a bright pocket square in his tailored suit, beat us with his slipper at the slightest provocation. The romantic story we made up was that he had been in love with the most beautiful girl in the whole world, and when she wasted quietly away from cancer, he devoted his life to celibacy and solitude. One of the tests was particularly hard for me, and though I could ace most of my English tests with my eyes closed, I turned that particular test in blank. I was Mr. Bae's favorite, but even I wasn't spared. The day after the test, he called out the names of the girls who had turned in blank exams, hitting them ferociously with his hard slipper.

When my turn came, he narrowed his eyes and said, "You go back to your seat!"

I shrieked and ran before he changed his mind, the cries of the other girls filling my ears.

During lunch and after class, I was inseparable from my best friend Oksoon, whom I'd met in the ninth grade. She was shy, with brown, almond-shaped eyes enhanced by long, thick lashes. She looked a bit like Woojung. And like Woojung, she never stepped one toe out of line. I think she didn't even know how to get into trouble. I could tell she wanted to be friends with me whenever our eyes would meet between classes, but she waited for me to speak first.

I bumped into her shoulder one day on purpose.

"Oops," I said. "I'm sorry! I'm Jeanhee, who are you?" She forgave me instantly and introduced herself. I told her, "Our friendship can begin in exactly one minute." I stared at the wall clock in the classroom until she burst out laughing with her pretty eyes with long lashes.

"You're so funny, Jeanhee!" she said.

I *smiled* back, and we became best friends, inseparable from that day on.

Because my hotel home was too seedy for me to entertain guests after school, I often went to visit her. Oksoon lived in the country, and I had to ride a bus along bumpy roads to get to her big house that included main quarters for her parents, a small room for Oksoon, rooms for her brother and sister, a field with cows, lambs, and goats, and a barn filled with farm tools. Like a fancy top hat, a red cement roof sat atop the house, and a blue metal gate adorned the driveway. Both her parents were tanned from working the land, but unlike my family, they were wealthy. At age fourteen, Oksoon wore a gold ring.

Oksoon didn't study hard like me, but on Saturday and Sunday afternoons, when I had more free time, we always spent time together. Since Oksoon was the youngest child in her family and I was the oldest, she let me boss her around and pick our activities. Her family welcomed me into their household, and her older sister, Mincha, was particularly kind. My siblings had never asked me about school or whether or not I was happy with my studies, so Mincha's curiosity about my life impressed me. Oksoon, however, was embarrassed by her sister's questions and often put her finger to Mincha's lips to signal her to shut up.

Mincha was six years older than us and was engaged to marry a rice farmer from a neighboring village.

"The matchmaker approved them," Oksoon whispered to me one afternoon. I shuddered. Marriage sounded horrible to me, and I couldn't believe Mincha had accepted it without complaint. She'd never even met the man.

"How does she know he's the one?" I asked. "Maybe he's mean, and he'll beat her."

"My mama and dad interviewed him," Oksoon said. "They approved him. He's good."

"I will never get married," I said. "Especially to a handsome man like my father!"

Oksoon giggled and told me I was crazy.

"Maybe so," I said. "But I'm not joking."

The rules of my school dictated that I only keep company with girls. I had two sets of friends, Oksoon, who never got into trouble, and another set of friends, four older girls, Youngsook, Jumsook, Moonsun, and Sungcha, who weren't serious about academics but were lots of fun to hang around. Older girls meant trouble in those days; they knew things most of us didn't. I wouldn't dare to invite them to my house. My mama would know right quick they were bad news. We often sneaked into movies to gawk at American stars and their on-screen adventures. As I became older, I grew increasingly fascinated by these films. The blonde women on the screen were glamorous and risqué. I thought the movies portrayed America as it actually was, and I viewed them as a window into my future life.

I was an obedient student. I didn't like to get into trouble, and I didn't want my teachers to beat me. The only times I took chances on getting caught were when I went to see American movies. Once, I borrowed a shorthaired wig from an older girl and sneaked into the theater, posing as an adult. Someone— I never found out who— recognized me and told the school board I was being tainted by American *filth*. When Mr. Sun summoned me to his office shortly afterwards, I shook. Mr. Sun was a heavyset man, with a mean, middle-aged face. To show he meant business when we broke school rules he never smiled. No one wanted to face him.

"Kang Jeanhee," he asked. "Were you at the movies yesterday after school?"

"Yes, sir," I answered, looking down at my feet.

Luckily, Mr. Sun was my father's friend, and instead of suspending me, he gave me a warning instead. "Next time," he said, "you'll be suspended for ten days and have your name posted on the bulletin board."

I bowed and backed out of his office as quickly as I could.

My fear of Mr. Sun wore off in only a few days. I was hooked on American movies and had to see more. Whenever the traveling movie distributor came to stay at my mom's hotel with new movies, I was the first to arrive to get a free ticket. I knew spying eyes from the school board were everywhere, and some students even worked as double agents, currying favor with the board and the teachers by telling on their peers. I learned to wait till the movie had begun, when theater was dark, and sneak in to the back row, leaving before the movie ended so my face was never illuminated.

I saw most films by Charles Bronson, Clint Eastwood, and Sir Lawrence Olivier, and also enjoyed *Dr. Zhivago*, and most memorably, *Gone with the Wind.* I wanted to become Scarlett when I moved to America. From what I could see, it truly was a land of glittering white teeth, beautiful homes, sparkling clothes, fancy cars, and tall buildings, and the films only made my daydreams more vivid.

When we weren't at the movies, my bad girl friends found other ways to take me from my studies. Since we had school every weekday and half a day on Saturday, we found fun Saturday afternoon and on Sundays. No one had a TV and only a few of my friends had radios, so we learned to enjoy activities that didn't require money. Hiking, visiting temples on the outskirts of town, and lounging around at each other's houses. We never talked about specific boys, but we were obsessed with them. Boys our age hung out at a nearby mountain park, and we sometimes went there to scope them out. Though they were too far away for us to see their faces, we lay in the grass each afternoon just to glimpse them from a distance.

One day, an older neighbor boy bravely came up to us and asked me about my little sister, Sunhee.

"You're too old for my sister, and she's too pretty for you!" I snarled at him, scaring him away. I came home that afternoon from the park to find my parents pacing beside the gate. My mother bit her nails, and my father scratched the dry skin on the back of his neck, gestures that surfaced only when they were angry.

"You whore!" my father yelled when I stepped into the yard. "What were you thinking? How dare you throw manure on our face? You've shamed us!" He pulled back his hand and slapped me across the cheek. He'd never hit me while he was sober before, and I had no idea what'd prompted this.

"I raised you better than this," my mama spat. "How will we hold our heads up on the street?"

"I didn't do anything," I protested. I pressed my hand to my cheek. Tears filled my eyes as I fell back against the wall. "I don't even know what you're talking about."

I tried to defend myself, but my parents ignored my pleas. In my dad's eyes, I was already a whore. It infuriated me that my father, who'd gambled away our family land, had questioned my integrity. I ran to the back of the house and cried into a pile of blankets.

"Why do you believe that liar?" I shouted, after I found out that the boy I'd insulted in front of my friends had told my mama and dad that he'd seen me kissing a boy in the park. My hate boiled over. My father had never once praised me for doing well in school. Every day I woke up at two a.m. on my own to wash my face with cold water, study for two to three hours, fall back asleep for an hour, eat breakfast, and head to school early to study some more before class began. He'd never acknowledged how hard I worked on the farm or how I protected my brothers and sisters. I'd been more of a father to them than he ever had.

My mama didn't defend my innocence either. I'd followed behind her, planting beans, working the rice paddy in my father's place, hauling buckets of water, and mopping the floor. I'd saved her life after she ate rat poison and never told a soul she had done it. Once, I picked pears for hours for a fruit farmer just to have a few to take to her so she could enjoy their sweetness. Her choice to believe someone else's words over mine was unacceptable. I knew then that she was never going to reward me for being a good daughter. I was merely someone for her to use. My body heaved with disappointment.

In the past, when I'd dreamt of running away, I'd always placed her in the center of my plans, scheming to one day make enough money in America that I could shower her with pretty clothes and a new house so she'd never have to work again. I'd shouldered the burden of her pain and suffering for as long as I could remember. I would've died for my mama, and she had betrayed me. I swore to myself that I was through trying to be good.

I cried until I fell asleep, and my parents didn't wake me for dinner. When I finally stirred from my heartbroken slumber, it was the middle of the night. The house had settled down from the afternoon's accusations. I picked up *War and Peace* from its place beside my bed and marched over to the neighbor's house. A cute boy, Heechang, lived there, and he had lent me the book. I planned to return it to him and give him something in exchange. I would make my parent's judgment official. I would become a whore.

Just as I was about to knock on Heechang's door, a girl's voice echoed from inside. Girls were forbidden to be alone with a boy who wasn't a relative, and Heechang didn't have any female relatives. At least, I didn't know of any. I paused on the path outside his house. Though Heechang felt like an older brother to me, I didn't actually know much about him. He was two years older than I, with a strong build and a handsome face. He had a black belt in Taekwondo and luscious long eyelashes. I walked with him often in the summer and during winter breaks. My mama had told me to because, according to her, he was a genius in math and could teach me good study habits. Despite all the times we'd walked together, I knew hardly anything about his personal life.

When Heechang and I walked to his school, we had to act

as if we were walking as part of a group because the school board wouldn't let a girl talk to a boy. Even if we had been allowed to talk, I was too shy to make eye contact. While I had had no trouble yelling at boys who were bullying me or my siblings on the farm, I was completely unable to talk to any boy who wanted to be my friend. Heechang's duty, agreed upon between him and my mama, was to make sure I learned proper study skills. I was scared to death when he invited me to a donut shop before we walked home one day. The entire time, I looked around for spies who might report me to the school. When he asked me a second time, I told him my mama wouldn't let me. I'd enjoyed talking to him, but the risk he posed to my *education* was too great.

Now, I stood outside Heechang's house, wondering if he had a girlfriend. My anger toward my parents had pushed aside my devotion to my *education*. I hid around the side of the house so the girl wouldn't see me when she left and get suspicious. I felt glad he had a girlfriend. Then he'd know how to take away my virginity. My revenge would be sweeter knowing my mama had introduced me to the boy who would take away my honor.

After a tired looking girl left Heechang's house, I softly knocked on his door, and when he opened it, he looked at me in surprise. Apparently, he had expected to see the other girl.

"I finished your book," I said, holding out *War and Peace*. "Thank you for lending it to me."

"Isn't it about twelve-hundred pages?" he asked, looking me straight in the eyes. "You read it in three days?"

"I love Tolstoy," I lied. "It was better than *Anna Karenina*."

The expression on his face told me he didn't believe me; he wanted a straight answer. The shy girl, who had hardly been able to look into his eyes during all the time he had known me, now stood on his doorstep in the dark, looking at his eyeballs. He found my actions strange.

"What's wrong? Why are you here so late at night?" he asked like an older brother. And, indeed, since he was two years older than me, I called him *Oppa*, the word girls used for older boys. The warmth in his voice burst my heart wide open, and when

I saw the worry in his eyes through my lashes, I started to cry.

"Come here," he said. "Tell me what happened."

He wanted to hug me, but I could tell he was afraid to touch me. He had considered me his little sister all the times he had escorted me to study, acting with utmost respect out of deference to my mama. He'd never made a move on me, and I would've refused to walk with him had he made me the tiniest bit uncomfortable. He put his hand on my shoulder, which shook with sobs. Any other time I would've jumped away and run to the other side of the room, but that evening, I clutched his arm. I did not want to go home.

"I want to sleep with you," I said. "I want you to touch me everywhere."

"What are you saying?" he said. "You can't come in here like this."

"Wasn't that your girlfriend who just left?" I asked. "Why did you let her in your room and not me? What's wrong with me?"

"What are you saying?" he asked. Every word that came out of my mouth shocked him. "You can't stay here, Jeanhee! You don't know what you're asking."

"Okay," I said, "Then I'll sleep outside your room. You can trip over me in the morning when you leave. I'm not going home."

"I should take you to your mama right now so she can lock you up. I'll be in so much trouble if you stay."

"I won't tell her. I promise!"

He stepped back from the door, and I stepped forward. He pulled a blanket out of a closet and arranged it on the floor to make me a bed. He waited until I tucked myself in to turn out the light. Soon, the dark room became chilly. He lay next to me under his own blanket, wrapped around him tightly as a barrier against me. I kept squirming toward him, hoping he would have a change of heart and give me what I wanted.

The darkness made me brave, and I asked him again, "Please touch me. I don't want to be a virgin anymore. No one will know, *Oppa.*"

My desire was too much for him. He took me in his arms and touched his lips to mine. I could feel the pulse of his heart through our shirts. When he slipped off my panties, I stiffened.

"Are you okay?" Heechang asked.

I told him I was. I had to do this. I would be the whore my father had called me. He would be sorry.

Snug against Heechang's body, I was no longer cold. After a brief flash of pain between my legs, my body relaxed. No one had ever touched me in that place before. The closest anyone had come was the monster man who'd groped me on the bus, and this felt different. I wasn't scared at all. Being close to someone felt wonderful. I was happy I'd gotten back at my parents.

From that night on, Heechang was my universe. He ended it with the girl I'd seen leaving his house. She came back several times, and I knew from her tears that he'd taken her virginity, too. I told him not to talk to her or open the door. I wanted to be near him every moment. He filled the void of affection and love I'd always felt. I was merciless in my possession of him. I'd found someone I could love who loved me back. And worse yet, I liked what we did in the dark.

For a while, I was happier than I'd ever been, but the situation quickly became more than I'd bargained for. I struggled to act normal in front of my parents and to face my friends, who became suspicious when I kept smiling for no reason. I wasn't spending as much time with them as I usually did, and I refused to tell them why. I was filled with such a strange mixture of elation and shame that I didn't even tell Oksoon at first.

The guilt weighed heavily on me. One day in science class, the teacher started the lecture by saying to all eighty-three of us, "I know which ones of you are not virgins just by looking at you. Shame on you!"

I wanted to die right there. I was certain he was speaking to me, and I sweat with shame the entire fifty minutes of the lecture. When the teacher finally left the classroom without calling me out, I almost peed my pants.

But while the science teacher was quick to condemn us, none of the teachers bothered to teach us about our bodies. When I saw a small, bloody stain on my underwear at school one day, I panicked. The first time blood had spilled from between my legs was when I'd lost my virginity. I'd thrown that underwear away, fearing my mama would discover what I'd done, but this time I was at school, and Heechang was nowhere nearby. None of the other girls had mentioned anything like that happening to them. We never talked about our bodies to each other. I spent all day worrying about how to tell my mama about the blood. I was sure it was because I'd had sex. When she saw that rusty, damning spot, she'd throw me into the street. I'd be ashamed and defiled, my future in America lost for good.

When I pulled my panties off that night, I mixed them in with the other dirty clothes, hoping she wouldn't notice. I stayed up all night, planning to confess what I'd done with Heechang, to repent and face the consequences. In the morning, I was surprised when my mama was kind and gentle.

She softly pushed my hair from my eyes and said, "This is an important day. You're a woman now. You'll bleed once a month about the same time every month. It's something we all must bear." She handed me a clean, white cloth to fold into my underwear.

When my period stopped coming each month, I grew concerned that I was sick. I pretended to use the cloth my mama gave me, not wanting to worry her that something was wrong with me. Only after reading a book about pregnancy did I learn I had a baby growing inside me. My mother had never told me this could happen, and I was mortified. I went to school for a month, hiding my secret, but the shame was unbearable, and one day I cried uncontrollably in front of the only person who knew I was seeing Heechang.

Oksoon!

She tried to comfort me, but when I let her feel my tummy that was now hard as a rock and bulging slightly, she cried, too.

"What should I do?" I asked.

Oksoon had older sisters and knew more about life. She dried her eyes and squared her shoulders. "I'll ask my sister tonight," she said. "She'll know."

The next day Oksoon pawned the gold ring her mother had

given her for her birthday. We skipped school, and she took me to the abortion clinic. I'd never been to a hospital before, and the sterile tables and surgical equipment frightened me. As I lay naked on the table, covered only by a thick cotton sheet, mortified by my blown up stomach, I cried. Then the doctor and a nurse came in, and the doctor examined me. He not only looked at my swollen belly, but also wanted to see my vagina under the hot, bright light.

He said, "Open your legs wide."

I didn't want to but I did, and he touched my private parts. A tingle from the bottom of my feet shot to the top of my head.

"You waited too long," the doctor scolded. "You should've come in sooner."

The attendants took me to a back room and sedated me, so I'd stop shaking. Then they started the procedure. Seconds later, a hot pain shot into my groin and down my legs, as if someone were twisting my guts into figure eights. I cried the entire time, both from the pain and from the embarrassment of lying exposed before two strangers. When it was over, Oksoon wouldn't look at me.

"What's wrong?" I asked, angry she hadn't asked me the same question.

"I told. I called your mama. I heard you crying and thought you were going to die."

"Oksoon!" I was weak but angry. "My mama is the last person I want to see. You broke your promise."

"I didn't know what to do. Your mama's not mad."

I didn't believe Oksoon for a second. I knew my mama would kill me. She and my dad had been livid over the mere possibility that I'd kissed a boy.

Oksoon left to go to school. She needed to make up an excuse for why she'd missed class. "Take care," she said, patting my arm.

Drowning with shame, I didn't even respond. If only I'd known that her hand on my arm would be the last gesture we'd ever share, I would've acted differently. Her family would never let us visit each other again. Even when I went back to Korea years later, her mother wouldn't give me her address. They didn't want her tainted by my shame. I was ruined in their eyes.

I lay in the hospital bed wondering how I could ever be normal after this. I'd have to explain my absence to the school board and act as though nothing had happened. When my mama finally walked into my room, her face was a quiet mask.

"We can deal with this," she said. "Let's go home." She helped me into my clothes and held my arm during the long walk home. Every step sent needles of pain through my abdomen. Tears dripped down my face and she didn't say a word.

Her cold treatment confused me. Was I such a disappointment that I'd pushed her beyond anger? Perhaps she was only pretending to be calm, afraid her anger would drive me to suicide.

By the time the pain from my abortion lessened, I'd already missed three days of school. The school board confronted my mama and demanded the reason for my absence. Except for serious illness or a death in the family, missing class was not tolerated, and the principal told her they would let me know if I could return to my studies. All I could think of was that girl in the courtyard, kneeling in the ice, crying. I'd surely behaved worse than her.

I waited days for word from the school. Every time the phone rang, I jumped. When I picked up the phone on the tenth day and Oksoon's sweet voice met my ears, my heart sped up with joy. I'd been so terribly lonely.

"Jeanhee," she said, crying. "I can't see you anymore. The school board and my parents have forbidden it. I'd get in trouble if they even knew I was calling you. I'm so sorry. I miss you more than anything. Your name is on the school's center bulletin board. It says, *Expelled: Kang Jeanhee*. You're the entire school's gossip."

I sank to the floor. My heart shattered inside me. I'd been getting hopeful, putting Heechang and the abortion behind me, determined to be a good girl and start fresh. Oksoon told me that either Heechang's old girlfriend or Jungsil, she wasn't sure which, had reported to the school board that I occasionally spent nights in his room. I was ruined. After I put down the phone, I cried harder than I'd ever cried in my life. My heart ached so much I wanted to die.

Later that day, I prostrated myself before my mother, vowing never to see Heechang again. "He is nothing to me, Mama. I'm so sorry. I want to change. I want to go back to my studies. I want to be Jeanhee again. Help me." I begged wildly, my mind unhinged by fear and sadness. I'd thrown away my dreams to get back at my parents.

My mother shook her head and walked away. I knew neither sympathy nor comfort for my breaking heart would come from her. I had fallen. I had destroyed my own destiny, and my parents, my school, and my entire culture had given up on me.

After a few weeks, I forced myself to stop dwelling on the past. When Heechang sent me a note through my little brother Younghee to find out what had happened and demanded to meet with me, I threw it away and refused to see him. The soreness in my chest didn't lessen, but I forced myself to think of the future.

"Those people who gave up on me have something else coming," I told myself. "I'll show them. I'm worth being loved and forgiven. I deserve a second chance."

I tried to believe these words but found it difficult when I was the one both preaching and receiving the sermon. My life had truly crumbled. I would never find a decent man to marry, nor would I graduate high school. My culture wouldn't forgive my transgressions.

When the self-pep talks didn't work, I shaved my head. As my hair dropped to the floor in row after row, so too did my past mistakes fall from my life. I found the gesture oddly freeing. It separated me from my broken heart. I thought about going away somewhere deep in the forest to live as a monk, but I knew I would not qualify because of my impurity.

As the dark fuzz on my scalp grew back in spikes, my *run away* plans took shape. The memory of the Hershey bar on my tongue hadn't left me. The abortion I could at least hide, but being expelled from high school had stripped me of my childhood dream of getting an *education* to help me have a better life like the dam keeper.

Still, I refused to throw away my childhood dream. As my

heart slowly mended, I conceived of new ways for my *run away* plan to succeed. I'd fallen, but I wouldn't stay down forever. If anything, I had become even more determined.

Chapter Four

The Youngest Whore in the Lucky Club

After I shaved my head, my own mother didn't recognize me. The silky black hair that belonged to her eldest daughter was gone, and my skull was now covered in dark fuzz. When she saw my shaven head, my feathery dome became another reminder that she had a bold, independent daughter, and that was a devastating blow to her as a parent. She hadn't raised me right. Something had gone terribly wrong since I hadn't turned out to be obedient and docile like her friends' children, who would never dream of degrading their families' reputations in such a way. She was so embarrassed she immediately bought me a wig, one cut in a school girl hair style—shiny, straight, angled one inch below the ears. Even the wig couldn't conceal my dishonor, however. I was still the subject of neighborhood gossip. Even so, the wig was a small, if inadequate, consolation to her, and I felt obligated to do anything she wanted as repentance for my transgressions. Even though only a blind person wouldn't have been able to tell it was not my real hair, I wore that hot, itchy wig for her. And even a blind person would have known I was passing them on the street because my steps were heavy from the weight of my guilt and sorrow.

My brothers and sisters knew I had lost my virginity to Heechang, and they naturally concluded that this was the reason for my expulsion. I let them keep their misconceptions. My mother never mentioned my abortion to anyone, not even to me after it happened, and the mere fact of it, marked by scars on my stomach, was enough shame. I didn't want the additional judgment of my siblings. Whenever they tried to talk to me, I hid upstairs and shouted for them to go away. I'm sure they wondered where the loving big sister who had protected and cared for them had gone. The hardest part for me was seeing them leave for school each morning in their starched uniforms. Their school was much less prestigious than Namsung, but whereas before I wouldn't have been caught dead in anything other than my own uniform, a mark of my intelligence and hard work, now I longed to join them, to have been able to wake up, all my transgressions forgotten and my mistakes wiped out, to start fresh and smile again like Woojung taught me, and graduate with my friends.

Despite how much I resented the unfairness, I shoved my uniforms, school shoes, books, notes, pencils, and even my English textbooks into a battered old book bag and resigned myself to my fate. I slipped my name badge into the front pocket of the bag and zipped it shut, sealing away all the symbols of my hard work. My *education*.

I didn't want any further reminders of my sorrow, but I had nothing to distract me. We didn't have TV or radio, and our rooms at the back of the hotel were very quiet. When I tried to read the novels that used to entertain and comfort me, the words swam on the page and slipped out of my mind quickly. I couldn't care about made-up peoples' lives when my own real life was ruined. I spent my days alone and crying, wishing I could get a second chance to complete my *education*.

Sometimes I helped my mother check in guests or answer phones when she was short staffed, usually in the morning when customers wanted to check out in hurry, but she only allowed me to do so if I wore that hateful wig. I told her once that I wanted to be a monk, to leave this life behind and bury myself in a peaceful life of prayer and solitude, hiding in a temple forever. I quickly gave up that thought, though, because I had never seen a female monk, and even if there were any, they were probably all virgins. Besides, I wasn't a Buddhist, and I didn't have the first idea of how to become one.

While I struggled with how I had singlehandedly destroyed my own future, I prayed. I prayed to Buddha, my ancestors, and my dead grandmother, every living thing and dead relative, Jesus, and any other deity I could think of. I pledged to make straight A's, to help my mama without complaint, even to try to like my father—though I promised that with such repulsed reluctance that my ancestors would never have believed I was sincere.

In my heart, I wasn't so ashamed of losing my virginity—I could always scream on my wedding night and pretend to be pure if I ever decided I wanted to get married. And while I'd never be able to explain away the abortion scars and stretch marks on my lower stomach and my husband wouldn't see them until my wedding night, by then he couldn't do much about it. He would be stuck with me.

What broke my heart was that my chance for an *education* was gone. I remembered that hot day in the field when I was five-years-old, begging my mama to send me to school so I could make something of my life. I knew now I would never be like the dam keeper. I wasn't even going to be like my mother, who at least was respectable. Instead, I could either become a prostitute, a servant, or some man's second wife, one who had no place in the family book and whose children would forever be known as bastards. And when that man was gone, I would once again be left to support myself— except I would be older and more worn down, and life would be even harder than before. My prayers began with hope, but always concluded with me denouncing Koreans and their restrictive, harsh culture that didn't allow young girls to make mistakes. I was never going to get a second chance. Not here.

Shaving my head wasn't only a badge of shame; it soon became a new beginning. I finally decided the time had come for me to push away the weight of my mistakes and move on. As my hair grew to be about two centimeters long, I yearned to begin my new life and leave my bad memories behind forever.

This was hard to do in our enclosed space at the back of the hotel. My mama cried every time she saw me. She blamed herself for my failure. And when she cried, I joined her, hating that I had broken her heart along with my own. She cried for my shame, and I cried for her pain.

"Jeanhee Ya," she wailed at me one day, "has your grandmother come back to punish me again? What did I do to anger her? I pray to her and offer her all of her favorite dishes— and yet she still cannot let me be." Only in her most distraught moments did she ask if I was following my dead grandmother's wish to revenge her.

"Mama," I said with a sigh. "Grandmother isn't doing this. It's me. I made the mistake, and I made it all on my own."

"Jeanhee Ya, you must promise me your grandmother's spirit isn't making you such a bad girl! I should have hired a witch to get your grandmother's ghost off your back a long time ago."

"Mama," I'd sob. "If you call a witch, I will be out the door and will never come back home. There's nothing wrong with me." I yelled.

I must have had something in my voice that told my mama I would follow through on my threat because she never threatened to call a witch again. However, my protest didn't cause her to cry any less. My choices were bleak. I could either run away from my shameful past or kill myself. Choosing suicide after bringing deep shame to one's family was a well-known practice then, and given the magnitude of my crime, it might have even been accepted. People would have grieved for me, but some would've thought I'd made the right choice.

My parents did not give me any more alternatives than society did. My mama couldn't have gotten out any advice had she tried because every time she saw me she burst into tears.

"*Algo!*" she would cry, her expression of regret and failure ringing in my ears as I dashed back into hiding so she wouldn't have to look at me anymore. My dad, for once in his life, held his tongue, though at times I could tell he was biting down on his lips to keep from saying something derogatory. Despite the pall of shame I had brought upon the family, he didn't want my suicide on his conscience. Whenever we were in the same room, he turned his face away from me and refuse to look at me. I was surprised that with all he had done to me, his simple gesture still hurt.

Still, the more my mother fell into hopelessness, the more I realized I could heal. I knew I would never be able to find a single school in Korea that would let me through its doors. Even the lowest ranked would turn me away, no matter my previous academic performance. I might as well have had a criminal record. Because I'd been expelled, I carried with me a shame that darkened my path on even the sunniest days.

Only, I refused to die as a high school dropout.

My thoughts ran rampant. What if I really did run away? What if I went away from Korea forever? No one here would miss me; they would be glad to have one less bad girl to pollute their perfect world. I would leave and go to a place where no one would question my past.

What if I went to America? No one there knew my shame. I would find a way to get there, and I would finish high school in English, putting the words together like a puzzle to make sentences, and sentences into paragraphs, and paragraphs into a new life. I would spend hours every day in the library. After all, I had been trained to wake up early and study alone. How hard could it be to learn? And it would be even easier if I was there, immersed in it— my favorite English teacher had once said as much to me.

*****

I knew my time for escape had come when we received a funeral invitation from a distant relative. Of course, my mama would attend the funeral, and she would be gone for at least a two-hour window, leaving me plenty of time alone. I grew nervous and excited as the date crept nearer, and when the hour finally came, I followed her outside into the street until the crowds swallowed her up, her thin body walking briskly away from me. When I was sure she wouldn't turn around, perhaps from having forgotten something to take with her, I went into the hotel to steal money for train fare, food, and a suitcase. I walked fast to the open air market and bought the cheapest suitcase I could find, then hurried back home to pack. After I had finished, I told my mama's workers I had stolen Yi-Man-Won from the register so I could *run away.*

Then I said, "Will you tell her not to worry about me, and that I will be back once I have made a success of my life? And that I will pay back the money I stole after I become rich?"

As my eyes welled up and my last sorrowful tears dropped at my feet and I endured the last cry of my sad, unforgiving life at home in front of our employees, one of them helplessly asked, "Do you have to go?"

I didn't answer, and apparently they saw my pain and determination and knew in their hearts I had to leave.

"Take care of yourself, Jeanhee Ya," one of the house cleaners whispered in my ear. "Don't trust anyone, and don't let anyone trick you into doing something you don't want to do or into giving them money."

She tucked 1000 won into my pocket, the equivalent of one dollar in American currency, and gave me an even rarer gesture of affection. A hug. "You buy food with this money when you get hungry. I know how much you can eat!"

After I said goodbye, I picked up the bag that summed up my whole life and took one last look at my home, knowing I could never come back, that I would never again be a part of my family. I could never be a normal sister and attend any of my siblings' weddings or graduations, and I could never celebrate holidays with them. I was unwanted.

The train station was only about a five minute walk from the hotel. Once I reached it, I walked up to ticket window and purchased one ticket. The whole time, I feared my mama would appear behind me, grab my neck, and take me back home.

The half hour wait for a train to Seoul seemed to last a lifetime.

Had wishful thinking caused me to imagine my mama coming to take me back home? If she did, I would cry because she'd saved me from going where I was headed. But then what? She would probably be nice and sweet to me for a couple of days, and then we would be right back where we had started, back to my dreaming about *running away*.

After considerable thought, I decided I didn't need to hurt my mother twice. I would just go away forever on my first try.

I finally got on a train to Seoul, our nation's capital that was four and a half hours away. I held my small suitcase tightly as I boarded and found a seat away from other people. Still, a man across the train car kept staring at me and my suitcase. I focused my eyes on the ground and tried not to draw attention to myself.

"Are you running away?" he finally asked me.

"Yes, I am," I answered, lifting my chin proudly. "And it's no business of yours."

He had no doubt expected me to lie, but my bold answer and the confident tone in my voice showed both him and me that I would no longer be ashamed. I had faced the worst, and a stranger's judgment on a train meant nothing to me.

Flustered, he asked, "Where are you going? Where is your mother?"

"I've already said that is none of your business, mister." I turned my face toward the window and refused to look at him again.

No one else bothered me. When I got off the train, I planned to surprise my first cousin Youngcha, the daughter of my dad's stepbrother, who lived with an American in Itawon, part of Seoul, the largest American Army base in Korea. I had met her only two or three times over the years, on holidays, but I remembered she was very tall and slender, with sleek black hair down to her tailbone. She also smoked and cursed and acted however she wanted, the exact opposite of how a Korean woman should. She had started out as a prostitute but had been pretty and clever enough for one of her customers to want her exclusively for his own. Now she was being kept by an American GI. Everyone at home knew she was a prostitute, but I'm sure some members of my family secretly envied her, even as they denounced her lifestyle.

I was excited not only to learn her secrets about catching a GI, but also about living in Seoul—it was the biggest city in Korea—and no one there would know of my past. No one would whisper as I walked down the street or refuse to look me in the eye, and I wouldn't feel my heart break every time I saw a Namsung uniform or passed an old friend who held up her chin and walked by me as though I were invisible. I could finally throw out my wig and act like a woman.

I wandered through the busy streets of Seoul, and my feet felt as if they had wings. Strangers bustled by, bumping into me as they pulled along their children or argued with their friends, their arms full of groceries. The tall apartment buildings, the street kiosks full of pushy vendors, the aggressive, busy crowds—all of it exhilarated me. And no one cared about me at all—which was exactly how I wanted it.

When I finally found Youngcha's house, I stopped and stared. Surely, she didn't live in this beautiful two-story house all alone. It was brick, built American style, with a black-shingled roof. A thick concrete wall topped by fierce-looking barbed wire circled the property, scaring off any thieves.

When I'd gotten over my surprise at her extravagance, I pounded on the metal gate that led into the yard, my heart racing. I hoped she was home so I wouldn't have to sit on the curb and wait. When she opened the door, she raised her brows, squinted her eyes, and stepped toward me, her gaze on my face.

"Hello Sister, it's Jeanhee, your cousin," I blurted, wanting to get out my introduction quickly in case she didn't recognize me and shut the door. "I've run away. And I need to stay with you for a little while—I want to learn how to meet an American GI. I want to go to America."

Youngcha was taller than I remembered—at least 5'9"— and still very pretty, though she looked a little sunken around the eyes. I would later see that she had dark spots on her face that she covered with make-up, and she never smiled—she just observed. I could tell, somehow, despite her fancy clothes and home, that her life had been a harsh one. Perhaps, she recognized the signs in my face, as well. Like me, she had been a runaway teenager.

"Jeanhee Ya," she said with a sigh, "what did you do?"

She stepped back to let me in, half reluctantly. She was not so far removed from her Korean roots that she would refuse to take in a family member.

I stepped into the house, my eyes wide as I took in an entire wall of bookshelves, a mahogany umbrella stand, and a black lacquer table.

"Do you live here all alone?" I asked. "What do you do with all these rooms?"

She laughed. "These aren't mine. I rent the upper floor from a Korean couple—come with me. I don't think they'll mind you stay for a while. They probably won't even notice you're here."

Youngcha's home was beautiful. In those days, anyone who could afford to rent such a place in Seoul had to be rich, so I knew her American GI must make a lot of money. As I later found out, he was a doctor, a truly exceptional catch even among GIs. I found it easy to get used to a life with indoor plumbing, an actual bed, and a refrigerator filled with meat and food and delicious drinks. I drank Coca Cola every day, and while it wasn't as good as the Hershey bar I'd been given so many years before, drinking from those glass bottles still felt decadent. Taking a hot shower and having my own tiny room off of the kitchen was also a novelty. The size of the place was big enough for my entire family though Youngcha often had it all to herself.

I fit into Youngcha's life easily and tried to be as little trouble as possible so she wouldn't send me home before I was ready to leave. I also made sure I went to bed early since I felt as if I was intruding on her time with her handsome GI, but I was never brave enough to talk to him. He was blonde with blue eyes, and he was very kind to me. I wanted desperately to say something to him in English, but my mouth seemed to go numb whenever I tried even the simplest words: hello, goodbye, good morning. No matter how carefully I listened, I couldn't make out a single word that spilled from his mouth. He spoke fast, his phrases and sentences tumbling one on top of the other until it was impossible for me to pick out even a single word.

Youngcha was a good hostess, perhaps in part because she didn't want to face my mother's anger if she didn't take good care of me. She always made sure I had enough food to eat and taught me what not to touch, such as the record player, a machine I had never before seen or even imagined. After she got over her fear that I would tell my family she was living as a kept woman, she became prideful, hoping I would let everyone know she had obtained wealth beyond what any of them could ever hope to achieve.

Youngcha didn't work, and her days were free. During the week, she either shopped or her friends came over, and they gambled, smoked, and ate the afternoon away. Weekends were her time with her GI. They went out while I stayed home alone. Youngcha really did look like a model—she had a sensuous, rhythmic walk that left men staring as she strolled down the street, and she had a closet full of beautiful, expensive clothes that all fit her perfectly. She also had more shoes and jewelry than I imagined one woman could wear in an entire lifetime. She kept her nails long and pretty, as only fallen women did. Her soft, pale hands did not tell the same stories as my own, of hard work in a rice paddy. And she held her cigarettes in the casual, glamorous way American movie stars did. On date nights, she was truly stunning—her lashes coated with black mascara, her red lips pouty with lipstick—and I could see why her doctor GI paid so much to keep her. She belonged in that beautiful home, in a beautiful life.

Every day, she asked me, "Jeanhee Ya, when are you going home? Your mother misses you. She calls me every day crying.

You can't stay here and drink my Coca Cola forever."

"Soon," I answered. "I'll go home soon. I just need a few more days. You understand how hard it is there, don't you?"

She would frown, and say, "Yes, I know. I know it's hard. In a few years, you can find a GI. Right now, you're too young. Go be with your mother."

She believed my story that I intended to return home and even gave me extra spending money for being a good girl. What she didn't realize was that I was using her as a stopover on my way to the Air Force base in Osan, about two hours away. According to her, that's where the educated GIs lived.

My cousin quickly tired of getting daily calls from my mother, and I knew I would have to leave on my own before Youngcha put me on the train herself. I made the most of my time, asking her ten thousand questions about GI bases, English grammar, anything I could think of that would help me get to first Osan and then to America. I didn't write her answers down; I didn't want her to get suspicious about my plans. Instead, I kept them in my head and repeated them to myself as I lay in bed at night. After a few weeks, I'd gathered enough information about where to go and how to meet a GI. I told Youngcha I was leaving, and she seemed relieved.

"You're always welcome here, but this is better. You need to be with your mama. She misses you. Here," she dug into her bag, her perfect nails clinking against tubes of lipstick, and pulled out some money. "Take this for your bus fare. And some extra— for whatever you want. Do you need me to take you to the bus station?"

"No," I said. "I can find it. It is too far for you to go. Your GI will be home soon, and I don't want you to miss him."

"Are you sure?" she said, reluctance in her voice.

I nodded. "Yes, sister. Thank you for letting me stay."

I bowed to her and headed out to get a taxi to the bus station. Taxi driving through Itawon traffic to the main bus station in Yongsan scared me. I looked for a seatbelt to tie me, but it was nowhere to be found. So instead, I clutched the edge of the seat with my right hand while holding onto my purse with my left. The taxi driver zipped through the zigzag city and dropped me off at the corner of the bus station. I was so glad to be out of that crazy cab. He had gone so fast I almost forgot my worries about what I might face in Osan.

On the road to a place I had never been, I knew that once I got there, I would never be the same. I could never go back home, ever. I had dreamt of many things in my short life, but I had never imagined I would someday be one of thousands of hopeless, fallen Korean women making a similar trip, the only solution for their failure as good Korean women. I was just like the rest of them; I had failed to keep my virginity for my wedding night. I had given it away instead of waiting to reward my husband with his prized possession: Me. Little did I know that I was done with Korean men, too. Heechang was the first and last Korean man for me. They had given up on me, and so I gave up on them.

I had no regrets or guilt as I rode the bus over the bumpy dirt road, past the busy markets on the outskirts of Seoul to the small city of Osan. During the two-hour ride, I pulled off my wig and combed my fingers through my fierce spikes, now nearly an inch long. I can do this, I told myself, scheming how I would protect myself from pimps, Mama Sang, and prostitution.

I was determined to get out of Korea, and a ticket was waiting on me. I couldn't wait to get to Osan to meet the GI who would take me out of the country forever. I pictured my American high school, with tall metal doors and big open windows. The bookshelves there would be filled with thick English textbooks and brand new notebooks for practicing my writing. Garbed in a silky black robe, I would receive my diploma, my name scripted in black ink, in English, as Jeanhee Kang.

Before the bus arrived in Osan, I planned the letter I would write my mother bragging about how well I was doing and how my past didn't matter in America. I would send her packages filled with chocolates and Coca Cola, gifts for my siblings that tasted as sweet as the life I would have. Just before arriving in Osan, I chunked the sweaty wig into a bathroom trashcan at a rest stop.

The soft *thunk* as it hit the bottom, resting on the other trash, was one of the most satisfying sounds I'd ever heard in my young life.

I stepped off the bus in Osan on a sunny afternoon in April of 1974. The air was still cool and full of promise. The streets were busy but much less so than Seoul, fewer people bumping into each other as they passed by. Tall women in go-go boots and short skirts strutted down the sidewalks, and handsome GIs at street side cafés watched their swishing skirts until they disappeared around the corner. Older women called from their shops, yelling out, "Sister, I have just the blouse for you," and men in tie dye shirts and ripped jeans slapped five, their eyes bloodshot and tired. People who glanced my way gave me second looks but not because I was seductive like Youngcha. I could tell they didn't know what to make of my youthful face and unusually short, spiky black hair.

I had barely stepped foot outside the bus station when pimps started trying to pick me up. Men's voices bombarded me from all sides as I walked.

"Do you need a place to stay?"

"Little girl!"

"I got a high-paying job for you, girl, come with me."

I looked each one up and down and told them I was waiting for my sister. I wasn't going to go with just any pimp—most of them had mean, tight mouths that made me afraid of what they might do to me before I reached the brothel.

I had my eye on a stylish man with slicked back hair and a tailored suede vest when a smooth, low voice rumbled from behind me, "You need help with that bag? It looks heavy."

My suitcase wasn't heavy at all, but it seemed so when someone was ready and willing to carry it for me. I turned to look at the man. He smiled, showing one gold tooth in front. He wore a button up shirt and jeans, and unlike the other pimps who'd already spoken to me, he looked like an average Korean guy. He was about 5'4" and skinny, and he seemed kind. I gauged him to see if I could take him if he tried to violate me before he sold me.

I handed him my bag.

"I could use some lunch, too," I said, trying to act innocent.

I wanted him to think I was a fresh young flower with no knowledge of the world. He'd be eager to take me to a brothel if he thought I was a virgin and worth more than the experienced whore. Besides, I didn't want to spend the money Youngcha had given me if I could get a free meal first.

"What do you want to eat, little girl?" he asked. "My treat. I can always use pretty company at a meal. I'm Jinsoo."

"Toasted seaweed," I said. "And a big bowl of rice, please."

I didn't buy his comment about me being pretty—I knew I wasn't. While I was much improved from childhood and no longer crawling with lice, I was still no Youngcha. I followed him to a nearby restaurant and sat across from him at a table, ordering two lunches, soybean-kimchi soup with stirred fried squid, and washing it down with barley tea. When I was done, I wiped my mouth with my arm and sat back.

Jinsoo smiled his greasy smile again. "Were you starving, little girl?" he asked. "I know grown men who can't eat that much. Or that fast."

"I haven't eaten in days," I said, not wanting to explain that I had been hungry since the day I was born and always ate huge portions. "I probably would have fainted soon. Thank you for the meal, mister."

"If you can't afford food, then where will you stay?" His brow furrowed in what I could tell was false concern. "If you need a room, I can take you to Mama Sang. She'll buy you pretty dresses, and feed you, and give you spending money. You'll be like a daughter to her. Any friend of mine is a friend of hers."

"Really?" I answered. I gave him a smile just as fake as his own. "She must be a very nice lady to take in strangers. Do you think she will like me?"

Of course she will," he said. "She loves girls from the country. Where are you from?"

"Junjoo city," I said. I didn't want to tell him I was from Iri.

He paid the bill, stood, and picked up my suitcase again. "She's busy this afternoon," he said, "but you can stay in a hotel until tomorrow, and I'll take you to her then."

He was trying to pull a trick to get me to have sex with him—my cousin had warned me about that. But he was right. I needed a place to stay, and he was my best option.

I followed him down the road, passing through a busy marketplace and turning down several twisting streets until we reached a run-down old hotel, one that only a local could find. An old lady called him by name, and I decided he must bring all his aspiring whores here before taking them to Mama Sang. The room he rented was small, with peeling flowered wallpaper and cotton blankets and a pillow folded up in the corner.

He pulled out a cotton blanket and made the bed. "Come on over here," he said. "Be a good girl and repay me for that meal before I bring Mama Sang to see you."

"No." I shook my head. I stood in the corner away from him, ready to run if I needed to. He may have been used to trying out the new girls, but I was not just any new girl. "I'm fine over here, thank you."

His face hardened. He marched over to me, gripped my arm in annoyance, and dragged me over to the bed. I pulled back, no match for his strength. He pushed down on my shoulders, forcing me onto him. My heart beat quickly and I collapsed backwards, my back against the drooping blanket.

"No!" I yelled again. He pressed his chest against mine. Time to drop the innocent act. I spoke to him in a voice barely louder than a whisper. "I know you're taking me to a brothel, and that's fine. But you won't be able to sell me as a virgin if you have me first—and you'll get more money if I'm pure. And I will tell Mama Sang if you touch me."

"You're crazy. How do you know any of that?" He stopped, his face just inches above mine. He had specks of rice caught on either side of his gold tooth. I inhaled his nasty garlic breath and prepared to push him away and run, but to my surprise, he rolled over.

"You win," he said. "I won't touch you. But you'd better not run away. I have eyes all over this city. I'll find you, and you'll be sorry. I'll be back at ten o'clock tomorrow to take you to Mama

Sang."

He left, heading back to the streets to find another girl, and I locked the door behind him. Exhausted and full, I slept until the doorknob rattled. Jinsoo had come back to take me to a brothel. A new day had dawned, and the sun's soft rays streamed through the window. For a second, I thought I was still in my small room at Youngcha's. I listened for her voice or the voice of one of her friends. and when I heard neither, a pang of guilt slid through me. She would be so worried about me. What I'd done wasn't fair after all the kindness she had shown me..

Jinsoo lingered in the hall of the brothel where I was to live while Mama Sang spoke with me. She was at least fifty, her face weathered and weary; her eyes, sharp. I was sure she had once been a prostitute herself and worked her way up. She had more ambition and intelligence than the average whore.

"Hello Jeanhee," she said gently. "I'm Mama Sang."

My lie about my virginity had increased my value tenfold.

"Do you know what you will do in the brothel?" she asked. I'm sure she could tell I hadn't come from another brothel. While sadness marked my face, I did not yet have the jaded look that marks the life-long whore.

I nodded in answer to her question. "Yes. But I've only ever had one boyfriend, and I never went all the way with him. I wanted to be a good girl. I'm embarrassed to let a man touch me that way."

"You'll get used to it," she said. "It's not that bad. And life here is good. I'll buy you a bed, clothes, shoes, make-up, and other necessities, and feed you three meals a day. Once you've paid me back, you're free to go. I'm not sure whether the men will like your short hair, but I imagine you'll find some who prefer it."

"I want to meet a GI and go to America," I said. I needed to share my dream with someone, and I didn't find it odd that one of my only confidantes so far in life was an aging whore. "I want to finish high school there."

"If you want that so much," she said, her eyes sad for reasons I didn't understand, "I'm sure you'll get it. We have enough GIs in this town to bring the whole city to America. If you find one who'll make you his wife, you won't be the first or the last."

She paid the pimp and led me back to the brothel, a two-story building made of concrete and brick, with dark screen windows and two glass and red vinyl doors that opened onto the street. Mama Sang led me through the glass doors into the Lucky Club. The first floor was a nightclub, where the whores danced and solicited customers. In the daytime light, the place looked shoddy, the mirrored walls smeared with grime and dust, the air reeking of stale smoke and sex. Spilled alcohol created a sticky film on the floor, and my shoes stuck to the dirty tiles when I walked.

The living quarters were on the second floor. I followed Mama Sang up the creaky stairs. Some whores stayed there, Mama Sang told me, while others had homes nearby. The bedrooms each had a separate entrance and a common bathroom with running water for the shower next to washboards, soap and shampoo. Several whores lounged in a bedroom, gossiping and smoking when we walked in—they all smoked constantly—but they immediately stopped to check me out. Their long red nails and exposed bodies draped in cheap, gauzy clothes advertised they were for sale. Some were old enough to be my mother—their soft, florid curves barely constrained by their dresses—while others were still lithe, filled with the allure of youth. None of them had Youngcha's class, and they all looked, at first glance, like straight trash.

"Hey, green bean," one of them greeted me. "Heard you're a virgin."

"Were *you* ever a virgin?" another one asked the first whore. "I can't remember."

"Hush," Mama Sang said, and the other whores laughed. "One of you needs to take her shopping. Here's some cash. Give back the change, or I'll take it out of what you make tonight."

Youngmi heaved herself off the bed and gestured for another whore to join her. "Come on, Yuna. Let's get the little bean ready for tonight."

The other whores smiled kindly, all except for the youngest, Choi. She had sloped cat eyes and sharp, prickly cheek bones. She had clearly been the babe of the club until I got there, and she eyed me with fierce jealousy.

As we walked to the market to purchase clothes and make-up for my first night, I learned that Youngmi had been married before and had two children, but now she was the pimp's girlfriend. When she found out I had turned down his sexual advances, she laughed and laughed, and after that we became close friends—she watched out for me and treated me like a sister. Later, I would see that Youngmi wasn't a very good whore. She didn't like GIs, and because she was not very pretty, they didn't like her. She rarely had customers, and without income, would be stuck paying off her debt to Mama Sang forever. Though I couldn't understand it, her heart belonged to the grease ball Jinsoo, and she wanted to be with him whenever she could.

Yuna was pretty, quieter than Youngmi, and did not yet look like a whore. Her face was bright with the bloom of youth and hope. Her short hair was dyed light brown, and she wore much more make-up than Youngmi, who, by virtue of her age and status in the house, could refuse to wear it and not get punished.

"This life isn't so bad. We'll watch out for you until you get on your feet," Yuna promised. "Don't sleep with anyone until we look at them first. Some of those GIs are not for first-timers. And if your first time is awful, it'll be harder to get used to it."

We spent the afternoon buying cheap outfits and make-up. The gold high-heeled shoes they picked out pinched my feet and made me feel as though I might topple right over and break my ankle. I'd felt safer walking in the rice paddy with snakes than I did in those, but I was determined to learn to wear them. If I could carry water buckets up an icy slope in winter, I could certainly teeter around in heels. Perhaps to appease me, Youngmi and Yuna let me pick out a pair of white go-go boots. I felt chic and sophisticated with white leather wrapped around my ankles.

I had more trouble learning how to put on make-up. At first, I slapped it on like a geisha from hell, not understanding how the thick white powder made me prettier. I refused outright to put on lipstick. It tasted nasty and made my lips dry and tight. I couldn't see why any man would want to kiss me and get that goop smeared on his face.

My mama would have fainted if she had seen me if she even recognized me at all. I'd never before had so many outfits at once or spent so much money on myself. I could see why girls like me, who'd lived in poverty their whole lives, would see this life as a way out. Lying on my back a few times every now and then with GIs seemed like fair trade with my past, my heartbreaks. Even though the makeup made my face feel hot and tight, it also empowered me. When I looked in the mirror, I didn't see the old Jeanhee, the one left brokenhearted by a mother's sorrow and a father's disdain, but instead I saw the new Jeanhee, a young woman in search of a better future. I didn't plan to end up on my back for the rest of my life. I was determined to end up in America, on my own two feet.

The first thing I did when I returned to the brothel from my shopping trip was to speak again with Mama Sang.

"I just turned seventeen less than two months ago," I said, "I've never slept with a man. I promise I'll be worth your investment if you let me pick who I want to sleep with until I get used to it."

I wasn't lying entirely. I *was* a virgin of sorts. A GI virgin, anyway. She already knew about my *run away* dream, and she hadn't scoffed at it, so I thought she might be open to this deal, too. Plus, I knew there was no way in hell I would be staying in this whore town long. I wasn't going to become tired and jaded like the women around me. If I could meet a GI fast enough, maybe I wouldn't even have to sleep with anyone at all. Maybe my soldier could pay back Mama Sang and take me from her.

Mama Sang looked reluctant, but I kept talking so she couldn't interrupt me. "I'm scared to be alone in a room with those big men, Mama Sang. I'm afraid it will hurt. I want to pick someone gentle."

The truth was, I wasn't scared, but I wasn't willing to let anyone touch me unless I wanted to be touched. But I knew she could turn me down. She owned me because she had bought me from the pimp, and now I owed her even more money since she had transformed me into a perfumed harlot.

After we had eaten dinner and the sun had finally set, all the girls put on their make-up, slipped into sheer dresses, glued on false eyelashes, and secured wigs to their real hair with bobby pins. They talked casually amongst themselves about how much they were going to make, some teasing the others about their prospects.

"Youngmi, you'll be lucky to make enough to buy lunch tomorrow," Yuna said jokingly. "You don't even try to get the GIs to notice you."

Choi glared my way, her eyes slits. "I'm sure she'll make more than that little country chicken over there," she said, referring to me. "Who would want such a skinny thing? Not even for free, probably."

I ignored her and followed the other girls downstairs. Mama Sang still hadn't answered my plea and right then, Choi's curse sounded like a blessing. I hope no one wanted me. Not yet, until I was ready.

In the soft light of The Lucky Club, even the older prostitutes looked pretty. They had smoothed their wrinkles, wiping away the years of hardship hidden beneath their elegant scarves and hairpins. It was a scene right out of an American movie. I had been drilled with a price sheet, so I knew what the prostitutes did and what they made when they disappeared—five dollars for blow jobs, ten for a short time—one time sex—and twenty for a long time, or an overnight sleepover. If a GI wanted anything kinky, he paid more money. When Yuna first told me that, revulsion rolled through me.

"Yuck!" I said. "This is disgusting. If somebody wants something kinky, he'd better marry me. What does kinky mean, Yuna?"

"Shee! Jeanhee Ya, shut up," Yuna said. She looked around to see if anyone else had heard. "You'd better not let Mama Sang hear you say that."

She smacked me lightly on the shoulder. "You have to pretend to enjoy it, or you'll never pay off your debt. You'll be here forever, like Youngmi."

Later, she giggled to me about how far some of the girls went in the bedroom to make more money. "I'd never do those things, and neither will you."

I wasn't sure what she meant, but I didn't want to know. I was already so embarrassed by the list of prices that my head felt light and fuzzy. I kept thinking, *What now? What have I done?*

I couldn't believe my cousin hadn't shared these details with me. Maybe she'd thought I was too innocent to hear it. I'd imagined looking pretty and sweet to lure my GI husband, but I hadn't imagined the actual sex act. I was in complete shock. I'd been so cavalier about my plan—and now I was stuck with it, do or die. My determination didn't fade, though. I had to stay, or I would never make it to America. Besides, while my mind was my own, my body belonged to Mama Sang—at least until I paid her back.

Here comes Mamasang comes by to instruct Yuna and Youngmi to escort me to the club room downstairs about seven o'clock, where the rest of the whores sat around several tables near the dance floor. I had on a baby blue miniskirt, a shiny pink sparkly halter top, black fish net hose, and a brand new pair of white go-go boots. Clothes different from any I'd ever worn before. And when the other whores danced suggestively up against the GIs, trying to get them to buy a drink or an hour's worth of pleasure, I was appalled. I tried not to look at the funny looking GIs and decided I'd best not get up too many times so they wouldn't notice me. Walking in tall boots was hard to get used to, and I had no guarantee I wouldn't fall flat on my face.

Night had transformed the filthy clubroom into a shadowy den of pleasure, the grime concealed by soft lighting and a disco ball turning overhead, with multiple beams of light flickering on and off, on and off. The DJ played five fast songs in a row, and then one slow song. Over and over. I had no idea the names of the songs, but after hearing them so many times, I still remember a line or two of the lyrics, even today. *Funky music, California dream,* and *lay your head something, something,* the last line in the slow song when they all ground their bodies tightly together and acted as if they were in love.

Laughter and raucous voices spilled out onto the streets—all overwhelming the softer, more private noises coming from the rooms above. The other whores taught me how to entice a GI with my eyes, holding his gaze seductively until he approached me. I had never been to a club or a dance before, so I just watched their moves in amazement, I had always wondered why my school had made night clubs off limits... and now I understood.

After that, I let the other girls pull me onto the dance floor, and they laughed at my shyness. I didn't know how to shake my hips or move around like a mad woman as they did. No one our age back home was ever allowed to dance. In fact, I'd never seen *anyone* dance. I couldn't possibly move my body like that, and I wasn't comfortable mimicking sexual positions the way the other girls did to excite the men.

Still, I accepted any drinks the GIs sent my way. If I wasn't going to make any money for Mama Sang from prostitution, at least I could boost her liquor sales. I never once drank any alcohol, though. I hated the flavor, and the smell of it turned my stomach. It reminded me too much of my father, what a terrible beast he became whenever he'd had too much to drink. I never wanted to be like that. Eventually, the bartender caught on and sent me water or Coke while still charging the GIs for liquor. I could drink Coca Cola all night. By the end of the evening, I was so tired even the caffeine couldn't keep my eyes from slamming shut when my head hit the pillow.

As the days and nights went by, I got used to my new life and started getting braver in the club, dancing baby steps to the disco songs, flirting with GIs, and laughing at the mysterious jokes they told in English. I learned how to cross the floor in my go-go boots without stumbling or walking too stiffly, catching a man's eye and then looking away, knowing that in a few minutes he would send over a drink and perhaps join me for conversation. I spoke hardly any English, but that didn't matter. They just wanted someone to listen, to laugh at certain points or make a sympathetic face and stroke their arm. I spoke probably ten words of English and beyond that had to pull Yuna over to translate for me. I could say *yes* and *no, hi* and *how are you*, or tell a man he was handsome. I could also ask for a food and drink, and, of course and recited Mama Sang's price list. Many of the girls in the club spoke less English than I did, and we relied on body language more than anything else. Sometimes, the nights flew by, and sometimes they dragged. It all depended on my mood and how many GIs I had to fight off to keep hold of my *virginity*.

During the daytime, the other girls whiled away the hours smoking and gambling, but I never joined in. I was never judgmental, though, because I didn't want any of the girls to think I was being disrespectful and beat me up. Instead, I spent a lot of time with Youngmi at her home near the village, getting to know her kids, her mother and father, and her friends who weren't prostitutes. They were all poor, and they accepted me as a runaway, a young girl who could never go home. At night, of course, I went back to the club—I didn't want to have to explain to Mama Sang why I wasn't working.

*****

The longer I delayed in picking a man, the higher my price went. The GIs were intrigued by me. They thought I must be something special for Mama Sang to allow me to hold out for so long. Some of the GIs were shy and just wanted to talk though I never understood what they said. I just nodded and said, "Hi" and "Thank you, thank you" when they bought me drinks. Others used body language to communicate, sliding a hand up my thigh or caressing my neck. Those were the ones I hid from in my room. If Youngmi or one of the other kind whores saw this, they would come and intercept the GI so he wouldn't get angry at having wasted drinks on such an ungrateful girl.

The higher my price rose, the angrier Choi became. She'd walk by and blow yellow smoke in my face, letting me know she could tear me up anytime she wanted. She couldn't stand the men flocking around me instead of her, and life would've been insufferable without Youngmi and Yuna to keep her at bay. I also knew not to look at her man—and I didn't care to, anyway. He didn't look like a prize to me. She was also angry that the other prostitutes treated me like a little sister. None of them liked her, and whenever I walked by, she would quack or cluck likes a chicken, hissing, "Hey, country chicken, why don't you go home? Go back to your farm. No one wants to sleep with a skinny thing like you." If she'd been the only whore in the house, I would have left Osan and gone home.

One night, my eyes accidentally caught those of her GI, and he immediately walked over to me. "Hi, little virgin girl," he said. "May I buy you a drink?"

Before he had even ordered the drink, Choi slapped my face so hard my eyes teared up. She dragged me by my hair toward the front door, swearing violently. I struggled against her, but despite the shortness of my hair, she had a firm grip on it.

"Little bitch!" she yelled. "I told you to stay away from my GI! You no good yi *ssipalyon, kalboya*! No one wants you here!" I had rarely heard those words spoken and had certainly never been called a *fucking whore* before. My face turned red and my heart pounded. That crazy mean whore who hated me scared me to death.

"I'm going to kill you!" she screamed. "I've been waiting to beat the shit out of you from the day you first walked in, you little country chicken. Let me show you how a *real* bitch fights!"

Screaming bloody murder, she practiced every curse word she'd ever heard on me, swinging at my face, my ear, and my forehead and kicking me wherever she could while Youngmi and Yuna tried to prevent her from hitting me. The other whores and Mama Sang tried to pull her away from me, but she lunged forward again in a final, mad-as-hell effort to shove me out the front door, screaming, "Go home, you fucking bitch!"

Unable to stop, I tumbled through the plate glass, my arms wheeling, helpless to stop my fall. I landed on my side and curled up in a pool of blood and glass. Choi shoved a GI out of her way and stormed up to her room. I struggled to my feet and brushed glass off my dress. The entire club fell silent. Her man looked on impassively, not running after her—perhaps he was used to this kind of behavior.

Youngmi pulled me up and lifted my left hand gently. A

jagged shard of glass was imbedded deep in that arm, and blood poured from the rough wound. I looked right at it. My vision swam, and I nearly fell back down. Youngmi put her arm around my shoulders and murmured in my ear. "Jeanhee Ya, Jeanhee Ya, you're fine. You'll be just fine. We're taking you to the hospital, sweet bean."

Yuna ran into the street to hail a taxi, and Youngmi ushered me inside. The three of us sped toward the hospital, their clients forgotten. The town only had one hospital—the first floor was the emergency room, and the second was recovery, childbirth, and surgeries. As soon as we stepped through the doors, the pungent odor of rubbing alcohol filled my nose, making me cough. I cried, not because I was in pain, but because I was scared of the blood that soaked my clothes and dribbled from my left arm. The shard of glass gleamed evilly from my bicep.

Youngmi held my right hand as Yuna hovered nearby. We didn't have to wait long before a doctor and a nurse rushed in with a needle to numb the area and pick out the glass, dropping the bloody shards into a tin tray. I watched in disgusted fascination as the doctor's needle and thread wove in and out of the cut, stitching it closed with jagged black sutures. I had received yet another scar in my year of trauma. When they had finished, they wrapped my forearm in fluffy white gauze. I was told to keep it clean. Mama sang, who had shown up while they were stitching me up, looked on.

Youngmi paid them, and then Mama Sang turned to me, her voice frantic, "The police will be looking for you. Please, please don't tell them your real age, or we will all be in big trouble. I will lose the club, and Youngmi and Yuna and all your friends will be out on the street. You must lie. Promise me, Jeanhee Ya, promise now."

I nodded silently, and we turned together to leave.

A squat policeman confronted me as I walked out the door. "You must come to the police station," he barked. "Right now. And we don't need your friends. Just you."

The police station was less than a hundred feet from the

brothel. Prostitution was legal in Korea, but underage prostitution was not, and the police liked to crack down.

The station held six desks and six policemen, and the head of the police station sat me down in a chair across from his desk and hammered me with questions. He was heavy-set and middle aged, and walked as if he owned the town.

"How old are you?" he demanded.

"Eighteen," I told him, trying not to let my voice shake. I had never been in trouble with the police before—I was terrified. What if they put me in jail? Or worse, what if they sent me home?

"You shit girl!" He slammed his fist on the desk, and his face turned red. "You are a lying *Galbo*. You tell me your correct age, or I will throw you in jail—and you won't last a day with the murderers and rapists in there."

"I-I'm seventeen," I said, singing like a bird and crying desperately. This was probably the easiest interrogation he'd ever had. "I'll go home. Please! Don't send me to jail."

"What year were you born?"

"1957, sir."

"What day?"

"February 22, sir"

"How long have you been working in that whorehouse?" he asked, slamming his fist against the desk again, this time so hard the vibration shot straight through the brown metal into my newly stitched forearm.

I wiped tears off my face with both palms. "I-I got here two weeks ago, and a pimp sold me to Mama Sang. But she never forced me to sleep with any GI, or let them touch me. I'm just living there. Please, sir, please. Let me go home."

Of course, I had no plans to go home, but if he put me on a bus I'd have no choice. If my mama had been ashamed of me when I ran away before, who knew how she'd feel if I came back. I had no going back home plan. So... no. No way in hell would I go back home to face Mama's brokenhearted looks.

The police officer, apparently satisfied, sat back and folded his hands over his gut. "You can come back tomorrow morning after I arrest Mama Sang. You'll have to be here to press charges. Don't go back to the club."

"I'll take her to my house and watch her," Youngmi called from the door. She had been standing outside, watching us through the window. She'd followed me to the station, but the police hadn't allowed her to come inside. "I'll bring her back tomorrow and help her get a bus ticket home."

"Why should I let her go with you?" the officer asked Youngmi.

"Because I'm her friend," Youngmi said.

"You're another whore at the Lucky Club?"

"Yes, sir," she answered.

"I don't know why I should trust a whore." The officer sneered. "But I can't take her home with me. I have children. Take her and bring her back tomorrow, or I'll arrest you both."

I was shaking by the time we reached the sidewalk outside. "Youngmi, what do I do?" I asked in despair.

"We're going to see Mama Sang," Youngmi answered, putting her arm around me. "We'll work it out."

"What if the police are watching us now?" I pulled back, panicking. "She'll be so mad at me. I don't want to see her."

"We can fix this, but you have to follow my lead." Youngmi's face became stern, and for a moment she looked like my mama. But apparently she still needed assurance from me, for she asked, "Okay?"

"Okay, sister." I said, and I nodded.

I'd had too much trauma in one day to keep asserting my will. Once we reached Mama Sang's house, I stayed behind Youngmi, my eyes downcast.

"Mama Sang, the police want you to report to them in the morning. Jeanhee will not press charges if you wipe out her debt and mine," Youngmi said. "Let us go free. And give her *Sasip* manwon for the damage." She pointed at my stitches and bruises on my face.

I gasped—that was more than six months' pay for an average Korean back then—the equivalent of $450 American dollars. I was sure there was no way Mama Sang would hand over that much cash, but she started counting bills immediately and handed over a stack, fuming the whole time. The gentle manner in which she'd always treated me was completely gone. If she could have beaten me right then, I'm sure she would've.

"You country girl from Jolla Do," she snapped. "I should've known your kind. This is my savings for the whole year. I was good to you. And this how you pay me back? You whore. You'd better watch out, or I will tell every Mama Sang in town about you"

"Get out!" she shouted. "Both of you!"

Youngmi and I backed away.

"Don't let me see her anywhere near my club again, or I'll lose my brothel," Mama Sang hissed at Youngmi before she slammed her door.

Youngmi and I walked to her home without saying much; she knew I wasn't feeling good enough for conversation. But she caressed my short hair once we arrived and said to me, "You are going to be okay."

I slept like a baby lying next to her children that night, sleeping through the night for the first time in two weeks.

I went back to the police station to see the officer the next day, but I refused to press charges against Mama Sang. He was angry and tried to intimidate me into backing down, but I stayed calm. Little did he know that I'd been coached by Youngmi. We had rehearsed the dialogue.

"Don't be scared when he yells at you," she'd said. "That's how they talk. Remember—he's not going to beat you up. You didn't do anything illegal, so he can't send you to jail."

I wouldn't go back on my word to Mama sang, not after she'd paid me off. When the officer realized I wasn't going to press charges, he asked me if she paid me to refuse.

"She did, didn't she?" he asked.

And I answered, "No, sir. She didn't force me to sell my body, either."

I could tell he was still wondering if I'd been paid off, but I stuck with what Youngmi and I had rehearsed. He seemed disappointed that he couldn't arrest Mama sang, and he made me promise I'd go home. I tried my hardest to look meek and repentant, and then I lied and told him I would call my mama as soon as I left the police station.

"Be sure you do," he snarled. "If I ever see you again, I'll arrest you."

For months, I worried that the cop would dart around a corner and take me into custody, but when I finally ran into him, I found our exchange oddly pleasant.

"You're still here?" he asked, amused. He must've been having a better day that day than he was the first time I'd met him.

"Yes," I said. "I met a nice family, and they are taking care of me. I'm a good girl now."

I could tell by his face he didn't believe me, but he nodded. "I'm going to pretend I didn't see you today. And don't let me see you again, or it's off to jail with you."

At first, I stayed in Youngmi's hillside home, a nicer house than the one where I grew up, but not by much. Youngmi, her mother and father, and Youngmi's two children, Junho and Sooki, all shared two rooms and a small outdoor kitchen. The children reminded me of my brothers and sisters, whom I missed deeply, and I was good to them, doing all the things with them I hadn't gotten to do with my own brothers and sisters because we were too poor.

We went to the movies, to the park, and on boat rides on the reservoir. I bought them toys and snacks and Coca Colas, and they liked being around me.

Youngmi was sweet to me, too, and treated me as if I were her prized possession. She was proud of how she had rescued me from Mama sang and had gotten our debts wiped clean, and I was happy for her, too. With so many mouths to feed and no husband, she'd had no choice but to sell her body. Her grease ball pimp boyfriend, Jinsoo, drifted in and out. He always smiled at me, the one he couldn't get, and occasionally, he would reenact that night of his unsuccessful conquest, trying to lure me into the bedroom.

"Little girl, you still owe me for that lunch," he would say.

"And there is a special kind of payment I want—not cash."

"Go away, grease ball!" I would shout, laughing, and he would laugh, too. I'm not sure he would've slept with me even if I'd let him. We'd become friendly and developed an odd mutual respect for each other. I ended up loaning Youngmi a lot of the money I got from Mama Sang, because she needed it more than I did. I never asked her to pay me back; she was the reason I was free of Mama Sang, and she was letting me stay with her.

During all of this time, I never once forgot my goal. As happy as I was to have gotten out of the brothel and still live in GI town, I needed to get to America and finish high school. I couldn't stay in Youngmi's house forever, and I needed to hang around the bars so I could meet a GI. So I came up with another plan.

Even with what I had lent Youngmi, I had enough money to get my own place, and since I was no longer afraid of the cops, I rented a little room with a kitchen near whore alley, only two blocks from the GI base. Though Osan wasn't a huge city, the nights there were vibrant. GIs were everywhere, and bars adorned every corner of the alley. I was finally on my own—with no supervision—and I liked my freedom. I had been liberated from my upbringing. No one knew me, and no one judged. I had no one to answer to or to tell me what to do.

Since Youngmi often stayed with the grease ball, I hung around more with Yuna, who was now on her own as well. She told me that Mama Sang had never recovered from the police interrogation and had gone bankrupt after I'd taken her money, so she let all the girls go.

Yuna was from the same region as me, Jolla Do, so we had a special affinity for each other. I followed her from bar to bar as she worked, and she shooed all overly-friendly GIs away from me.

"Not him," she would say. "He's no good for you." Then she would shake her finger at the man flirtatiously. "Talk to me, handsome soldier. You stay away from her."

I always listened to her because I wasn't ready to sell my body. I had trouble keeping the GIs away, though. They followed me as if I were a magnet, offering to buy me drinks and meals. I still hoped to meet a GI on my own, without prostituting myself.

The first GI Yuna approved for me to meet was quiet and kind—he didn't force me. Instead, we got to know each other over several nights, always with Yuna watching over me to make sure he didn't pressure me before I was ready. When I finally consented to sleep with him, he rented us a hotel room.

I was scared and unsure of what I was to supposed to do, yet I knew I was about to have intercourse with a man I'd probably never see again. Even so, I let him kiss me on the lips. He touched my boobs as he undressed me, and soon my underwear dropped to my feet. He picked me up, laid me on the bed, and said something I couldn't make out. I guessed he was getting hot and heavy and ready to take me. I was about to sell myself, body and soul, for $20.

I kept reciting to myself, "This is for my second chance at the America dream. I can do this."

I lay there like a board, trying to remember the tricks Yuna had taught me to please a man. But he was too big, and after a few tries, he gave up.

I cried, and he said, "I don't want to hurt you. It's okay, Jeanhee. We don't have to do it."

I refused to take his money, and I didn't talk to him again. He wanted to try again, but I refused.

"I know the perfect guy to teach you," Yuna said, when she heard what had happened. "He used to come visit me, and he's real nice. He's even asked about you several times. He'll show you what to do. And he won't scare you away with his big thing. You have to relax, though. GIs like sex, and if you don't pretend to like it, too, you won't make it to America. So you can't tell them you don't like sex. No man's going to marry a girl who can't keep him happy between the sheets."

She was right. If a GI was willing to marry someone who wasn't a virgin, then he surely expected some excitement in the bedroom. My money was running low, and being surrounded by whores made it easier to justify my decision. I sold my body to that man for $20, giving up my childhood notions that physical love was to be between one man and one woman for life. I don't know how I had held on to that belief anyway, considering my father's example, but somehow it had remained.

The GI was good looking, with blond hair and piercing blue eyes. Afterwards, he told me he was married, and I knew he couldn't take me to America. He started crying when I told him to go away, but I didn't understand his tears. He could find another Korean girl to please him. GIs willing to marry Korean girls were harder to find, and I didn't have time to waste.

Later, I lay in the dark and thought about what I'd done. I was already a fallen woman, so what did it matter? I hated men, especially my father, who, it seemed to me, had directly contributed to that $20 stamp on my soul. I could never be a normal Korean woman again, not after that night. I'd be a bad girl forever. Maybe, I thought, my grandmother was riding on my back. Whatever the reason, everything I'd believed was pure was gone forever.

I decided I wouldn't give myself to a man for free ever again. They would either pay me in cash or pay me in marriage. Either way, I would profit. I worked as a prostitute for two weeks, sleeping with two more men before Yuna introduced me to John.

"This one looks sweet," she said. "Maybe he's the one for you, little bean."

John had just arrived in Korea and was only two years older than me. He wore cowboy boots, blue jeans, button-up shirts, and a ten-gallon hat. He was the funniest GI I'd ever met. Though I already smiled a lot, thanks to Woojung's teachings, he was the first man who had ever made me laugh out loud. We couldn't have long conversations because of the language barrier, but he used every technique he could think of to tell me what he was thinking: body language, drawings, pointing, and mimicking. One time, he stood against a wall and pretended to be a clock, moving his arms at angles and tick-tocking loudly, sending me into peals of laughter. He didn't care who else stared as long as I giggled.

He wasn't a big man, and he had a shock of dark hair and hazel eyes, unlike all the blond-haired, blue-eyed GIs I'd been chasing, and he persisted in pursuing me. He'd been in Osan for only two weeks when we met and had been in the Air Force for only six months. I could tell he was lonely. He was from Mexico, Missouri, a place I had never heard of but thought sounded fabulous merely because it was in America. He didn't have a woman of his own yet—and he didn't hesitate in telling Yuna he wanted me.

"Yuna, you can't keep Jeanhee forever," he said. "I want her. I'll take good care of her."

"You might not be able to afford Jeanhee," Yuna said cleverly. "After all, she is a virgin—men ask me for her every night, and I send them away. They're not good enough for my Jeanhee."

"How much?" John finally asked.

"Two hundred dollars a month, plus her expenses," Yuna said. "No less!"

"Done," John said, and he shook her hand. "I would pay more than that."

Then he scooped me up and twirled me around, laughing, and Yuna laughed too.

"You two are big innocent babies," she said. "You deserve each other. Neither of you should be out on the streets."

John joined me in the little room I had rented, and even though we had a room and a kitchen outside, we didn't have a private bathroom. The outhouse was nearby, but John would have to shower on base. I had to go to a public bath house for a bath. We were happy with each other, though. He always called me *honey,* and I thought it was because he thought I was sweet like honey, but later I found out that's what some Americans call their loved ones. He constantly told jokes, and neither of us cared that I didn't understand half the words he said. He kept talking, and I kept laughing. I was completely relaxed with him and felt close when he touched me.

Unlike my innocent trysts with Heechang or my cold couplings with the three previous GIs, we learned to make love in a way that made me feel connected to him, as if I were a part of him. He also taught me how to French kiss. The first time he did it, I pulled back, confused. I thought a kiss was a smack on the lips while both of my eyes were closed. I also made sure to take my birth control pill every day and was glad the prostitutes had shown me how to get them—I'd been too embarrassed to buy them when I was with Heechang. Back then, I hadn't known enough about my own body to even realize I could get pregnant.

As I spent more time with John, I regretted my past actions less and less. I knew within our first week of living together that John would marry me one day. Though he didn't know it as soon as I did, he soon came to realize our destinies were entwined. I'm sure he expected to return home after his tour of duty to marry a buxom country girl who'd never heard of kimchi and could bake perfect apple pies. But I'd known my future all along, and with John I believed I was getting so much closer to it.

America was where I would attend high school with American students.

Chapter Five

Back in High School

There was no more nightly action or hanging around bars trying catch the perfect GI to take me to America. I had found my GI. *John*. We were together every chance we got. After work and on weekends, he came to find me at my small rented room. John, with his big nose, hazel eyes, dark hair, fair skin, and American English, was my GI. I could never fully understand him, but I was able to figure out most of what he tried to say from watching the movements of his hands, fingers, or feet. We used make-shift sign language, taking turns trying to understand each other, and most of the time I didn't need Yumi to translate everyday stuff.

We both wanted to be together. Just by being next to each

other and holding hands, waking up with yawns, shivering when the air was cold, fanning our faces when the weather was hot, and rubbing our tummies when we were hungry, we managed to communicate. When I ate faster and enjoyed more portions than John, he was happy because I was full and happy. We worked out the differences in culture, language, and customs as they fit into our lives, and it worked for us. We both knew I was his girl, and he was my GI. And whenever the two of us were together, jittery butterflies roamed around us, and everything felt right.

I pieced together phrases in English, and he learned a few words in Korean like *eat* or *I love you*, and *good bye*. Cooking was a challenging task; I knew how to boil ramen noodle soup, and I cooked it every day. My mama had been too busy using me as second man to work the farm and had forgotten to teach me how to cook. Perhaps, she thought I would never develop the skill she had perfected of cooking just enough to go around. Or maybe she feared that if I knew how to cook, I would've cooked more just so I could fill my ever hungry belly.

John was so infatuated with me, he never complained about my lack of cooking skills. We went to movies on the base often, and I loved every one we saw. The actors spoke English words I didn't understand, but seeing those films was one of the privileges of being a GI's girl I would not turn down. I would always ask for popcorn, with lots of hot, creamy butter, a Coca Cola, and, without fail, a Hershey's Bar. I would unfold the silver foil slowly and drop those perfect rectangles into my mouth, one by one, remembering the day I had first tasted the heavenly sweetness in my mother's rice paddy.

After the movie, John would take me to the NCO club— the noncommissioned officers' club—and feed me hamburgers and French fries with lots of ketchup.

"Slow down, Honey," he would always say as I gobbled my food. "Nobody is going to take it away from you."

My eating machine habits were hard to lose. When I was growing up, I never got enough food, hugs, or affection, but now I was getting plenty of all three. Every chance John got, he said,

"Thank you! Thank you!"

Kissing or even hugging in public was forbidden in Korea—no citizen would ever dare show such affection—but John loved displays of affection and spread them around everywhere we went. I slowly accepted this, but made sure no Koreans were around first. Otherwise, I would be taunted by the words, "You whore!"

My mama used to tell me that words would never hurt me, but I know she didn't mean it because whenever someone called me a *whore,* it hurt my mind and my heart.

Two other words I couldn't quite understand but had to learn were "Excuse me!" if I passed even slightly too close to an American. Even if I didn't think I was passing too closely, I had to say, "Excuse me!" and I had to say it back if they said it to me. "Excoosemeeee!"

Between saying "Thank you!" And "Excuse me!" all day long whenever we went to the base, I became tired of repeating the same words over and over; I couldn't help but think to myself what strange people Americans were, saying the same words again and again all day long. For Koreans to say one word or the other would take their whole lifetimes, even to just say it one time. I never heard any of that from my dad or my mama, but if I did anything sweet for John, he would say, "Thank you!"

I could be setting his big, shiny black GI boots neatly together in formation next to my shoes, and he would say, "Thank you, honey."

Within a short time, John had given me more hugs and kisses than I'd had during my previous life, and I decided I liked the sweet sensations this strange looking American with the big nose gave me whenever he hugged me. Now, I not only wanted to go to America, but I also liked American culture, with all those hugs and kisses. They warmed my heart. I wanted more of them, so I did things just so I could get one or the other or both as often as I could.

I didn't need John to go down on bended knee or to hear the swell of violins to know he loved me. His smile lit up my heart, and I smiled back. I began to miss his hugs and kisses while he was at work, and I couldn't wait for him to come home to me every day. After we'd been living together for about three months, I noticed he was grinning more than usual, and through a mixture of hand movements and broken English, I asked him why he was so happy.

"Did you meet another girl, prettier than me?" I teased.

"Jeanhee, I want to marry you. I want to take you home with me to America," he said.

I didn't understand much of what he said, but I knew *married* and I knew *to America.* Smiling so big I thought my face would split, I threw myself into his arms.

"*Chungmal!*" I cried in Korean. "Yes, I'll be your wife and go to America with you. John, I am so happy!"

He may not have understood my words, but he understood I was ecstatic. Later that day, I got Youngmi to translate for us.

"Jeanhee says she needs one more thing, or she won't marry you." Youngmi laughed.

John looked worried. "Why? Did she change her mind?"

"Silly GI." She smiled. "She wants a maid. She doesn't want to do chores anymore."

"Maids are cheap here." He relaxed and smiled at me. "Jeanhee can have two, if that's all it takes to win her love."

The news was almost too much for me—a GI was going to marry me and eventually take me to America. I was going to high school. In America. I danced around our tiny room in a circle until I got dizzy. John was so tickled.

He set me down with a sad little expression, and I asked him, "What's wrong?"

"Honey, I don't have a ring to give you. At least, not yet."

"A ring? I don't need a ring." My hands were covered with frostbite scars and wrinkles from all those years of working in the fields with my mama. A ring wouldn't look good on me, anyway. "It is okay, I don't need it."

John hired a marriage broker to start the paperwork the following week. The papers were written in English. First, however, they had to interpret Korean forms from the Embassy in Seoul, and we quickly realized our wedding plans would be more difficult to pursue than I'd initially imagined. Because I was only seventeen, I needed my parents' permission to marry. The day the marriage broker told me this news, John came home and saw my face clouded with fear. I felt as if the ghost of my grandmother sat on my chest, smothering me. Already, my father would be less than glad for his shamed daughter to come home. There was no way he'd allow me to marry an American.

John didn't seem as worried about it as I was, but then he'd never met my father. He wanted to meet my mother and brothers and sisters and offered to accompany me on the trip home, but I wouldn't let him. I didn't want him to see where I came from. I knew my family would give him the cold shoulder. Koreans like Americans, but marriage between the two races is looked down upon. No decent Korean girl would ever dare marry an American GI unless she had faced what I had. Once one crossed that line, there was no going back.

I wouldn't broadcast to anyone that I was marrying an American GI, nor would my family. They would keep it a secret as long as they could. I couldn't bear it, but I packed my little satchel for a one-night stay and called home to tell my brothers and sisters that I would be arriving on Friday by train. I told them I was not coming home to rejoin their lives but to get my father's permission so I could leave Korea forever.

"Is this what you do?" my mother screamed back at me, so loud I almost dropped the phone. "How could you? You've shamed this family enough, Jeanhee Ya! You can't go and marry an American! What else will you do to run me into an early grave? You disappear for months and return with this? You worry me and then you kill me!"

I waited until she calmed down and then said, as neutrally as I could, "What will I do if I return home for good? Can you find me happiness? There's no place left for me in this country. Tell Dad that if he doesn't sign this permission slip, I'll terrorize him tenfold. If you think I've ruined the family name already, just wait. I can do much worse!"

Eventually, she agreed to make sure my dad would be home

when I arrived, and I rested easier, hoping my threats would force him into signing the slip.

The train ride home was very different from the one that had taken me to Seoul. Instead of being excited for the next step in my journey, I was filled with shame. I wished I had a mask of a pretty girl's face—maybe Oksoon's or Woojung's—so I could hide behind it. Despite my conservative clothes and a fresh face wiped free of make-up, I felt as if everyone who saw me knew where I'd been and what I'd been doing.

While I was living in Osan, the shame had receded. Most of my friends were prostitutes since normal Korean girls wouldn't dare be caught with me, and around them I felt almost normal while I was living with John. Returning to my home town where my family lived by Korean traditions they had been taught from birth, I recognized that I had become a different kind of Korean, a different person, and that person could never go back home to live with them again. I was no longer welcome there. I had become an outsider. This last trip home was necessary, however. I must make it in order to leave the country that hated me for what I had become. So I accepted it.

By the time the train chugged into the station, I shook from head to toe. I was sure my brothers and sisters had learned my secrets and wouldn't show up to greet me. I had protected and loved them for so long; I couldn't bear the thought of their disapproval.

From an independent woman betrothed to a handsome GI to a washed-out, used-up girl without self- worth, I might as well have been wearing go-go boots and a tube top, my face white with powder, the words *bad, dirty girl* written across my forehead in permanent marker when I finally stepped off that train. I thought again about how no decent man in Korea would ever want me. Despite my faith in John, I felt ashamed that my own culture had so thoroughly rejected me. I wished I could take a train back to Osan that same night. I would hurry and find my father, beg him to sign the permission slip prepared by the American embassy, and then return to John's strong arms by bedtime. I wouldn't have to sleep even one night under my parents' roof.

I clutched my bag and did my best to walk tall and proud as I marched across the platform. Before I'd even scanned the crowd, my fears receded.

"Hi, Sister!" Meehee shrieked, running towards me, her eyes wet with tears, her crazy hair as big and uncontrollable as ever. I couldn't believe how tall Junghee had gotten and how Sunhee had turned into a young lady. Familiar chatter filled my ears, and as I hugged each of them, I saw in my siblings' eyes how worried and upset they had been by my seven month absence.

Sunhee ran her fingers through my hair. "I'm glad you decided to let your hair grow out again, sister," she said. "When you left, I thought I had three brothers instead of two."

"Sister or not," I said, while my siblings fought over who would carry my bags, "I can still take Junghee if need be. So you all had better behave while I'm home."

"Sister! This is heavy!" Junghee complained. "Did you fill it with bricks?" He couldn't stand it. He wanted to know what goodies his sister had brought for him.

I smiled at him. "It's filled with presents, for you and the others and for Mama."

As I wove through the crowded streets towards the hotel, I almost felt as though I'd never left. Only when I looked down at my simple dress did I remind myself I wasn't wearing my school uniform, swinging my book bag against my shoulder. At least my sisters' uniforms no longer sent pangs of regret through me. I was glad they were still in school. Even if they never went to America, with an *education* they'd be more likely to find better husbands, ones with a stronger work ethic and more compassion than our own father possessed.

As we neared my old home, my brothers and sisters became tense, darting secretive looks back and forth. Junghee's lips tightened, and Meehee crossed her arms over her chest. Our pace slowed.

Finally, I stopped walking.

"What's going on?" I demanded. "Why do you all look so nervous? Did Dad tell you I couldn't come home? He doesn't want to see me, does he?"

"No, sister." Junghee looked away. "He knows you're coming, but he doesn't care. Mama's gone. We didn't tell you because we didn't know how to reach you in Osan. Mama wouldn't give us your address. She ran away."

"What?" My question was more a breath than a word. "Run away? She wouldn't leave you. Never. What happened?"

"Dad brought home a second wife," Meehee broke in, bursting into tears. "Mama won't come home. She comes to work and then leaves."

"Meehee, stop crying," I scolded, slipping quickly into big sister mode. "It'll be okay."

I gritted my teeth the rest of the walk home. Every step sent a jolt of anger through my body. I couldn't believe my father had done this. My mama had worked hard for all of us. I was livid. He only cared for himself. I forgot for an instant the purpose of my trip, that I had come home to get permission to marry John. All I could think of was giving my father a piece of my mind and running his new whore out of town.

I stormed through the hotel door, dispensing with niceties and confronting my mama's workers standing behind the reception counter.

"Where is she?" I asked.

"She who?" they said in unison, playing dumb.

"It is good to see you, Jeanhee Ya," one woman said. "Your mama will be happy."

"She, who? That young bitch my dad brought home. Is she in our home? Is she in our mama's room?"

I could see in their eyes they knew exactly whom I was talking about. They looked down and kept their mouths shut.

"I'll look in every room in this hotel," I said. "I'll find her and throw her into the street."

"She just wants money. Then she'll leave," another one of them said. "She's so young. She doesn't have anywhere to go."

"Oh, no!" I yelled. "No whore of my dad's is going to take the money I send to my mama."

I shoved past them into the kitchen, dropped my bag on the tiles, and grabbed the biggest butcher knife I could find. Its wooden handle was worn smooth from years of being gripped by sweaty hands, but the blade was shiny and sharp, and a thin string of gristle clung to its glistening edge. When I stormed toward our rooms in the back, my brothers and sisters hung back, their eyes wide. Once again, I was crazy Jeanhee, going forth to protect the family, but this time my mission was slightly more important than retrieving a lost skate. My father had been irate by how I'd dishonored the family, but I found his behavior to be infinitely more wounding than mine had ever been.

A man taking a second wife wasn't an uncommon practice in Korea, but it always devastated his first wife and children. The government wouldn't sanction the second wife, and the couple couldn't be legally bound. Usually, she was a fallen woman who'd lost her virginity or worked as a prostitute and couldn't find a decent man to marry. Sometimes, a second wife was taken when the first couldn't produce a son. Either way, she had no legal authority. Usually, her husband would give his word that he would take care of her, but that only occurred if the estate were distributed before his death. Otherwise, the second wife was left with nothing. The first wife was none too eager to give her rival a handout.

As soon as I entered my mama's room, I halted. My father's new wife, a tall, skinny woman much too young for him, cowered in the corner. Mascara coated her long eyelashes, and red lip gloss brightened her lips.

"Get the fuck out of my house," I hissed, holding the butcher knife high. "I'll slice you in half and throw you into the river!"

I swung at her, close enough that she should be deathly afraid. Then I noticed her quivering lips. In her face, I saw myself and my friends, Youngcha and Youngmi. Somewhere was a family who had chosen to throw away her love and leave her with nothing. She had been unlucky enough to land my father, rather than an American GI. I didn't want to judge her, but I had to protect my family. Hopefully, in some way, she would understand that.

I ignored these thoughts, however, and continued my rant.

"If you don't leave right now, bitch, I will kill you!" I yelled. "This is where my mama lives!"

"Sister!" Junghee cried, running behind me into the room. "Don't hurt her! You'll go to jail. Sister, stop!"

I knew he wouldn't try to grab me while I was swinging the knife, so I pulled my hand back and said to the woman, "This is where my brothers and sisters live. You want my dad, you take him with you. We don't want him, and we don't need you. Get out!"

One of my mother's workers grabbed me around the waist, and the other twisted my wrist until I dropped the knife. Between sobs, my dad's second wife threw a few short skirts and some silky lingerie into a suitcase.

"You're crazy!" she shouted, holding a framed picture to her chest. Mascara ran down her cheeks. "You're a crazy girl!"

"That's right!" I yelled back. "I'm crazy, and if I find out you've come back, I'll get that knife back and finish what I started!"

Within a few minutes, she was out the door and back on the street. My mama's workers let go of my arms, and I turned to face my brothers and sisters, my heart still pounding in my chest.

"Where's Mama?" I asked. "I want to bring her home."

My brother told me she was staying in a motel nearby. Tell me where she is!. Changhyundong motel on Main Street. All my little brothers and sisters cried," will you bring our mama back home, sister?"

I will be back with Mama! I nearly ran to find Chanhyundong motel. A little old lady in front office told me my mama's room number. I walked in her room without knocking. My poor mama was laying on the floor with little wet towel on her forehead crying as she was staring out the smeared windowpane. When she turned and saw me, her face crumpled.

"Jeanhee Ya, my daughter," she cried.

We wrapped our arms around each other, something we rarely ever did, and tears wet both our cheeks.

"Mama, I'm going to America," I told her. "I'm marrying a GI, and I'm going to live in a nice house and have nice things and never be hungry. Every month, I'll send you money so you'll have plenty of food and be able to afford somewhere to live if Dad brings home another young slut."

"I won't go home to your father, Jeanhee Ya," my mama said. "He's had that woman in our house. I won't go there." She shook her head vehemently. "I've put up with enough from that man. I never made a worse decision than telling him I'd marry him. I used to love him."

"You must go back," I said, taking my mama's hands in my own and looking her in the eye. "Junghee,Sunhee, Meehee and Yonghee need you. If you don't raise them, she'll take your place. Do you want a woman like that raising your children? What will happen to the girls with a mother like that?"

I knew she'd never put herself before her children, and she knew I was right to remind her of that. I helped her pack her things, and we returned home together. Meehee and Sunhee had already removed all traces of my father's second wife. Somehow, they'd even excised the smell of her cheap perfume.

I turned to my mama again.

"This is your home," I said. "Don't let anybody run you out of here ever again. You tell him to leave and take whatever whore he brings home with him. One day, I'll buy you your own home with a garden full of flowers you can water with running water. You'll wear pretty clothes, and I'll shower you with jewelry to show off to the neighbors."

I got choked up and had to stop. Even with all that had passed between us, I still loved my mother with a daughter's pure love. I would always care for her.

My father didn't come home that night. I didn't want to spend more than one night away from John, so I hoped he'd be back in the morning. I sat with my mama and brothers and sisters, and we talked long into the night. I gave them the Hershey bars, M&Ms, Snickers bars, and cookies I'd packed in my suitcase, and they gobbled the exotic sugary treats by the fistful. I also brought them a number of popular black market items including Vaseline, Maxim instant coffee, Spam, toothpaste, soap, and shampoo. Most of these, my family had never seen before.

Although it was an unknown rich country, America was where all Koreans wished to go. I felt certain braveness would be required to challenge the English-speaking world. I wanted my family to be where they were, at home without change, without facing what I had faced. I was happy my brothers and sisters still had a chance to be Korean, to grow up as they were supposed to as Koreans, to live as Koreans and die as Koreans. I didn't want my brothers and sisters to change. I wanted to protect them so that no Korean man would ever tell my sweet little sisters, "You are a whore. You married an American; you must have been a prostitute!" as I had been yelled at by Korean men on the street in Osan, You whore! You Dirty Trash! I knew I no longer will hear their taunting once I left Korea.

My skin had become thick in the few months I had been gone from home. I had grown up fast; getting my goal accomplished had made me do so. I would never tell them how I met John, and they would never ask for fear the answer would be one they never wanted to hear. I could handle it, but not my family. I wanted them to stay as they were with their values intact, their minds unjaded. My brothers and sisters didn't have my willpower, and they were happy with their life and Korea.

I was the only one who could tackle the challenge that lay ahead. Eventually, I'd lead them to a better life if they wanted to join me. I didn't want them to face what I had already dealt with, and the new challenges I would face once I got to America. Unknown factors would mold me, but I was certain I could handle it. I was equally certain they could not.

I told my brothers and sisters about John, that he was just nineteen years old and was a redneck from hell who dressed in cowboy boots, cowboy shirts, and Wrangler blue jeans when he wasn't in uniform. I wished I'd brought a picture of him, but I described him as best I could, telling them how funny he was and how nice. I told them I had an electric stove and had learned to cook Ramen noodle soup. I told them I was going to America to finish high school.

"Will you come get me one day, sister?" Yonghee, the

youngest asked, his eyes shining. The rest of them didn't ask. Immigrating to another country was an unthinkable dream to them, they didn't want to see outside their walls, their home, and Iri City.

"Yes," I said. "I'll get you all. We'll live together in America." I said that but hoped that he would change his mind about wanting to join me by the time he grew up.

After the younger kids went to bed, my mama put her hand on my arm and looked at me intently. "Jeanhee Ya, tell me. Are you happy?"

"Yes, Mama" I answered. "I'm going to be rich one day in America, but first I am going to finish high school. First, I have to study all the time to pass the test in English. Once I get to register in high school, I will send you a picture of me sitting in an American high school, Okay?" She didn't believe me, but she was happy for me just because I was going to America.

"If you are happy, then so am I," she said. "I don't want your life to be as unhappy as mine has been. I don't want you to struggle as I have."

"One day, I'll make enough money so neither of us has to struggle," I said. "I promise you that."

Even if she didn't agree with my decision, we parted that night with a certain understanding.

The next morning, my father stumbled in the door.

"You're still around?" he sneered. "You have no right coming back here for anything. You're a shame on our *chosang*, our family tree. If you marry an American man, we'll mark you out. You'll no longer be my daughter."

"That's fine," I said, pressing the paper into his hand. "Sign this, and I'll be gone forever."

I didn't tell him what I really felt—that I'd never wanted to be his daughter in the first place—for fear he'd storm out without signing the slip.

Once my father sealed the paper with the Kang family stamp, I clutched it to my heart as if it were made of gold. Nothing stood in the way of my going to America and finishing high school now.

My brothers and sisters walked me to the train station, and my mama came, too. As I climbed through the train car's door, unsure of when I would see them again, they waved and shouted their goodbyes.

"Don't forget us!" my mama cried out. "Jeanhee Ya, don't forget!"

They waved until I couldn't see them anymore, and I spent the train ride thinking how my childhood was over. I was relieved to arrive back in Osan. There, I was no longer Jeanhee Ya, shamed daughter, but Jeanhee, soon-to-be bride, who would soon start her life over in America. I tucked my permission slip into a small box in my small apartment, checking it at least once a day to make sure it was still there.

Finally, in September of 1974, John and I took a morning train to the American Embassy in Seoul, holding hands all the way. People stared at us as we climbed the embassy steps. I'm sure they assumed I was a prostitute.

The marriage ceremony was brief. I couldn't understand most of the words except when the judge asked, "Will you be John's wife?"

"Yes," I said, lifting myself up on the balls of my feet and nodding, so happy I could jump to touch the moon.

Then it was John's turn to answer if he wanted to be my husband.

"Yes, I do," he said. His smile started in his eyes and spread to his lips, filling his face with joy.

With those words, I changed from Kang Jeanhee to Mrs. John Burch. I smiled through the ceremony and for the rest of the day. I knew John loved me regardless of my past, and I was one step closer to enrolling in an American high school and getting my diploma. After that, I'd figure out a way to be rich. I was going to have everything I'd ever wanted growing up.

The official stamped our paperwork, officially proclaiming us man and wife, and I felt like a new person. I wasn't as excited about marrying the love of my life as I was about finishing high school. A diploma appealed to me much more than babies or housekeeping.

Once we got home, nothing really changed. Our routine remained the same, and we joked with one another as easily and happily as before. Three months passed, and then one day John slipped a slender band with five small diamonds onto my finger. He hadn't been able to afford a ring the day we got married, and I hadn't complained. Wearing a ring to signify marriage was an American custom.

Once I saw it there, sparkling on my finger, the enormity of our decision hit me.

"Are you sure?" I asked.

"Yes," John answered. He looked at me tenderly, his hazel eyes soft. "So sure. I love you."

"I love you, too," I said. And though I wasn't sure how he would fit into my childhood dream of completing my *education*, it was true. As long as I was on the track to America, I was happy. I'd learned from my mama's mistakes—having a flock of five dirty kids with my deadbeat father, working her ass off to care for us— and I didn't want a life of poverty. John was kind and clean and never raised his voice or treated me as if I were less than he. He thought I deserved the world, and he wanted to give it to me.

I liked showing my ring off to my friends. I became their idol, no longer innocent Jeanhee; I was a ballsy, brave young girl from Iksan si, Jollado, on her way to America to finish high school. I was living their unthinkable, impossible but optimistic dream now, not for an *education*, but for an escape from poverty and prostitution. Though most of them would never make it out of Osan, I gave them hope.

After John and I married, I became anxious to go to America, but John wanted me to stay with him while he finished his tour. I begged him over and over again, in broken English, to please send me.

"John, please. I want to finish high school. I'll be waiting for you when you come home. Please, John? Please? Please?"

"Jeanhee, we don't have enough money to send you to America yet. We'll have to wait and see."

I beseeched him literally every chance I got, and one day his answer finally changed.

"Okay, okay," he said. "I've been saving money to buy your airplane ticket. I'll send you when we have enough. I asked my parents. You can live with them until I can come get you."

Almost six months passed before John had saved enough money to buy the ticket and another six months went by before the government processed my Visa and passport. The passport had my photo, but they had spelled my name wrong.

"Chin Hui?" I said with a frown. "My name is Jeanhee, not Chin Hui."

"We're not asking them to change the spelling," John said. "It would probably take them another six months."

I couldn't think of a single reason why it would take them six months to correct my name, but I figured it wouldn't matter: I would correct people as I went.

Two nights before I was to leave for America, I felt I should at least let my mama know that I was going. So I called her. I knew Osan was too far for them to travel to see me off, and even if they could, my dad would not let them come say goodbye. I didn't even ask. Instead, I told them I was leaving from the air base, and she wasn't allowed inside to wave goodbye.

"Mama," I said, cradling the phone. "I'm really going. Remember everything I promised you? Don't let Dad bring home any more whores. If he does, use the kitchen knife to run them off. I'll send you money, Mama, I promise. It may take a while, but I'll take care of you. Please tell Sunhee, Junghee, Meehee, and Younghee that I'm leaving Korea."

I could have talked to them directly, but I was too sad to say goodbye. As it happened with most of our conversations, Mama started to cry, but not because she was angry or sad this time.

"I knew you'd get to America," she said. "Make me proud, Jeanhee ya. Okay?"

I can never live with them. The thought bounced around inside my head as I made her promise to tell my siblings that I loved them. I would make them proud of me one day. After using the public phone where I couldn't cry openly, I hurried home to cry my eyes out. The fact that I would forever be a stranger to my own family made me cry more than my unsaid *goodbye* to my brothers and sisters.

I went to the market with Yumi to buy new clothes to take with me to America. She helped me pick out things that would have looked good on me while I was trying to catch a GI, but I said no. I wanted somber colors, school girl clothes for women my age. She finally agreed. As if she were my sister, she was both sad and happy for me.

"Jeanhee ya, chalga," she said. "I'm going to find my GI one day, just like you did."

"Okay." I nodded my head. "I know you will, Yumi."

I packed my underwear and bras, the shirts I'd purchased from the market, two pairs of bell bottom pants, and shoes, and then I threw away all of the slutty clothes, including my white go-go boots Mama Sang had paid for me to wear. As I tossed all of it into the dumpster, I said goodbye to what I wanted to forget, what I had done while I wore them. I would keep what had happened to me in Osan a secret forever.

Next, I purchased two dictionaries: one, Korean to English; and the other, English to Korean. Then pencils, notebooks, and extra erasers. I was going to need lots of them. I guessed I would make a lot of mistakes in English. I packed and unpacked everything before packing it again while John watched, sad but happy. Happy only because he saw how happy and excited I was to be going to high school in only three days. I would go to an American high school as soon as I arrived in America.

The country was so far away from Korea, I figured the school might not even ask for my transcripts from Korea. I would deal with that when I got there. I must get there first and register for school; then I would deal with the paperwork.

On October 16, 1975, John handed me two twenty-dollar bills to put into my purse in case I got hungry at the airport when I changed planes. He told me I would get off in Alaska and change planes, then fly on the same plane the rest of the way to St. Louis.

His face was downcast, but he obviously believed this journey would make me happy..

"Don't lose the money. You might get hungry at the airport." His voice grew husky with sadness. "Put it in a safe place."

"I love you," I said, wrapping my arms around his neck and kissing him over and over before giving him one final hug. His tears wet my cheeks.

"If you get lost, find a soldier or someone who looks like an airplane pilot with a uniform on," he told me. "Make sure he's in uniform, not civilian clothes. Remember what I said about strangers."

He tucked a small, folded piece of paper into my hand. "This note will tell anyone who you are and where you need to go. It has my mother's name and telephone number on it. I'll see you in six months. I love you."

I was sad to leave him, but I knew he was in the harder position, being left behind. I was starting my adventure, excited to have a second chance to fix my mistakes, and proud of myself for showing my family and friends I wasn't a loser. As I stepped onto the plane, I felt as if I were literally climbing aboard my own dream. I was so giddy that I missed a step and stumbled. The stewardess helped me find my seat by a window. My body sank into the soft seat, and I buckled in. I'd never been on a plane before, but I wasn't afraid. My heart pounded with so much excitement, I thought it might jump out of my body. I would soon be flying over the Pacific Ocean on my way to America.

When the plane took off, I looked down at my home country. My husband would miss me, but my country wouldn't. Koreans saw me as damaged. John hadn't wanted me to leave, but he knew Osan was no place for me, not even for the last six months of his deployment, and he was happy that I would spend time with his family and finish up my *education* at his hometown high school. I waved to John from the plane until he was no more than a speck on the tarmac.

The flight would be long, but I was too excited to sleep. I had never been on an airplane, and I looked around to see if I knew anyone, but my fellow passengers were mostly Americans, along with a few older Korean women who had mixed blood children by their sides.

I saw the word *lavatory* and needed to know what it meant, so I took out my dictionary. I carefully watched how to buckle my seatbelt and positioned myself for the long flight. Then I studied the picture of John's parents, memorizing their faces, hairstyles, and smiles. I imagined what I would look like in an American school. I was excited that I wouldn't have to wear a uniform. The plane took off like a bird in the sky and flew for what seemed forever over the white clouds, and then darkness fell over the plane, and I slept.

When I woke up, I looked out the window to see an iced ocean.

The plane stopped in Alaska, but I didn't leave the gate to get food, afraid I would miss my connection, afraid someone else would take my seat if I was gone too long and then I would never find my way to John's parents.

When I finally stepped into the terminal in St. Louis, I looked around the corridor by the exit sign. John had promised me his mom and dad would notice me when I got off the plane. I had memorized their pictures, and yet I looked at the pictures, and then at the crowd, until I spotted a group of people waving at me— and I knew he had been right. A family of four rushed toward me holding my picture.

"Jeanhee?" they called out, as they did what I was doing, looking at a photo of me, trying to match it up. They were all much bigger than I, and I thought they must be very wealthy to be so fat. I bowed to his mother and his father.

"Hi! I am Jeanhee." As I bowed, they tried to bow as well. Then they grabbed me to give me hugs. Big hugs, from big fat people who were my husband's family. I couldn't figure out why John was so skinny and thought that maybe they hadn't given him enough food.

John's mother hugged me, then his father, his sister Tammy, and Randy, John's younger brother. They stared at me and tried to engage me in conversation, but I hadn't learned enough English yet to get beyond the niceties.

John's father grabbed my tattered satchel from the luggage carousel, and his mother led me to a station wagon and directed me to the backseat. I wanted to jump and dance around and yell, "I'm here, America! I finally made it!" but I didn't want my new family to think I was crazy. So I kept quiet.

John's sister and brother positioned themselves on either side of me, and the car settled lower to the ground. I wondered how it would have enough power to travel the four hours John told me it would take to get to their house from the airport. Exhausted from the plane ride, I immediately fell asleep. I woke up a couple of times, but the air had grown chilly and night had fallen, with only some streetlights beaming soft yellow light. I fell back to sleep, not sure how long I slept, jerking awake when the car pulled into a gravel driveway.

"Come, Jeanhee," my mother-in-law said. "Welcome to Mexico, Missouri."

John's father picked up my bag for me and led me toward the house. It was a trailer, with metal sides. I'd never seen one before, and I thought it might be a train car they could move whenever they needed to. Inside, the trailer was dim and messy. John's room was tiny, containing minimal decorations and a narrow bed with graying sheets. I peered curiously into the other rooms. They weren't much different. This wasn't how I thought America would look. I had expected every home to rival Woojung's, with high ceilings and grand windows to let in sunlight and fresh air.

In the morning, I saw that all of the other homes in the neighborhood were trailers, too, some built right on the ground and others propped up on wheels. Either way, they all looked the same. I'd always assumed everyone in America was rich, but the street where my new family lived looked as if it were a far cry from my wealthy, stargazing dreams.

I didn't waste any time. With a mixture of sign language and broken English, I let John's mother know I wanted to start school right away.

"Don't you want to rest a little, Jeanhee?" she asked. "You

just got here."

"No," I said, shaking my head. "I want to start today."

After breakfast, John's father left for work. John's brother, Randy, and his sisters, Marsha and Tammy, bustled around the house, preparing themselves for school. When they were ready, John's mother drove us all right up to the main entrance in the station wagon.

The school was a large brick building, the only high school in the city, and had what seemed to be infinite classrooms. I wondered how I'd ever find my way around inside. Students milled about on the fresh green grass, idling and chatting before they entered the classroom and began their school day.

I was back in school in America. I was back in high school. Just to be able to put my foot in the door in a high school again was worth everything I had given up. I would give up everything I had now just to be able to walk back in school, to be able to study. I didn't care if I understood a single word in English. The point was that I was back in school. I was able to study side by side with other students in an American school. I was as excited as I had been when I first charged into first grade at the age of six, more than a decade earlier.

The girls wore make-up and nail polish; the boys had on T-shirts and jeans. Not a uniform in sight. I even saw a couple leaning against the doors, kissing. We would have gotten suspended for even holding hands at my old school. I could tell right away that no one here would be made to kneel in the snow as punishment. I wondered if the teachers even struck their students when they acted unruly. I was too busy staring at them to notice they were staring back.

John's mother accompanied me to the office to help me register for classes. The administrative workers smiled at me, nodding a lot, trying to be encouraging. They registered me for English, history, home economics, math, speech, and study hall. They asked for a transcript from Korea. I hadn't expected to be asked for it since I was in America. I lied and told them I would get it soon. John's mother was worried about my English, and I was worried about my transcript. I could not tell them I had been expelled. And no- way I would tell them what I had done to earn the chance of my life time, my second chance. Even if I could, I wouldn't. *Not now,*

A blonde student escorted me between classes, and I went over the route we took in my head over and over so I wouldn't get lost the next day. I couldn't believe how often we changed classes, once each hour. In Korea, we sat in the same desk for three or four hours at a stretch and the teachers came to us. Here, we went to them. And the classes were much smaller. Instead of eighty, no more than twenty students were in each section. Students daydreamed and passed notes during class. I was usually too afraid to even look away from the teachers back in Korea, but in America students seemed to have no fear.

In most of the classes, I was lost. The teachers talked much too fast, and I never knew what page we were on, though they'd often come by and show me. I decided to focus on English and home economics, two subjects where I knew I could make some progress. Every day, I was shocked by something new. Kids made out in the hallways. The library was bursting with thousands of books, more than a person could read in a lifetime. The large, sunny cafeteria looked like a fancy restaurant. I took my Korean-English dictionary with me everywhere, determined to learn as fast as I could.

Despite my best efforts, I still didn't speak enough English to make friends. My inability to communicate made me feel invisible. Still, it was better than the invisibility of social shunning I'd experienced in Korea. My favorite teacher was the special English teacher the school brought in from another city. She at least halfway understood what I said. She may have pretended most of the time, but it made me feel better that she understood me a whole lot more than the other teachers. I could understand her more because she spoke very slowly. I wished I could ask other teachers to do the same but I didn't want to be disrespectful. "How dare you request that?" Korean teacher would have reprimanded me. After so many years of corporal punishment being common practice, I was still afraid of teachers in America.

During study hall, I went to the library and pieced together a few single paragraphs that described my new life. My teachers never pronounced my name correctly, not even once, but it didn't bother me. I was in an American school, studying English every day. If the teachers would just slow down, I was sure I could understand more of their lessons. A one page letter to John took me hours to write. I asked John's mother to send it to him, along with the cowboy shirt I made for him in my home economics class. In his letters back, John always said how proud he was of me.

I was the first Asian student in the school's history, and my name, picture, and an article about me appeared on the front page of the school newspaper within two weeks of me starting classes. I clipped it out and sent it to my mama. Later that month, I received a full-page letter, the very first I'd ever gotten from my dad, expressing how proud he was of me, how sorry he was for being an unfit father.

Dear my daughter Jeanhee,

This is your father. I saw your picture in American High School. I had it framed and hung it in my bedroom wall. I am so proud to have a daughter like you. I always knew you were the smartest of all my children.

I want you to know I didn't mean what I said when you came back home to get my permission to marry GI. I was angry, just angry about losing you to an American man. You are my daughter, no matter what.

My dear daughter, Jeanhee, I am truly sorry for being an unfit father for you while you were growing up. I am drinking less now; I quit gambling for good after you paid off my last gambling debt before you left Korea. I just want you to remember you are my daughter no matter how far you are from home.

From Your proud father

Kang Palhyung

I cried as I read it over and over, a one page letter from my dad. I held it to my chest. My dad *did* love me. I was his daughter still.

I forgave my Dad. That letter washed away all the wrongs he had ever done to me. My hate vanished because he wrote me from his heart.

After a few weeks, I started to dress more like the American girls, in Levi blue jeans and flowery shirts. I didn't get to eat Kimchi and rice; Mexico, Missouri had no oriental grocery stores. Besides, I didn't know how to cook rice, so it didn't matter. Lunch was challenging enough for me. While I understood what each option on the food board cost, I didn't know what the words actually meant. All I recognized were *hamburger* and *French fries* from my meals out with John, and so I asked for those every day. The portions were big, and I never left lunch feeling hungry. One day a boy came up behind me while I was eating and poked me in the shoulder. He lowered his face to mine and said, very slowly, "Why do you eat the same meal every day?"

He drew out each word so that I actually understood what he was saying. I don't know why it bothered him so much that I got the same food every day, but after that I became more adventurous, ordering tacos, fried chicken, and mashed potatoes.

The longer I went to school, the easier it was for me to communicate with John's family, and they embraced me as a daughter. Whatever fears I'd had about them doubting John's choice quickly disappeared. They were as open and loving as he was, and they took me bowling, out for McDonald's on special nights, and to visit his grandmother. Like John, she was funny, and it often felt as if I understood her better than anyone.

One time we went all the way to Branson, Missouri, and Tammy was so excited she couldn't sleep the night before. Her dream was to become a country singer. I didn't understand country music with its twanging guitars and plaintive melancholy voices, but I pretended I was having fun. I knew how important it was to live a dream, even a small one. Plus, Branson was better than Osan.

I liked pretending to be a normal teenager again. I had not forgotten my past. Only a year before I'd been working in Mama Sang's brothel, brushing off overly friendly hands and coldly discussing the prices for various sex acts.

I was not ashamed of what I had done to get where I was, to be able to study again. For that matter, I would study even harder to forget my past, all my extra hours at the library with two dictionaries in my hands, Korean to English and English to Korean, using them back and forth to help me understand simple questions or words and to understand sentences, paragraphs, pages, and then entire chapters. My studies took countless hours, but in comparison to what I had almost missed out on, having a second chance to be back in high school meant everything to me. I didn't mind spending hours trying to figure out foreign words. I didn't care if I failed all of the classes. The most important thing to me at that time was just to be able to be back in the classroom, to be with other high school students again. The simple pleasure of carrying my books and walking down the halls searching for the right classrooms was to die for.

"This is what I had worked for back in Osan!" I wanted to yell to the people of Korea thousands of miles away. I had reclaimed my dream. I deserved this second chance. My heart burst out of defiance, screaming, "Look! Look at me, you Koreans! Anyone… all Koreans out there, do you hear me?"

I studied all the time, every chance I got, in the American school among the Americans. If I could only understand what everyone was saying, especially the teachers, I could do so much better. My English teacher was so impressed, he gave me an A for effort, no doubt. I was so proud of that grade. It gave me hope I could do better in the rest of my subjects.

Time flew by, and soon John finished his tour in Korea and returned home. When we picked him up from the airport, he was tired but beaming. He wrapped his arms around me and kissed me firmly on the mouth before hugging his mom and his sisters. I was glad to see him, and he held my hand in the car ride back to the house.

"Jeanhee, your English is so good," he said. "I'm so proud of you."

Not long after he got back, he broke the news that we were moving to Luke Air Force Base in Glendale, Arizona, his new base. I didn't mind a bit. I'd held out coughing up my Korean high school transcript as long as I could, and the school administration was growing weary of my excuses. Besides, life in Missouri wasn't what I'd envisioned. My dream of a pretty home and delicate, beautiful clothes was nowhere in sight. From a material standpoint, John's family's trailer wasn't much better than the house I'd left behind.

High school in Glendale was tough. They already had a great number of Latino students and the administration couldn't afford to find a special teacher to help me with my English. In addition, John and I were broke. He worked two jobs, and we barely paid our bills on time.

Besides trips to McDonalds, we never went out for a dinner. But even though our apartment was small and we frequently went without good food, I didn't complain. My home life was glorious compared to school. Without a special teacher to help me with my English, my classes were too difficult, and after a few months of struggling, I gave up. I was heartbroken. Dropping out felt like being kicked out of school in Korea all over again.

John pressured me to have a baby and be his wife, two things he wanted more than me getting my *education*. I think his parents must have told him I had a second agenda in marrying him, and he wanted to affirm my commitment by starting a family.

When my period finally stopped, John was overjoyed. My world, my dream of finishing high school in America, ended in a hopeless dream. He hugged and kissed me and laughed and then called his mother. I cried. I was still unable to communicate fully with John; to him, my tears were happy ones. I locked myself in the bathroom and cried some more. I'd gone through this before.

"This is a happy time for us, Jeanhee," he said. "Every married couple wants to have a baby. I've never met a woman who wasn't excited to be a mother. What's wrong with you?"

I didn't speak English well enough to tell him there were plenty of women like me who didn't want to be mothers. I came to America to finish high school; I needed to graduate in order to validate myself. I'd run away from failure when I'd gone to Osan, hoping to get a high school *education* in America since Koreans had denied my second chance. The words were in my head, but they wouldn't come out right, so I kept them to myself.

In my frustration at being unable to communicate, I cried even harder. The only solace I found was the few other Korean women I met on the base who were married to GI, but John became increasingly possessive and tried to isolate me from having friends.

"You don't need to be around them," he said.

"They're my friends," I choked out, putting my hand on my taut, growing belly and sobbing like crazy. "I'm like them."

"No," he said, "You are *not* like them."

I still had both sets of dictionaries, now tattered with use, and I looked up the word for *abortion* under A from English to Korean. After I found the word from Korean to English, I showed it to John, my finger trembling as I pointed to the word.

"I want this, John. I don't want a baby." I didn't care how much it hurt, or what it cost. If I had a baby, I would never live out my dream.

He jerked the book from my hand and placed it on the table. "Hell, no. That's illegal here, Jeanhee," he said angrily. "That is my baby. If you ask a doctor about that, they'll throw you in jail. We don't do those things in this country."

I had a deathly fear of being deported to Korea and having to return to Osan and work in a brothel again, or worse, live with my mother and face the shame of failing twice.

My first son Joshua was born after sixteen hours labor. I cried a lot during labor, not just from the pain of contractions but also in fear of unable to be a school girl again. A little tiny baby was all mine. Cries After she wrapped him tightly in a blanket, the nurse let me hold him-- a precious life, all mine-- and his life was depending on me. I was his Mommy. I didn't quite know how to be a mom; I was trying to grasp of what all must take place.

Just a year before, I had been trying to pass exams in high school; becoming a mommy was overwhelming. We couldn't afford disposable diapers, so washing dirty diapers, feeding the baby every two to three hours completely wore me out. I forgot to eat most of the time. I was overwhelmed and exhausted looking at the tiny being that was all mine. I was not eating well, and I became anemic. The doctor told me I had to eat liver every day for the next six months. Two months after Joshua's first birthday, I had another son, Jason. With two babies, little money, and poor English, I felt trapped for life. I understood for the first time my mother's hopelessness. My life wasn't supposed to be like this. Two babies, a poor husband, and I was still a high school dropout. This was not part of my dream.

Despite my depression, John still loved me. He wanted to make me happy. So, in an effort to save our marriage, he submitted a request to be deployed to Korea again, this time to Kusan Air Base, about an hour away from my old home. U.S. citizenship was automatically awarded to me as the wife of a military service man about to be deployed overseas. I was so happy and proud to become an American citizen. I was so proud to be an American. It was surreal to be part of Meegook, the country I had been dreaming of coming to since I was eight. , I will forever call America my country. I became an ever proud American citizen in 1978. I felt it was justified since the Koreans gave up on me and the Americans didn't. They said I could vote for president if I wanted to and enjoy the same freedoms all Americans do.

As the plane took us back to the country I had left in my quest to go to high school, I was happy to return home. At least it was a change from my unhappy life with John, the life I didn't want, where I felt trapped. I would feel better when I saw my mom and sisters and brothers again. My babies would like to see their aunts and uncles and grandma. I cuddled my baby boys as the shores receded into the sea.

I was happy to see my brothers and sisters and my parents again. I thought perhaps my dad would accept me back since I had babies, his first grandkids. And I was right. This time, my visit was much different, more like a family reunion. No one in my family was ashamed of me anymore. They were so proud that I had gone to an American high school, and in their minds, I had finished. I kept my dropping out and my unhappy life with John from them. No one had to know I hadn't graduated. My dad had the picture I had sent from the high school classroom in his office to show off to the entire neighborhood. I was his daughter again.

Because the American dollar was strong in Korea, we once again lived lavishly, in a large home with a full-time maid, and I slowly pulled out of my depression. I reconnected with some of my girlfriends I had hung out with before I was expelled from high school. They hadn't changed; they were the same as when I had seen them last. They visited me in Kunsan often. However, I could never find my friend Oksoon. I rode the bus to her home to find her, but her family refused to give me her whereabouts. I cried and left my phone number in case they changed their minds, but I never got a call back from Oksoon.

My father was too proud to visit my home in Kunsan, but because of my sons, his first grandkids, he let me visit him often. He loved to play with Joshua and Jason, and I was told that when I wasn't around, he even made gaga sounds and tickled their tummies to hear their giggles and sometimes bought them sweets from a nearby store. I cannot remember even once when he ever bought me anything, presents or birthday wishes, let alone gave me praises, when I was growing up. Perhaps he had gotten old, realized his mistakes, and wanted to make up for it with my babies. Who knows? Still, I was happy for his change of heart.

John's deployment only lasted one year, and before long we were sent back to the States. This time, my family came to the airport to see us off. My mom and sisters waved and cried, and said, "*Chalga, uynni.*"

This time, John was stationed at Lakeland Air Base in San Antonio, and we returned to the miserable poverty of GI life once again. John's new status as a *drill sergeant* meant he received a higher paycheck, but it wasn't that much higher. The upper-level officers encouraged him to project a stronger persona in order to transform the new GIs into obedient machines, and John brought these lessons home with him. He practiced his commands and sang marching songs in our bedroom, and I rolled on the ground with laughter whenever his voice grew deep and harsh and his face became an unfeeling mask.

Quickly, though, his behavior stopped being amusing. He started barking out orders for me, trying to run me like I was one of his basic trainees. Despondent, I wondered where the fun-boy filled with sweetness and light had gone, the one who used to tick-tock like a clock and tell me jokes to make me smile. He must've gone to the same place that hopeful girl who dreamed of America had gone.

After three months of non-stop fighting with John, I knew it was time to make a move. I'd already been looking for a way out, panicked that if I stayed with him I'd never finish my *education*. His change in personality gave me a way to leave without guilt. Despite my threats that I'd divorce him if he didn't change, he didn't take my complaints seriously. I knew that if I stayed complacent, I'd be stuck in that life forever. By this time, I spoke enough English to tell John what was on my mind, and we had the same conversation numerous times to no avail.

"John, I want a divorce. I don't want to be your wife anymore. I want to finish school."

"We'll work things out, Jeanhee. We're fine."

John was in denial. He couldn't believe I wanted divorce. The naïve girl he had married and brought to America to give her a good life could hardly speak good English. He didn't see the changes in me. He thought I'd get over whatever I was angry about soon.

"I won't discuss this anymore," he said. "We're not getting a divorce."

Eventually, John turned away whenever I brought it up, always involving himself in some household task and refusing to answer my pleas. By that time, I'd met a good Korean friend, Miye, and when I finally packed my bags and moved out, she not only let me live with her, but she also helped me get a job at the restaurant where she worked. I had never worked at a job that paid for actual physical labor, not sex, yet Miye said I could learn, and I did.

Miye and I were like real sisters; we could share anything. With a beautiful oval face and a perfect smile, she could've easily been Miss Korea. Instead, she had been alone in America like I was. Like many GIs, once her husband got home, he regretted taking a foreign bride soon after she arrived in the States, and he left her for an American girl with yellow corn silk hair. Miye still hadn't gotten over him. She wistfully told me how every morning he'd say "Konichiwa," which meant *good morning* in Japanese. She'd whisper this magic word to me in the mornings, and her eyes would grow unbearably sad. If he ever asked, and we both knew he wouldn't, she would have taken him back in an instant.

We worked as waitresses at a popular Chinese restaurant called The Golden Wok in San Antonio. Its authentic noodles and vegetable dishes were so good a line formed out the door at dinnertime, and on good nights, I made as much as two hundred dollars in tips. I got along fine with the chef, who was from Hong Kong and spoke no English. He smiled a lot, his smile revealing several missing teeth. However, I did not get along so well with the chauvinistic Mexican manager, Luciano.

One day after the lunch shift, Luciano took off his shirt to show me his physique. I knew he was trying to impress me, but I couldn't help laughing at his bravado.

"Too dumb to get a high school diploma?" he asked with a sneer. "Dumb little Jeanhee, you'll always work in a restaurant."

When I started night school to study for my GED, he laughed at me. He didn't take rejection nearly as well as that grease ball pimp back in Osan, and he made it his life goal to punish me, making me clean the toilets, and afraid I missed a spot, bringing me an old tooth brush to use on the tiny cracks. He also mocked my nail polish. His jibes made me furious.

I didn't care how I got my high school diploma, and at twenty-two, a GED was now my only option. I was so proud and happy to be back in the classroom, even though it wasn't much of classroom. It was located in a local church building, and twice a week I went there to meet with eleven other high school drop outs of varying races. I was the only Asian, studying for my long-awaited high school diploma. A GED.

I made a pact with Miye to get back at Luciano for harassing me constantly, and so one Friday, the busiest lunch day of the week, we clocked in and then clocked out five minutes later, shouting, "We quit, Luciano! Enjoy the lunch crowd!"

As we knew she would, the owner, Lily, called and asked why we'd quit without notice, and we told her what'd been going on with Luciano. He was fired that day, and we got our jobs back. Lily reluctantly rehired him back as a kitchen worker after he begged piteously for a second chance, and so the next day, when we clocked in, we found Luciano in the kitchen making eggrolls. He refused to look us in the eye. To me, his demotion was a small but satisfying victory. I walked up to him as he tried his best to prepare egg rolls and asked if I could show him how to roll the dough faster.

"Go away!" he snarled without looking up.

Despite the joy Miye brought into my life, my family life continued to fall apart. John and I had agreed that he'd take custody of my two little babies until I got on my feet, and I gave him my wedding ring back to help pay the bills. I also paid for the lawyer to represent us in our divorce. I didn't know at the time that I was listed as the defendant even though I'd asked for the divorce and paid the fee. We had no possessions to fight over. All I wanted from the settlement was my freedom. I didn't want a husband who was going to end up dragging me back to Mexico, Missouri, to live in a trailer next door to his mother.

My heart still ached with regret over missing out on my high school *education*. My status as a *high school dropout* hung over my head, heavier than ever, and I believed time was running out. I had unfinished business within me.

While I waited for my divorce from John to be finalized, I continued attending night school, hoping that once I got my GED, I could go to college and experience an actual classroom again and enjoy what it is like to be single in America. I was depressed because of my broken life. My childhood dream, my high school dream, was nowhere near. I had been trapped in my marriage, and I had lost my brave optimism. Living a life I didn't want and having kids wore me out. I just didn't see myself as either a wife or mom.

After spending four years with John, I couldn't fit into any of my clothes. I had gotten fat. I needed to do something about my double-stacked-tummy, so I bought a book titled *How to Lose Weight* and learned what exercises would slim me up quickly and inexpensively.

Be a runner, it read. The next day, I went out and bought myself a pair of running shoes, a couple pairs of running pants, and a tee shirt from Wal-Mart. I also bought a tape recorder with an earplug for music. Next, I found some fun, upbeat music to listen to, nothing with a sad tone. I couldn't understand too many songs lyrics in English, so I chose Mozart & Beethoven, classical piano concertos that made me smile, and several of their symphonies. I made myself jog every morning while I listened to my new favorite music.

I initially started with one mile, extending the distance as I got used to running. Soon, I ran from three to five miles a day religiously. I found my daily runs exhilarating and discovered, as sweat dripped from my entire body, that all my worries had melted away along with all the fat from my body. I became hooked on my daily jogging routine. It made me happy about life and about myself. I was on a runner's high. And little did I know that jogging would be my favorite workout for next thirty-plus years.

Chapter Six

My Long-Awaited "Education" Dream

I was at an officer's club on Lakeland Air Force base with Miye on our night off when Robert first came up to me. Dressed in a one-piece hunter green flight suit, he was exceptionally tall, slim, and good-looking. I soon learned that as a young man, he had run away from home after rejecting the wishes of his wealthy parents and foregoing college.

He had immediately joined the Air Force, where he served in the Vietnam War. After ten years overseas, he decided to become an officer and finished his bachelor's degree through the University of Maryland's overseas program for active GIs. When I met him, he was just one month shy of finishing the United States Air Force's Officer Training School. He wanted to be a pilot, but because of his age he didn't meet the requirements and had to settle for becoming a scope dope—a flying radar controller on an AWACS spy plane.

Robert was the exact opposite of John in every way. Well-bred, he came from a wealthy, successful family from Syracuse, New York. His father worked as a chemical engineer for the Bristol-Myers Company; his younger brother, Jeff studied at Harvard Business Law School and was engaged to a classmate pursuing the same degree; his youngest brother, Adam had a full basketball scholarship at USC; and his mother was professor at Syracuse University. I was drawn to this well-educated man with piercing blue eyes that conveyed caring warmth I had never felt before.

As a six-foot-two, blond-haired, blue-eyed lifelong bachelor, Robert was apparently as surprised as I was by his infatuation with me. He said he had never before met a woman he wanted to come home to every night. During all the years he had spent in Vietnam, the Philippines, and Thailand, he had never found a woman who tempted him into giving up his carefree, bachelor-lifestyle, but as he later told me, he fell in love with me the moment he saw me smile at him. That was the only time Woojung's lesson got me into trouble.

We went on a date the next day. Over the next few weeks, he took me to eat at fine restaurants and showered me with compliments, saying how beautiful I was. He was a perfect gentleman at all times, probably because he knew I had just gone through a divorce and he wanted to earn my trust first. So much time had passed since John had shown me any tenderness, I hadn't even realized how much I missed it.

A few days before Robert was to leave for Tyndall Air Force Base to begin his final training, he took my hands in his and squeezed them gently. Then he reached into his jacket pocket and pulled out a round-trip air ticket to Panama City.

"Jeanhee, I love you. Will you fly to meet me?" he asked. "You'll never want for anything. I'll take care of you while you get your GED, and I will even send you to college if that's what you want. I'll help you get your children back, no question about it. And after Panama City, I'm deploying to Korea. I put in a request to go there in hopes you'd come with me. I know you miss your family."

He kept on talking, not let me getting a word in edgewise. I could tell he wanted to convince me. "And in case you change your mind, I bought you a round trip ticket so you can return to San Antonio if you choose. You don't even have to sleep with me."

For once, I was speechless. I took the tickets, but put up my hand when his face glowed with happiness. I couldn't believe I had just been offered such a gift by a man I hardly knew. I enjoyed my newly single life, and now this man wanted to put me in another cage. My mind raced with the idea that if I accepted the tickets, I might be forced to give up the freedom I had worked so hard to get. Then again, his magical words were the kind that any woman in her right mind would swoon over.

He promised me security and love, but he couldn't promise me what I truly needed— the freedom to pursue my dreams without a man tying me down. He wasn't part of the plan. But at the same time, I was deeply tempted.

"I'll keep the tickets for now," I said. "But that doesn't mean I'm coming with you. May I have some time to think about it?"

"Of course, sweetheart," he said. "I'm a patient man. I can wait."

I certainly didn't want a second husband, but that's what I ended up with, almost before I knew it. On graduation night of officer's training school, Robert's parents flew in from Syracuse for the ceremony, and he insisted I be there to meet them. At the celebration dinner with his parents' watchful eyes on me, I was filled with a sense of pressure and uneasiness. They were nice and welcoming, with the same air of serenity and class Woojung's mother had so effortlessly conveyed, but I caught them looking at me several times with confusion. What did their handsome, accomplished son see in this little scrap of a woman?

Robert's mother was beautiful and blonde; her make-up was flawless, and her hair was pulled back into a perfect, sleek ponytail. Her dark coral lipstick accentuated her egg shaped face and fair skin and showcased her gleaming white teeth. Her ring was the biggest rock I'd ever seen, sparkling against the bright lights and radiating in a thousand shimmering lights. She had beautiful hands, and her nail color matched her lipstick.

Robert had been a bachelor for so long, and now this tiny, shy little Asian girl had somehow caught their son's eye? They didn't understand. Though to be fair, neither did I. Roberts's intense emotion for me had taken me by surprise, as well.

Robert and I stayed together his last night in San Antonio at the Hilton hotel on the River Walk. I reluctantly gave him my promise that I would join him, but I warned him I needed time to think. He held me so tight in his arms for so long, I feared he might smother me with his hairy chest I so loved to caress when we were lying naked in bed. When I had finally decided I was ready, we had fallen into bed naturally and effortlessly, our bodies working together in tandem, and now we couldn't keep our hands off each other.

I thought about Robert's offer all night. I barely knew him, really. Despite the fact that we'd already spent our first night together, we had only dated for four weeks. I stayed up late looking for a world map in the books at the hotel. I didn't even know where Panama City was. Although my life was in disarray and without direction, I knew I didn't want to marry again. I was still without my sons and got teary-eyed at the most unexpected times, whenever I saw small things that reminded me of them and how deeply I missed them. John barely let me see them because he was so angry at me. He hoped I would change my mind and go back to him if he used my babies as bait. He told me he still loved me, but he had a cruel way of showing it. If I went with Robert, I didn't know if I'd ever see them again. Could I give up my children for security? Or could Robert really help me get them back?

I asked my friend Miye for advice. She wasn't much older than me, but she acted like an older sister and was eager to take care of me. Although she didn't want me to leave her, she told me to go.

"You have nothing to lose," she said with a sob. "Keep your ticket, and if he turns out to be horrible, come back. You can always live with me again."

She held me as she said this, and though I cried, too, I could tell she hurt more. Maybe she wished a man like Robert would fall for her. She would've accepted his proposal in a second and would never have looked back. Almost any woman would.

A few days later, I called Robert.

"Hi," I said, unsure of what to say next. "I've thought about your offer, and I've decided to take it. I'm coming to Panama City."

"I'll make you so happy, Jeanhee," he answered, his voice choked with emotion and so happy. "I promise I will be so good to you, you won't be disappointed."

Miye cried as my plane pulled away from the gate, waving me off in time with her sobs. I cried with mixed emotion. My heart ached at leaving Miye, who was still grieving for her ex-husband, and my head whirled over my uncertain future. I knew I wasn't ready for another relationship, but if we always made the right decision, the word *regret* would never have come to exist in English or any other language.

When I got off the plane in Panama City, Robert walked toward me in tears. After a long hug, he put his hands over my eyes and led me to the parking lot. When he took his hands away, we stood in front of a brand new red Firebird. He pressed the keys into my hands and let me drive it home.

"This is your car," he said. "You can take it anywhere you want to go."

Grateful and confused, I kissed him long and hard in the front seat of that beautiful car. His gift was generous and I was grateful, but what would I ever achieve for myself if I kept taking handouts from men?

We ate dinner at a restaurant perched on the shore, the gentle crash of the waves underscoring the seriousness of our conversation. As the sun set, Robert poured out his heart and tried to convince me I had made the right decision in joining him. Eagerness filled his eyes as he poured our champagne and made me promises I knew he would keep.

"I'm going to register you for school tomorrow, and then I'll find the best lawyer in town. We'll get Josh and Jason back. I want us to be a family, and they're young enough to accept me as their father. We can make this work, Jeanhee, I promise."

He was true to his word, and I soon started school on the base, taking a business English class and a typing class. Robert got me a maid and rented us a beautiful condo on the beach, a fully furnished bachelor pad more than a home for a couple, with two bright red L-shaped couches in the living room and sleek black appliances. The furniture was beach themed, and the curtains were made from a pretty palm tree print in green and beige, with beige carpet throughout the entire condo. It was very cozy.

We went out to dinner every night after his training class on base, and every weekend he asked what I wanted to do, and that's what we did. He never tired of being tender toward me and making me happy every single day. In his eyes, I was precious.

I, on the other hand, didn't feel as if I deserved so much attention. I knew that if he knew the truth about my past, he wouldn't even look at me. I wondered from time to time if I should reveal my secret, but I decided to stay silent. Keeping what had happened in Osan a secret was a necessary measure for me to stay where I was. Why spoil a good thing?

In September, as he was about to finish this three-month training before his deployment to Korea, he asked me to marry him. I wasn't ready to say yes, but I couldn't say no to this man who I was sure was the sweetest one in the whole world.

I looked him in the eyes and listed my shortcomings. "I don't know how to cook, and I hate housework. I'm independent and follow my heart and fight back when I feel I need to. I would be a terrible wife, Robert.

"Shh." He pressed fingers to my lips. "We already have a maid, and we'll get a cook. Once we get your children back, you can join me in Korea and see your parents. Jeanhee, I love you. Be *my* Jeanhee, will you? We'll be a family, and I'll be the best daddy ever to your boys."

"Robert, you are the sweetest man I've ever met." My eyes welled up with tears, but I still wasn't quite moved enough to say yes. "I don't deserve this kindness. I'm not sure I'm even ready to be married again. I don't know if I'm really in love with you."

"Okay, Sweetheart." To any other man, my words would've been a crushing blow, but Robert just laughed them off. "Then learn to love me. I'm willing to wait."

I said *yes* then. I didn't know what else to do. He had promised all the right things, and he followed through. He helped me get custody of Joshua and Jason, and he treated them like his own sons. Soon we were on our way to Korea, where I took a job at the *Education Center* on Osan air base, working as the field assistant for the Los Angeles Metropolitan College overseas program for GIs. Robert would have let me stay home, but I wanted to keep busy.

During the week, I worked hard. My job at the *Education Center* was a dream job, one of the most sought-after positions on Osan Air base and the highest paying position for a Korean. Because I was also a US citizen, they paid me more than five times what the average Koreans in the office made, and some had been working there over twenty years.

I had a full-time maid to take care of my kids and do all the housekeeping, and I wore designer suits to work every day, suits that fit me perfectly. The designers came to my house in the evenings for my fittings. I was the person on base all the Koreans wanted to be. I wouldn't dare spill my secret to anyone. Only six short years before, I had stood outside the main gate selling myself on the street to any GI who would have me as just another twenty-dollar prostitute.

*****

I received my long waited high school diploma soon after I went to work at the *Education Center*. I passed the GED test in English and was the first Korean to ever have a high school diploma after being expelled from a Korean school on Korean soil. If they had offered a second chance the way Americans did, would more follow in my footsteps? I was even more proud of being an American citizen and cried tears of joy for my redemption. I wanted to yell and scream at the Korean culture that had been so quick to give up on my *education*, saying,

"Look, Koreans! Look at me!"

"I did it!"

"I had proved every one of you dead wrong!"

I immediately bought the most beautiful mahogany frame I could find for my certificate and hung it right behind my desk on the wall in my office, for everyone to see. They couldn't miss it unless they were blind. No one passed me without noticing my certificate. To many, it was just a GED, but to me it was the redemption of my dark past wrapped with a large red bow, the gift of my life, everything I had done in a single piece of paper.

Getting my high school diploma in Korea, the same place that had refused me an *education* nearly six years before, felt right. Working at the *education center* also gave me an opportunity to take college classes at night, and since I worked for the school, they waived my tuition. Me? Studying college courses in English with Americans? It couldn't possibly be real, especially since I was in Korea, the country that had denied me an *education*.

I still had a chip on my shoulder from being expelled from high school and having to get a GED instead of attending an actual graduation, and yet my missed dream came back to me in a rush during the classes I took two nights a week. As I held my heavy textbooks, my notebook, and my pencil case in my arms, my desire to get an *education* came back just as strong as it had been when I was five, but this time, nearly twenty years later, the meaning of the word *education* had taken a turn. I no longer just wanted to eat fluffy white rice wrapped in toasted seaweed every day. I now wanted redemption, the second chance I was never given by my own culture.

My gut instinct had been right, no matter how I tried to fight it, however. This was the wrong time for me to be married. A little over a year after we moved to Osan, I divorced Robert and shattered his heart. I wasn't miserable, and we never fought, but I was filled with a deep restlessness that tortured me day and night. I hated myself for it, but what I wanted was more important than accepting his love and settling down as his wife.

"I'm so, so sorry, Robert," I said with a sob. "I wish I could live with you and be your wife, but I can't. I have to find myself. I need to be independent. Please understand. I'm so very sorry. If I ever do decide to settle down and be married, it will be to you or someone just like you. I am thankful for all you have done and for your loving me with all your heart.

"Nothing you did or didn't do left me unfulfilled; I simply need my freedom. I want to be single, free from being married. Please... I beg you. Hear my heart. I truly wish I could bypass this part of my life and stay married. But I can't."

"I love you, Jeanhee," he said. He cried and stroked my hair. "Will you think it over? If I did anything wrong, I can change. Will you please tell me what I did wrong?"

"Robert, you didn't do a single thing wrong," I answered. "It's me. If I could ever change for anyone, it would be for you. But I met you at the wrong time in my life."

"I'd never keep you from anything," Robert said. Then he begged, "Please come back to me one day. I'll take you back. I'll wait as long as it takes. Just don't divorce me."

But I stood steadfast in my belief that for me to start my future, my relationship with Robert had to end. He did everything he possibly could to delay it. I finally had to find him and drag him down to the law office to sign the divorce papers.

I wanted to be on a campus, reading, learning, and making friends. I wanted my dream, born so long ago thanks to a Hershey bar in a rice paddy. I knew I'd probably never meet another man who loved me like Robert did. I also knew I only had one chance to make something of my life and get an *education*. And I had to hurt him to make that choice. Korea had given up on me once, but I was not going to ever give up on myself. I knew that soon I would fly back to America with my sons, still chasing my second chance.

When I found out that Josh and Jason could no longer attend school on the base because we were no longer military dependents, I knew it was time to take that next step toward my dream. What did I want the most before I got too old? What did I need to do to make up for the mistakes that had hurt me the most?

I wanted to reclaim my dream. I wanted my second chance back, and this time, I was going to succeed at being a student, carrying my books on campus somewhere, anywhere.

No, not just anywhere. I wanted to get my *education* in America, to graduate with my peers. The kind of degree I got didn't matter, and neither did the school I attended or my major. I just wanted to get a degree in a ceremony, wearing a black robe. I wanted to go back to America and attend college. The day I received my *education*—the day when I could say to my old friends from Namsung, the ones who had turned their backs on me, that I was just as good as they were, would be the proudest day of my life. I was no longer ashamed of my Osan experiences. My achievement would overshadow that part of my past and show the world that anyone can change her life if she tries hard enough, no matter what mistakes she might make along the way.

My marriage to Robert had lasted a little over a year. When it ended, I felt free. If I were a bird, I would have flown all over the place, forward and backward and around the world, both wings stretched as far out as they could go, looking down to see where I wanted to stop for food and water, on to the next destination without boundaries—no bags required, just enough energy to keep soaring. And I always had energy to spare.

Marriage as a permanent state of being had never crossed my mind; somehow, I had connected the institution to a life full of heavy baggage, my years wasting away while I lived with a person who would only hold me back. Living happily with a man, content and warm in his love, had not been on my list of dreams growing up. I wanted to see what was out there for me, what I was capable of doing, good or bad. I wanted to taste adventure without being committed. John and Robert had made me forget what I most wanted, and I had spent seven years of my life feeling lost and unfinished. If I were going through a quarter-life crisis, I listed my mistakes from age fifteen to age twenty-four in my head: I'd been married twice, divorced twice, with two kids and nowhere to go. So what now? What had I missed? If I started over, what would I want most? I felt as if time were running out for me to fix my past mistakes, pressuring me to live my life to the fullest right now. I just didn't feel my destiny was to be someone's wife—not yet, maybe not ever.

I wanted to know what other women my age did when they weren't married; I wanted to experience normal life and put away my past, living where no one would know about what had happened to me unless I told them. I didn't want to have already promised forever to two different men. Even though I felt lost and confused, I soon also felt as if a great weight had been lifted off of my shoulders. I *could* change the course of my life before it was too late. I wasn't satisfied with my GED, but I *could* still go to college to graduate and wear that black silky robe. I wanted to celebrate at the finish line with my classmates, just as my Namsung peers had done on the day of their graduation. My goal was to focus on being myself without the heaviness of a being a *Mrs.* Robert Kennedy on my soul. Even though my mind felt forty-something, my heart was still fifteen—and my burning desire to be someone, to better my life, had not faded, no matter how my life's circumstances had twisted my path to their will.

The time between leaving Robert and his signing the divorce papers opened up a whole new world for me. I had never been in the dating scene, going out to dinner and meeting new men for nothing more than an evening of fun. I had never known the anticipation of waiting for a date night with a new almost-stranger each week. What colognes did they use, and what should I say during dinner? How do people make normal small talk? I found it exhilarating. I still wanted the companionship of a man, but without the commitment. I wanted to feel butterflies in my stomach, to desire someone and dance a little if I wanted, not the way I had danced back in the Lucky Club when I was trying to catch a GI to take me to America, but just enjoying the rhythm of the music. I did go out a few evenings with some of my new friends on the base to the very same clubs I had cruised when I was selling my body. However, because I was Korean, many of the GIs assumed I was still a whore and pushed themselves on me.

Sometimes, I pretended I didn't speak any English and just smiled and backed away, but what I really wanted to yell was "I am not a whore anymore! Now I am just Jeanhee, and I am not for sale!" But that would not have made sense to an intoxicated GI in the wee hours of the night. I didn't really mind their coming on to me for the wrong reasons, anyway. After all, that life had taken me to America. And I still had a bit of the old Jeanhee in me. I still drank Coca-Cola instead of alcohol as I watched the whores in action as they flirted and sashayed.

I spent my nights staring at the ceiling, dreaming of walking across a beautiful tree-lined campus, studying the afternoons away in the library, surrounded by other people who loved knowledge as much as I did. I didn't think for an instant what it would mean to be a poor, single mother in America. I knew my determination would see me through, just as it had so far.

Soon after the divorce, I told Sooncha, my best friend on the base, that I planned to return to America. Sooncha was five years younger than I—a baby in my eyes. She acted young, too, always silly and smiling, twirling her long dark hair as she laughed at her own jokes. She even called me *sister*. Sooncha was unfailingly sweet, her big heart shining out through her dark eyes. She had caught her GI's attention when she was a go-go dancer at the Officer's Club, and now she and Thomas were married. Tom, as she called him in her thick accent, worked in Robert's squadron, and that was how Sooncha and I had first met.

"It's time for me to go back, Sooncha," I said. "I'm free now. I can finally start college. I'm just not sure where to go. I don't really want to go back to Texas or Arizona, and definitely not Missouri."

"I know what you can do," Sooncha said. "You all can come to Oklahoma and live with me and Tom for a while. I will be lonesome since Tom will be flying all the time. I am sure Tom will say yes." I was sure he would, too. He absolutely doted on Sooncha.

When Sooncha told me the next day that Tom had agreed, we were both so happy. We sat over bowls of kimchi soup and made plans for our new lives, chatting the afternoon away. Sooncha was uneducated, but her youthfulness, pretty smile, and dancer's figure made up for it. Everyone who met her loved her. I mostly talked about college, and she talked about having a car to drive and spending Tom's money when he was away flying the AWACS spy plane. Neither of us could even say *Oklahoma* correctly, but we knew it was in America, and that was enough for us.

"Home of AWACS spy plane, Tinker Air Base, in Oklahoma," Sooncha said, excited and jumbling the letters. Then she laughed. "Who cares how you say it? I am going to America."

She had never been there, so she was thrilled, reminding me of myself when I was her age, nineteen. I was glad she had fallen in love with her GI before her face took on the ragged, worn look of a whore. Tom would be enough for her, and she would have a normal, happy life in America. She wouldn't be constantly restless and yearning for something more as I was.

Sooncha and Tom left the following week, leaving me their new address and phone number. Within a few weeks, I had sold all of my furniture, the American goods so loved by Koreans going first and for the best price—the TV, my electric stove, the plush sofa. I didn't need to buy plane tickets, since the Air Force would fly me back, and so with my savings and the money I made from selling our things I knew I would be able to get by for a little while even if I didn't find a job right away.

At the end of November 1983, I prepared to board a plane and leave Korea once again, this time for a new life in Oklahoma and with the goal to go to college. Robert came to say goodbye and hugged my boys with as much emotion as if they were his own sons. He gave me one last hug, as well, the same deep hug he had given me that day in San Antonio when he'd asked me to join him in Panama City.

"Good-bye, my Jeanhee," he said to me, with deep sadness in his voice. I had broken his heart. He wanted to say more, but my tears stopped him. I cried for my inability to accept his unconditional, undying love, and he cried because he was losing me forever.

"My Jeanhee, I'm glad you are going to live with Tom and Sooncha, so I won't worry so much. Take care of our sons, Josh and Jason."

He hugged them tightly again and then hugged them some more. "Goodbye, boys. Take good care of your mommy for me."

"Why aren't you coming with us, Daddy?" Josh and Jason asked, pulling at his hand. They didn't understand that we had divorced, and they looked at him with confusion. Robert broke down, crying uncontrollably, and turned away.

Leaving Robert was one of the hardest things I had ever

done, but remaining his wife would have been even harder and unfair to us both. I needed to finish my *education* on my terms. Not as a wife, not as a daughter. Just as Jeanhee. I'd dreamed of it for too long to compromise now. I didn't need a beautiful house, or sheer clothes, or fluffy white rice every day. I would get that myself, one day in the future. During the plane ride, I closed my eyes and imagined I soared over the clouds by myself, swooping and diving over the dark ocean below.

A bumpy landing startled me out of my dream of flight as we touched down in chilly, windy Oklahoma City, Oklahoma. Tom and Sooncha were waiting to pick us up, Sooncha bouncing up and down on her toes. She yelled, "Sister!" over and over in excitement as we neared the exit. We hugged, and then she scooped both of my boys into a big hug as well.

Tom drove us to their new home in Midwest City, in a sedate, middle class neighborhood. I was glad to see I wasn't going to have to live in a trailer again, at least not right now. Josh, Jason, and I were soon settled in Sooncha's small guest bedroom, all three of us sharing a bed and me waking up with a foot in my face more often than not. We were crowded but comfortable, and Tom really was gone a lot of the time. He very carefully kept from mentioning Robert to me, both for the sake of their friendship and at Sooncha's request, but he also seemed genuinely interested in helping us. Perhaps, he felt as if he were doing Robert a favor by pointing me in the right direction.

One day he told me about welfare, a new concept to me, and also told me about a nearby community college where I could start classes toward the degree I had been bugging him about ever since we had arrived.

"Jeanhee, you won't even need a car since an apartment complex is within walking distance," he said. I was elated, but he kept on giving me good news. "And that's not all. Since you're a single mom, the government will help pay for your tuition and books."

"Really, Tom?" I looked at him with my mouth hanging open. "Are you joking?"

"No," he answered. "I'm dead serious. And, the government

will give you money to live on, too. Not a lot, but it will help pay your rent."

My head spun. I knew my American dream was the right one now.

"Do I have to pay anyone back, Tom?" I asked.

"No," he said. And then he kept going. "They will also give you food stamps for you and the boys, to help you buy groceries."

"No way," I said, laughing. "Now I know you're joking. What would we do with stamps? We can't eat those."

"No, silly." He laughed back at me. "They'll give you a book filled with little cards you can spend at the grocery store— for milk, bread, and vegetables. Any grocery store will take food stamps."

"I love America," I said gleefully. "Let's go to the school now."

Tom laughed again. "You'll have to wait until Monday," he answered. "If you're going to be a real American student, you need to learn they don't go to school on weekends."

I could hardly sleep because I was so happy to learn that not only would I be able to go to school without having to buy a car, but also that my finances would be taken care of as well.

Tom and Sooncha took me to register at Rose State Junior College in Midwest City on the following Monday for the spring semester starting in January of 1984, and I spoke good enough English by then to register by myself. That made me very proud.

I squeezed Josh's hand as we walked out of the administration building where I had met with a financial officer who had approved the Pell grant that would cover my tuition and books. I couldn't stop thinking about how great America was. Because I was poor with two boys to raise, the government was going to pay for my *education*.

"Mama is going to college," I told my boys happily as Tom drove us home. "And you'll go one day, too."

We registered the boys at an elementary school near where I had rented a one room apartment on the way back from the college. The school bus would pick them up and drop them off each day, so it worked out perfectly.

The next day, Sooncha drove me to register for food stamps and government assistance at the welfare office in Oklahoma City. I wasn't ashamed of being poor. I needed help to finish my *education,* and I would rather take it from my new nation than from a man I would be stuck with forever just for financial security. My boys sat on either side of me in the wide front seat, gripping my hands. The building was tall and its glass windows reflected the city around it. People bustled in and out of its doors, some in suits, and some obviously very poor.

We sat in hard metal chairs, waiting to be called for our interview. Most of the others waiting were black, although a few white people and some Native Americans were sprinkled among them. They stared at the stained white walls, their faces blank. They didn't feel the hope I did. I was here to get help so I could better my life. They were here to survive.

Josh tugged at my sleeve and whispered into my ear, "What is this place, Mama?"

"A government building." I didn't know what to say about welfare or how to explain it to them without confusing them. So I said, "We are going to talk to some nice people who will give us a test that we must pass to go to school in America."

"Are all these people going to school, too, Mama? That lady over there looks awfully old to be going to school."

"Yes, Joshua." I looked over at the old lady with gray hair in the corner. "Her, too."

When the woman at the desk finally called my name, I left Sooncha and the boys in the waiting room and met with my caseworker, Melissa. She was blond and in her early thirties, and she wasn't yet jaded like some of the other caseworkers. I could tell she still truly believed she could make a difference in someone's life, and she would—my life. Her warm smiled reached all the way to her eyes, making me feel relaxed. I knew she would help me right away even though I had been expecting to meet a mean case worker who looked down on me, treating me like a beggar asking for a handout.

She shook my hand firmly, still smiling. "Hello," she said. "I'm Melissa, and I will be your case worker. Now, how do you say your name?"

"It's Chin," I answered, "but I prefer to be called Jeanhee."

She made a note on my file, asking as she wrote, "Are the boys yours?"

"Yes, ma'am," I answered.

"You can just call me Melissa," she said. "No need for *ma'am.*" She had overheard what I'd said to my son about why everyone was there, and after she asked me the basic interview questions, she questioned me a little bit more because she was curious.

"So, Jeanhee, you want welfare to help you go to school? Have you applied for grants and scholarships yet?"

"Yes, I have a Pell grant," I answered honestly. "But that only helps with tuition and books. I'm not ashamed to ask for help, and I'll find a job as soon as I graduate."

"Do you have a car, Jeanhee?"

"No. I'll take the bus if I need to go somewhere, or my friend will drive me. I can drive. I have my license, but I can't afford a car right now."

"You'll have to meet with me once a month for an interview in order to keep your aid, but I can come see you instead and bring your paperwork if you would like, so you don't have to come in. That way you can take care of your boys and do well in school, okay?"

Melissa sat back in her chair and thought for a moment. "I can tell you're not just looking for a free meal ticket. I see a lot of people like that, some who want it for a lifetime."

"Thank you, Melissa." I reached across the desk and clasped her hands in mine. "Thank you so much."

I was overwhelmed by the chance America was giving me. If Korea had offered welfare, my mama wouldn't have had to struggle so hard, and we wouldn't have walked such a slim line between starvation and survival while I was growing up. I was also relieved. Going from a life as Robert's wife, with a live-in maid and the prestige of being married to an officer in the Air Force, to asking for hand-outs was a huge change. Anyone looking at my situation from the outside would have thought I'd fallen a long way. Yet I wasn't ashamed. The boys and I could get by on very little as long as I was able to pursue my dream of getting a college degree in America.

Melissa came to my apartment each month after that to visit with us and get an update on my life, to check on the kids, and to review the condition of my apartment. She also needed my signature on the required paperwork. When she learned I ran at least five kilometers every morning, she soon learned my routes and would even stop me along the way.

"Jeanhee, stop!" she would shout. "Stop for a few seconds! I need your signature!"

With a smile, I would jog backward to her car, sign the paper, and get my aid for another month. She would make small talk as I signed.

"You're making me breathless, and you're the one running," she'd say with a laugh, or, "I wish I had the same motivation to run every day as you do, Jeanhee!"

She forgot about checking my apartment or checking on my kids after school. I think she probably thought I was a good mother, a responsible person. After all, she had never seen a welfare recipient run every morning to relieve stress to start the day. I often wonder now if she was harmed in the bombing in Oklahoma City, and I wish I had thanked her more often for being so sweet to me.

Being on welfare let me breathe more easily at night. America wouldn't expect anything in return for its gift of support, like a husband would. I wouldn't be tied down with chores and more children and responsibilities. Now that I had my high school diploma, my next goal was to slip on that impressive black graduation gown and walk down the aisle to claim the paper with my name written across it in bold, scrolling letters. I would frame it and hang it next to my GED, a map of my past.

I was happy to share my college life with my sons, but I got an idea in my head that I could be a kid again, too, even though in reality I couldn't turn back the clock. I wasn't quite as young as the other students, who didn't have two boys to raise, but other than that I felt as if I could fit right in and relive what I had missed. I walked tall and proud, as if thousands of miles away, on the opposite side of the world, they could see me walking into class and learning English. The fact that I was attending a junior college didn't matter to me. I was back in school, and I was going to pass every class and enjoy what I had missed.

As I walked to class that first day of college, clutching my notebooks, textbooks, and sharpened pencils, I recalled that skinny little girl, barely six-years-old, walking beside my mama to my first day of school in Korea. I may have changed and lived a colorful life, walking a journey few dared to make, but my dreams hadn't changed one bit.

"This is my time," I said aloud to myself as I walked. "Nobody is going to take it away from me this time, I am going to pass and graduate. I will show them all that I *did* deserve a second chance, and that I am worth so much more than they gave me credit for."

I had originally wanted to enroll at the University of Oklahoma, home of the Sooners, a four-year college in Norman, but I just didn't have the money. The higher tuition would have meant choosing between my *education* and a home for my boys. As it was, we had times now when we would barely get by.

I asked my counselor about OU one day anyway, however, telling her I could not afford to attend and asking if my grades would transfer if I could save up the money to go there once I completed my associate's degree. She recommended the ROTC program for the U.S. Air Force, and that seemed like the perfect idea. I would get my degree at the junior college, then switch to the university, where ROTC would pay my entire tuition and even spring for my books and some of my expenses. In return, I would serve a stint in the U.S. Air Force.

The idea was almost too good to be true. I visited the OU campus one day and fell in love. I knew I wanted to be a part of it. It motivated me to study even harder, and I started to mark OU symbols on my notebooks as a reminder of why I was studying so diligently. I might as well have been chanting the phrase *Go Sooners!* over and over at football games along with tens of thousands of other fans, all dressed in red and white.

But I could wait. For now, I was just so happy to be back

in the States, doing what I most wanted to do and sharing the love with my boys, watching them grow, and filling their minds with learning. An *education,* going to school, and being a good student would one day make them rich, I said, trying to drill the concept into their heads. We had only a limited budget from the welfare checks and food stamps, so we could only purchase certain items, but I felt it was a privilege to receive government assistance. I managed the savings I had brought from Korea wisely by not spending money on things we didn't need. I didn't consider our life as poor even though the life I could have had if I had stayed with Robert would have given me a life of luxury in comparison. Yet the process of being part of an *education*al institution, studying to pass my classes, and tasting campus life was worth everything I had given up.

My boys kept me grounded, and during this time I realized I had to truly take on the responsibility of motherhood. I was still deeply remorseful about my abortion, and I had an extra love for Josh especially because of that guilt. I was happy John had lied about abortion being illegal in America. I couldn't imagine my life now without that smiling, happy boy. I sometimes wondered who my other baby would have been, if it would have been a girl or a boy, and whether or not it would have had my eyes and stubborn drive, but I didn't let myself dwell on those thoughts for long. I placed that awful memory from my past in the same mental box as the rest and vowed I would never share it with anyone.

My sons and I did everything together. I didn't know much about how American mothers raised their children, like showering their babies with kisses and reading them stories at bedtime. I hadn't been taught the importance of physical and verbal affection growing up, but I tried to mimic what I'd seen other families do for fun. We played soccer in the park and hide and seek in the apartment; we swam in the complex swimming pool and watched TV together at night. At Christmas, I bought a small tree from the store that already had lights on it and gave them the few small presents I could afford.

During the week, I dedicated myself not only to my own studies, but also to theirs. I tried to instill Korean-style discipline in my boys. On the first day of school, every year, I sent a note to each teacher that read: *Dear sir or madam, you have permission to spank my child if he doesn't behave.* I read it to my boys before I tucked it into their backpacks for their teachers, just so they knew they had better listen and do what they were told.

Since I had decided to major in elementary *education*, I enjoyed the opportunity to practice a few lessons with my boys. I taught them every day, focusing especially hard on math. I had fun teaching Jason especially because he never had to be shown anything twice. He had done simple math beginning at age four. Josh, on the other hand, had a hard time with numbers. Studying didn't come naturally to him, though he tried so he could make me happy. I made them finish their homework right after school and gave them extra math problems as well as a page or two from some workbooks I had purchased from a bookstore to keep their minds in study mode. Even on weekends, I made them spend at least an hour or two studying. I told them that in Korea, kids went to school every Saturday, too.

After they were in bed, I studied. I was sure some professors only gave me a passing grade because they saw how hard I was trying. They all knew I had difficulty understanding English, but they also knew no one worked as hard as I did. I felt immense pressure to pass every test. I often stayed up most of the night studying beforehand, especially for the ones that tested intelligence rather than memorization. I often felt stressed out and weighed down with all of the responsibilities I faced as a single mother and a full-time student, unable to communicate fully with anyone except for Sooncha. Turning in my thesis in English was the most nerve-wracking moment I had ever experienced. I just knew I wasn't going to pass. Despondent, I wrote at the bottom of the last page, *Dear Professor, this is the best I can do. English is my second language. Jeanhee Kang.* I left my grades at their mercy.

As I struggled with the stress of school, my boys, the responsibility of managing the meager money we had by not spending any most of the time, thinking about the future rather than my present circumstances helped me find balance. I had not bought a single outfit of new clothes. I spent the money that was left each month on my boys. They needed it more than I did. I didn't have time to mope around or be depressed. I needed to focus on getting rich; every day was a step in that direction. My daily jogging routine became an obsession, a way to release stress that didn't cost anything but a pair of running shoes. One day, when I was watching television, I saw *The Bionic Woman* on TV, running so fast I almost couldn't see her. I wanted to be that woman—powerful, strong, and determined. My daily runs balanced me, releasing bad feelings and rejuvenating me with new, positive energy. My worries about passing tests in English dissolved by the time I finished my run each day; I might never be able to teach anyone in English, but I would get some kind of a degree, and majoring in *education* seemed a fitting goal for my *education* dream.

My plan to help me pass was to just try as hard as I could and hope the professors believed in me as much as I believed in myself. I looked at every subject as the one to pass. English was extremely hard to understand at times, so I would ask my professor which subject he would cover at the next class meeting, and I would read the whole chapter beforehand to at least familiarize myself with the foreign vocabulary. At least then I knew what pages the professors would use for their lectures. Then after each class, before my memory wandered off, I would go back and read each chapter again to keep me familiar with the words I didn't understand in hopes they would finally register in my memory bank. If I didn't know how to pronounce a word, I was sure it would definitely show up on a test. So I would write it, then rewrite it ten more times, until I could write it without looking in the dictionary. Sometimes it took me writing it twenty times.

Then I would go back and try to pronounce the words by looking at their syllables in my dictionary. I had already learned that some tricky letters don't make sounds. The longer words were harder to memorize, and the routines I'd developed were the only way I knew how to make them stick. If I were to fail, it wouldn't be from not trying, not studying enough. I put in my time. I knew my odds. The only experience I'd ever had in an American school consisted of the few months I spent in high school in Missouri back in 1975 and the one semester night class I'd taken along with GIs back in Osan. I still spoke very limited English. I wasn't exactly accustomed to carrying on conversations with anyone besides other then my two husbands, and in college, the speaking terms were quite different, making it difficult for me to understand the academics, as well as the professors.

I did not mind the hard work. I was on campus, studying as much as I could and realizing my dream—and this time, I wasn't letting it pass me by. It didn't matter to me that I couldn't really relate to the other students; they had no idea what being a single, foreign mother on welfare meant, socially or personally—but around them, I acted my age, like a carefree girl, and no one ever visited my apartment to learn what a frugal, stretched-thin life I lived. I separated my lives completely. I was a carefree young adult by day then came back to reality at night as a mom to my two boys.

Still, I kept my GPA at 3.25, higher than many of my peers who had lived in America all of their lives and spoke English without hesitating or stumbling or mixing up the verbs. I never missed one class and was always on time, except the first time I experienced the switch to daylight savings time. No one had told me that even existed, and the first time I heard the concept I didn't understand it at all. I laughed and thought someone was playing a joke on me. The whole nation just decided all at once to change the time? How could they do that? It didn't make sense. I had never been in America when all of the clocks switched over, and in Arizona, where I had lived briefly with John, they didn't observe daylight savings time at all.

So I arrived on time, as usual—or so I thought—to psychology, a subject I believed was very hard, especially because I was a little afraid of the teacher. She seemed a little mean sometimes, a little harsher than necessary, and so I was always afraid to speak up in her class. As I walked in that morning, everyone else was walking out. I stopped, my face falling in confusion. Had the professor rescheduled the class and forgotten to tell me? How had everyone else known? I was dumfounded; *there goes my grade point average,* I thought. Then the teacher smiled, immediately understanding what had happened.

"It's okay," she said. "I will not mark you absent for today.

It happens to at least one student each time."

I was embarrassed but grateful, and I was never afraid of her again.

Other classes besides psychology were also a struggle for me, no matter how hard I tried. I was forced to change my major from secondary *education* to elementary *education* when it became apparent that a required class, zoology, was just too hard for me, naming all of those amoebas along with every other micro-living thing one could see only under a microscope was way over my head.

On the first day, the professor announced loudly, "You are in the wrong class if you are not pre-med, especially if you can't pass my test."

Then he showed slides of those micro animals, pushing a button every second to bring up a new one in his slide show. The only word I was fast enough to catch was *Amoeba.*

"For the final exam," he went on to say "you must name all of the microorganisms in this slide show. If you can't, you are in the wrong class."

As he continued to press that button, I went out that door and straight to the counselor's office to change my major from Secondary *Education* to Elementary *Education*— a choice that did not require zoology.

I did better in English than I did in science. I befriended my creative writing teacher, Susan Mansour, who always took a group of students under her wing, and I made more progress with her help than I ever had before. I soon found it easier to talk to people, easier to express my thoughts in English. One night, I was shocked to realize that I had actually been *thinking* in English, instead of Korean, an unsettling but wonderful feeling.

Between raising the boys and studying, I didn't have much time to socialize. I was too busy soaking up my dream of studying at an American college, exhilarating in every new thing I learned. I was finally fulfilling my dream, and even though I was poor, I was so happy. The nine years since I'd been expelled from Namsung might as well have been a lifetime. I had certainly already had enough adventures to fill up one life, maybe two. And I knew that no matter what life threw at me, I could overcome that, too. Though, perhaps, I would not have been so optimistic had I known about the monster who was about to enter my life.

Chapter Seven

Redemption

My goal in returning to school wasn't to outdo the other students. I developed to do list as a desperate measure to find redemption for my failure in school in Korea, as a Korean girl gone bad. It was my own personal war against Korean culture and the only way for me to justify the depths to which I had sunk in Osan. I did it as much for those who had denied my *education* as much as I did it for me. No one would expel me from my American college. I would graduate, and I wished that I had all of my old teachers' and friends' addresses from Namsung so I could send them all a copy of my diploma from America.

I took a music appreciation class as an elective to help my grade point average and met a tall, dark-haired young student from

Kuwait named Hamid. He was in and out of class; his attendance was terrible. I wasn't sure whether he was there for an easy A or to find some pretty girl to make his victim. And I was sure he was younger than I.

As our fingers tapped out simple songs, filling the air with wrong notes and jangling discord, he would raise his eyes to mine and look me over. He always smiled at me with beautiful, perfect teeth and asked how I was, held doors open for me, and brought me cups of coffee. He was silly, always joking, and when he first asked me out I didn't take him seriously.

I was intrigued. I didn't have many social skills when it came to meeting men. I had gone straight from my Korean school days, where we were forbidden to even look at boys, to life as a prostitute, to the position of wife. Besides, dating wasn't on my agenda.

"Hamid, how old are you?" I finally asked him point-blank one day. I knew I had started college late, so I had to be at least a little older. Besides, he still had that young, baby-faced look about him, whereas I could clearly see in the mirror that I had developed an unmistakable jaded look—tightness in the cheeks, a certain shadow in my eyes. But he was untouched. I didn't see that we'd have a single thing in common.

"Old enough to buy you dinner," he said, smiling back. "Come on, Jeanhee, let's go on a date."

Eventually, I gave in. Part of the attraction turned out to be the fact that we were total opposites. He was not only five years younger than I, but I was also right about his experiences in the world. While I had been getting knocked around by life, he had been catered to by his father, his every need met. As long as he passed his classes, his father made sure he had a generous allowance not only for living but also for entertainment. Of course, sometimes even passing his introductory classes was almost too much for him. He liked to stay out and party and then sleep late before getting up to do it all over again. I was a dedicated mother of two with clear goals, a deeply disciplined woman who never drank or partied. I wanted to graduate early, while he was only in college to please his father, who thought an American *education* would guarantee his son a comfortable future. We could not have been more different.

A larger part of the attraction between us was physical. He was breathtakingly handsome, almost like a movie star, and I couldn't deny his charm and good looks. He had creamy brown skin, thick black hair, and gleaming white teeth. As soon as we kissed for the first time, I forgot all my mama's lessons about how she should never have married my dad for his looks.

He liked to twisted my hair around his fingers and trace the curve of my neck.

"Jeanhee, you're teaching me the ways of the world," he joked. "I never thought I'd be with an older woman. And such a pretty one. Look at your smile. We will make beautiful babies, sweetheart."

At that, I smacked his hand away. "You make me sound like an old grandma. I already have two babies. Three, if I count you. I don't need any more."

Hamid was nothing but fun and joyful at first, always laughing, always having fun doing whatever he wanted without worrying about what came next. I would have thought he never saw a cloud in the sky, even when rain poured down. He took me to movies, out dancing, and to nice dinners. The warm thrill of excitement that rose within me whenever Hamid called or appeared at my elbow exhilarated me. I wanted his carefree life. His formal manners and sincerity reminded me of Korean men, yet another attraction for me, and he was unfailingly kind to my boys.

Carried away by his charm, I ignored most of our more divisive differences from day one. I knew he was an Arab, but I didn't know what that meant. I didn't realize the vast chasm between Islam and Christianity, didn't realize how little respect he had for Americans and their culture, two things I worshipped. As he slowly revealed his opinions, I didn't see how he could be so bitter toward a country that had so much to give, but I forgave his views as coming from inexperience. He hadn't suffered in his homeland like I had, didn't realize that being in America was a gift.

Yet his consideration in small things, like taking me to the grocery store, or to the clinic when the kids were sick, made our cultural and age differences seem to melt away. He even allowed me to use his car when I needed to get to stores nearby. Or at least I told myself they did. I was reluctant to bring another man into my boys' lives because they still asked for Robert sometimes, but I wanted them to have a man around, and Hamid seemed pleased to take on the role.

A few months into our relationship, Hamid changed. One minute he would be smiling and jovial, and the next a black cloud sat on his brow, usually sparked by my having other men as friends. We spent less time whispering love talk and more quarreling over our differences and perceived offenses. As our relationship deepened, so did his moodiness. Any silly thing seemed to set off his rage without warning. His face would turn red, and he would clench his teeth. When he started mumbling a mishmash of English and Arabic, I knew we were in for another dogfight. I wasn't exactly an angel, either. A feisty, stubborn person at heart, I refused to let him off the hook for any wrong he did me. I was never going to let anyone treat me as *less than* again.

His temper and our arguments always blew over. Within a few hours, Hamid would be sweet again, our lives filled with new hope and the promise of a better future. That would always be followed by a night of make-up passion that scorched the sheets. I had never made love like that before; our passion made me certain I loved Hamid and kept me with him even when all the signs should have sent me running in the other direction.

Then Hamid started turning against not just America and the small annoyances that are part of life, but also against me. He found ways to say mean things—just so he could make me crumple in tears things such as "Stupid, Jeanhee, you're never going to get out of this crap junior college. You should have stayed in Korea and grown rice" and "You're lucky I took you in—you've already been used up and rejected by two other men." Or "Look at yourself in the mirror. Look at those wrinkles beneath your eyes."

In his worst rages, he would rant about the American

infidels, talking about the Bible and how Jesus was just another figure, not the Son of God, and he always wanted me to agree with him. I was not a Christian, but if what he preached from the Koran made him act the way he did, I didn't want any part of Islam. I sure didn't know any Christians who acted like him, so I figured their religion must be the superior one.

He kept trying to break me, brainwash me, leave me a shell who would always bend to his will. Despite the vow I had made after leaving Robert, that I would remain a strong, independent woman, something in me started to crumble under Hamid's ill treatment. Sometimes he hit me, but usually the words he used were worse than any beating.

The first time he smacked me, leaving a red-hot hand mark across my mouth, I flew into a rage. I feared I might kill him. But then he begged me to forgive him, telling me he hadn't meant it, that he just had a temper. That he would *never* do it again.

"Jeanhee, I love you. I'm so sorry," he sobbed. His body crumpled in on itself with remorse. "Why did I do that? I would never hurt you. You just made me so mad—so mad. Don't leave me. I'll never hurt you again."

By the time he did it again, I was already getting too tired to fight back. I found myself believing his mean words more often than not, his claim I wasn't even worthy of the air I breathed. I lived under his control and allowed my kids to endure his tyranny. They knew when to go hide. As soon as we raised our voices, they would scurry into their bedroom and shut the door behind them, then cower there, quiet as mice. Sometimes, I found them under the bed or in a closet. I always found them crying.

He didn't have to hit them for them to become afraid of him. All they had to do was hear a certain tone in his voice, see his face turn red with rage. They cringed whenever he walked by and they refused to hug him. That only made him more angry.

Mostly, though, we managed to fight only when the children were gone, sparing them from witnessing our most terrible moments. Hamid did try to isolate himself in my bedroom to cool off sometimes to keep from fighting with me in front of Josh and

Jason. When I made him angry— something that happened pretty often—he would go into our bedroom, shut the door, and listen to Arabic songs for hours then He would switch and listened to English songs, starts with *"Hey, teacher, leave those kids alone!"* "You don't need any *education*!" I was thinking if anyone dares to play such a song in Korea, they will be stone to death before the day is over.

When he was out, I always told my boys we would be alone again one day, just the three of us. I told them that I would find a way out, and we would get away from this man, this devil. They stayed devoted to me, and I made sure to spend special time with them, picking pecans from the trees right outside our apartment and making a special chocolate pecan cake, playing math games to make them think and stretch their minds. Life wasn't good, but it wasn't unbearable. *Yet.*

I had a brief bright moment when the next step of my dream came in the mail—my acceptance letter for a full ROTC scholarship to the University of Oklahoma from the United States Air Force. When I ripped open that letter, on special University of Oklahoma letterhead, I cried out with joy. I was going to OU! The Air Force would pay my full tuition and also cover my books and spending money. In return, I would serve as an officer in the United States Air Force for four years. The country of my dreams since I was a child had already given me a second chance and was taking care of me and my boys. Now they were willing to give me another chance to finish college at OU? I would serve twenty years if that was what they wanted of me. I was one step closer to leaving Hamid for sure and to achieving something even greater than a GED and a junior college diploma.

Hamid became irate when I told him my future plans didn't include him. He also hated the thought of my serving a country he despised. I thought, *How dare you even think I would include you in my life after all I have gone through and given up? I didn't leave Robert for a kid like you who is just going to hold me back.*

On May, 10th, 1985, I prepared for my long awaited triumph, my redemption day—my junior college graduation a year and a half. I hummed as I got out of the shower and dried my hair, so excited to put on my silky black graduation gown. I was about two hours away from receiving my associate's degree in elementary *education* from Rose State Junior College. I could not believe what I saw in the mirror. The happiest day of my entire life was about to unfold right in front of my eyes.

I smiled at myself, satisfied with how I looked in the mirror, turning backward and forward as my robe swished around my legs. I pulled my hat down over my hair, trying to decide where to put the tassel. It tickled my face as I tried about ten different positions. I could have screamed with joy.

Suddenly, the door opened and shut, and Hamid's footsteps echoed as he walked briskly to where I was. When he saw how happy I was, he became enraged.

"You think that is good for you?" he snapped. "You don't look pretty. You look ridiculous."

He started the fight on purpose. He knew I had a temper, too, and that, eventually, I would fight back. When I ignored his first volley of words and got ready to leave, he pouted.

"Those professors passed you just to be nice," he said. "They felt sorry for you. You'll never make it at a real college. They'll laugh you right out of the classroom in OU."

"Please get out of my way, Hamid," I said. "I can't miss this. I have been waiting for it my whole life."

"I shouldn't let you go. You don't deserve to go. You'll just leave me. You'll find some other man to be with, to take care of you. Slut!"

"Hamid, please," I said, trying not to cry. I knew that if he didn't want me to leave, I wouldn't be able to go. He was much bigger than I, too strong. I knew from experience that I couldn't make him back down with either my anger or my sorrow. I had tried both before and failed, time and again.

""I'll do anything; just let me out," I said, anything to get him to move. "Please don't make me miss this day. I'm begging you."

He didn't answer, and my cries grew more frantic.

"Please let me enjoy my proud moment." I sobbed in fear of missing the ceremony I had dreamt about and worked so hard for, the moment I would walk up to receive my degree as the dean called out my name.

"I'll do anything," I said desperately. "Just please, please let me go to my graduation."

He stayed silent for what felt like an eternity. Then finally, he asked carefully, "Anything? Are you sure?"

"Yes!" I yelled. "Anything you want."

"Then go get your stupid degree." He smiled and pushed past me into the bedroom, then called back to me, "But don't think you deserve it."

I was free! I literally ran the whole way to school, my black robe flapping behind me. I barely made it to the ceremony on time, sliding into my seat with my robe twisted and my face flushed, but when it was my turn to walk, I was filled with nothing but pride. I walked as slowly as I could, savoring every second, every moment of receiving my diploma, thrilled with the sound of my name over the loudspeaker, my handshake with the dean. I even reveled in the polite applause of the audience, though I received much less than the other students. I didn't have a single family member there, and I had been so busy fighting with Hamid lately that I had forgotten to invite even Sooncha, who would have stood up and yelled for me. I was still smiling as I sat back down, fighting back tears of joy and holding the small scroll as gently as if it were a newborn child. I knew my heart would be filled with pride for the rest of my life and that I would willingly have given a million dollars for it.

When I got home, I hid my diploma instead of hanging it proudly on the wall. I didn't want Hamid to destroy it the next time he got mad at me, and I knew he was just spiteful enough to do it. But I knew that even if he tore it into a million pieces, he couldn't take away my actual graduation. I, Jeanhee Kang, was on record as a graduate of Rose State. I had my associate's degree. And one day in the not too distant future, I would have my bachelor's degree. I was sure of it. I dreamt of putting on an Air Force uniform and serving the country that had given me a second chance. But the celebration in my heart didn't last very long. Hamid had figured out how he was going to claim my promise to do anything, uttered so carelessly as a way to get to attend my graduation ceremony.

*****

At his insistence, Hamid and I moved to Baton Rouge, Louisiana a month after. I made the sacrifice because I thought I loved him enough to give up my hopes and dreams, still believing he would change. I thought I could find another school to attend once I got there. It didn't happen. Hamid quit school and lied to his father about it. In no time, we were broke.

I pushed my *education* dream aside for blindly in love and looked for a job to help pay our expenses. His violent episodes grew worse, and more often than not he was out gambling, smoking dope, or drinking. I was sure he slept with other women. I saw then that I faced my father. Whenever Hamid yelled at me or came at me with his fist raised, my father's face snarled at me. When I looked in the mirror, patting concealer around a black eye or a bruise on my collarbone, my mother's sad eyes stared back. I felt like a ghost. I couldn't escape. I couldn't protect my boys. I didn't know what to do.

As the weeks passed, Hamid became even more obsessive, claiming he loved me more than anything. When I threatened to leave him, he swore he would change. He wouldn't let me have any money or friends, and he wouldn't allow me to register at nearby LSU no matter how much I cried. He controlled everything, and even though we could barely pay our bills, he still found enough money to play nightly poker with his loser friends.

To make ends meet, I waited tables at El Chico, a Mexican restaurant about ten minutes from our apartment. Hamid couldn't stand the thought that some of my tips came from men or that I had to be friendly and chat with them as part of my job. He started showing up unannounced, sitting near the waiting room and following me with his eyes. Each night he would question me relentlessly about my conversations, accusing me of flirting and of lying about whether or not I knew those men beyond bringing them a tray of enchiladas.

The manager, Ali, who was from Iran, had sympathy for me and not the unwanted kind that included trying to get me into bed, like Luciano. He knew what was going on but turned his head and didn't talk about it. He didn't want to embarrass me. Whenever Hamid slammed in through the door of the restaurant and slumped onto the bench beside the door, my heart would pound. I was sure I would get fired, but my manager always said, "It's okay, Jeanhee. He's not bothering anyone by sitting there. As long as he's quiet, it's fine."

The manager eventually let me tend the bar to keep me from direct contact with customers. I couldn't mix a drink to save my life, but he gave me a Rolodex full of ingredients and told me just to follow the steps. He told me to take my time making them, too, so I could avoid the male customers. I could just pass the drinks along to another waitress to deliver.

Despite my nervousness whenever Hamid showed up unexpectedly, I came to like my job. It got me out of the house and away from Hamid. For at least a few hours a day, I could smile and be a happy Jeanhee without being afraid I would set off someone and get a black eye.

Our fights became increasingly more vicious—Hamid punched walls, broke doorframes, and made physical threats. Sometimes, he confined me to our bedroom for hours. He got tired of me calling 911 and started hitting me more carefully, just as hard, but with fewer bruises, and always where my clothes would cover the evidence.

I managed to find Robert's number through Sooncha's husband, Thomas. Robert lived in Florida and I called him, begging for help. He came to Baton Rouge within two days, in hopes of whisking me away, and ready to take me back in his arms as his wife and be a family again.

Robert said, "My sweet Jeanhee, you know, I love you so much, but I don't want to have another heartbreak. You must promise me one thing, and that is all."

"Okay," I said, knowing he knew I was a terrible liar and would tell the truth. "Ask me."

"You know I still love you. I'm ready to take you as my wife again and be a father to your boys and love you forever, but you have to promise me you'll never leave again. And you have to look me in the eye when you say it."

I should have begged him for forgiveness. I was close to being swept off of my feet again, to stepping back into the life of a commander's wife in Wallace Air Base in the Philippines, living posh and secure in a nice house with a maid and the cook. But, I couldn't bring myself to make him that promise. It wouldn't be fair. I couldn't say forever. As badly as I wanted to be swept off my feet and taken away from the hell of my miserable life with Hamid, I simply couldn't bring myself to lie to a man who loved me so much.

"I am sorry," I said. "I need your help, but I can't give you that promise."

"You need to leave Hamid, Jeanhee. I can't stand seeing you with a man like that. But I can't help you unless you'll come back to me." Robert and I both cried as we went our separate ways after a long hug, and I didn't talk to him again.

Hamid and I had only been in Baton Rouge for five months when the most vicious fight we'd ever had broke out. It erupted into a blur of screaming, with Hamid's face turning blood-red and the veins on his forehead throbbing violently. I thought he might scream himself into a fit, and I wished he would just fall down dead. He had gotten jealous because I had gone to church after a preacher going door to door in the neighborhood had invited me. After my first visit, I went every Sunday, comforted by the welcome I had received there and eager to get out of the house and away from Hamid, going somewhere I knew he wouldn't follow me.

One of the church members even gave me an old car to help me get to work and back. Hamid literally broke that car into pieces, snapping off the side mirror, bending the antenna, and smashing his fist into the windshield, the whole time yelling, "American infidels! Trying to buy you with their false prophets."

He became even more disgusted when he found I had gotten baptized without asking him. I huddled in a ball in the corner, covering my head, as he screamed at me and punched me with his fists. I didn't even fight back. I just cried, knowing anything I said would only make him angrier. I remember thinking blankly that this might be the time he killed me. But he didn't.

As quickly as he had turned on me, he wheeled around and slammed out the door. Holding my hand to my split lip, my eye socket throbbing, I ran to a neighbor's apartment to call 911. The whirring blue lights and the siren filled me with almost as much dread as Hamid did. Trembling and nauseous, I allowed the police to drive me to the station to make a statement, and from there they picked up my boys at school and took us to a battered woman's shelter in Baton Rouge.

We stayed there for a week. I hadn't realized so many others were in the same situation. We shared stories, went to counseling, and worked together to take care of our kids. All of us were scared, different levels of sad, and some of us were ashamed. We weren't sure where our lives would go next. I was the only Asian there. We spent lots of time in group sessions, sharing our feelings and experiences. All of the husbands and boyfriends of the other women sounded like Hamid, They would be sweet for a while, and then a time bomb would go off and they would explode with anger. All of the others had run away before but had been lured back, thinking that the next time would be different.

At one of the group sessions, our counselor told us that we often follow our parents' patterns and how children from abusive relationships often go on to be in abusive relationships themselves. That idea broke my heart. I didn't want to continue that cycle, and I didn't want my little boys to be abusive. I wanted them to grow up to become strong gentlemen who loved their wives truly, not cruelly. After that particular session, I said to myself, *I will prove that study dead wrong.*

But I couldn't stay at the shelter forever, so I had to think about my next move. I knew my friend Lee lived in New York. She had been my neighbor in Osan, and we had become close and promised to keep in touch although we didn't share the same sister-close connection I had enjoyed with some of my other friends. Still, I called her.

"This is Jeanhee. May I speak with Lee, please?"

"Jeanhee!" she said. "This *is* Lee. How are you, honey?"

"I'm so sorry I haven't kept in touch," I said, trying to keep my voice even. "I need somewhere to stay, somewhere I can run away. I've been with a bad man. A man who hits me, and I have to get away from him." My voice broke off there, but she jumped into the gap.

"You have to come here, Jeanhee! I don't have an extra bedroom, but the living room is big, and I won't mind your boys, either. Do you have a ticket? Here, write down my address."

The battered women's shelter agreed to help me run away by buying us a one-way bus ticket to New York, and my counselor told me daily, "Men don't change; abusers do not change. If he gets your number, do not answer the phone. If he finds out where you live, do not answer the door. And never, *ever* call him."

The workers there wanted us to get as far away from Hamid as we could, and I could tell they hoped I would be one of the few women to permanently break the cycle.

The small van owned by the battered women's shelter dropped us off at the Baton Rouge Greyhound bus station, where we would catch our bus to New York. Josh and Jason each clutched a garbage bag full of clothes and pillows we had retrieved with the help of the police escort back to our old apartment. I had trembled the whole time, terrified of what Hamid might say or do, but he mumbled incoherently at us, too afraid to do anything with the cops there protecting us. The boys wanted to say goodbye, but the police pulled them away. I didn't meet Hamid's eyes the whole time, and I didn't feel safe again until I was on the Greyhound, finally running away. This bus ride was different from the one I'd taken in Osan. This time, I was responsible for two more lives, not just myself. I was tired, and I held my boys tight, believing we would be able to survive in New York City.

That bus ride was the longest I had ever been on, twenty-three hours. The bus stopped in every little town and city along the way, taking short detours off the highway to let us eat fast food. We rolled from swamps to forests to plains. I was finally seeing more of America, but not in a way that made me proud or that I would remember with anything approaching happiness. We started off the journey tired, drooping, and scared, my boys wide-eyed and confused but trying to be brave. I felt so sorry for myself and for them. I kept asking myself what I had done to them, why I fallen for such a violent man. Why I had given up my dream for him? I could have attended OU in Norman, going to football games and cheering for the Sooners in a red shirt. Instead, we were on a Greyhound Bus, homeless, with no money in our pockets.

Lee met me at the Port Authority terminal, the main bus station in New York City late at night. The time was well past ten p.m., and we were exhausted. Lee greeted me with a warm hug and instantly welcomed my boys, telling me how much they looked like me. I never felt like we were a burden to her. Koreans always stick together and protect their own, and she was no exception. We took a cab to the Bronx after stuffing our belongings into the trunk. What an odd sensation to wake up the next morning to honking cars and the screeching grind of a garbage truck. The shining high rises I had seen in movies were nowhere to be found outside of Lee's apartment window, either. Our view was of a trash-strewn, traffic-clogged street, and above us were decaying old buildings with broken windows.

We lived at 179 Anthony Avenue in the Bronx, New York, on the seventh floor, in the heart of the Puerto Rican district. Lee had warned me about this place call Bronx. But never in my life would I have believed it. Paint peeled off the wall, the ceiling was cracked, and the linoleum was wrinkled and warped. Our door had five locks. Drug deals went on in the shadows on almost every corner. I didn't allow Josh and Jason to play outside unless I could watch them and never let them go downstairs alone, even just to check the mail. I wondered just who we were trying to keep out, though after meeting Lee's boyfriend I was glad for the extra security.

Lee was a classic beauty with smooth skin and an oval face who had turned to prostitution in Korea after losing her virginity and being shunned by society. Like me, she had married and divorced a GI, but unlike me, she had left her GI to become the mistress of Choi, a Korean mafia loan shark who was already married to a former Miss Korea.

At first I didn't believe her about her lover's occupation, but one night when we were all together at Kim's Korean restaurant in Flushing, Choi thought it would be funny to convince me. All seemed well at first, but I wondered why so many Koreans had bowed to him, looking scared. When the owner of the restaurant came to the table to see how we liked our food, Lee's boyfriend grabbed the man's neck and said, "If you don't pay me back what you borrowed, I will kill you and add you to the menu tomorrow."

Then he laughed loudly and looked around to see who else had been intimidated by his show of power. Over dessert, he casually told me he had once taken off a disrespectful younger Korean's knee cap with an ax to teach him to respect his elders.

I told him, "I still don't believe it, Choi!"

However, when I looked at his big frame and noticed the crazy glint in his eyes, I realized it could have been true. He was one ugly Korean; his face was still marked with scars from chicken pox in his childhood. He never went anywhere without an army of men to protect him.

Luckily, he came over only rarely. I also learned later that he didn't allow any white men to rent apartments there, though they did allow Koreans to do so because they paid their rent on time. My neighbor, Sonya, who lived down the hall on same floor, told me this. She had lived in that apartment all of her life. They had two little girls, Bianca and Maria, and a husband who worked as a security company in the Bronx. Bianca and Maria were in the same grades as my boys so she walked Jason and Josh to school every day and took care of them afterwards until I got home from work. We liked each other instantly, and because she felt sympathy for what I had gone through, she didn't charge me much to watch over my boys.

"I never had a son, Jeanhee," she said in her heavy accent. "While you are at work, I can pretend. I've got your back, girlfriend."

Sonya was Puerto Rican, short-haired and slim, but with a round butt she liked to play up in skin-tight blue jeans that left a little chubby love handle under her shirts. She was impeccably neat. Her apartment was always in order, and her daughters were just as impeccably raised. They were extremely polite, with their hair braided neat and straight, not a strand out of place.

I was grateful she could watch my boys while I worked at the job Lee had found for me with her in accounts receivables at Art Books Publisher on 32nd Street in Midtown, right next to Korea Town. We rode the D train from the Bronx to the heart of New York City every day, walked two blocks from the Empire State Building. I was like a fish out of water in New York, not sure how I would ever be able to reconcile my unfinished business—finishing my *education* and raising my two boys—with life in this bustling, crazy city. I had never seen so many people or so many taxi cabs in my entire life. The constant bustle made me glad I had a friend to rely on. I only left my job after my boss insulted me with relentless sexual advances, and shortly after that, Lee moved to a nice condo in Manhattan with Choi, leaving me to pay the apartment bills all alone.

After getting and then losing yet *another* job thanks to another boss who couldn't keep his hands to himself—a lawyer, this time, with a cocaine addiction that addled his thoughts so much I didn't see how he tied his shoes, much less won a case—I found my dream job at Gold Spoon Investment Company, on 29th Street on Broadway in the heart of Korea Town. I felt safe there somehow even though I was no longer a part of that rigid culture.

Their unwillingness to forgive my mistakes had defined my path, and I could never undo what I had done as a Korean woman. Korean men wanted nothing to do with me, they knew I had been married to an American man, meaning that either I had prostituted myself or was too liberated to fit into their custom of a wife walking two feet behind her husband. To them, I was a washed-out woman.

I was relieved to know I wouldn't be the one they would chase around. I also felt proud that they needed my assistance in doing what they lacked: knowledge of the American way of doing business with tough New York investors, realtors, and brokers who spoke English. I also found it nice to be around my own race. I would never truly be *Korean* again, but I was still a Korean at heart.

No one at work asked about my past, and I wasn't about to tell if it came up. All they knew was that I had finished college in America, and that was something none of them could have done. Koreans had given up on me, but I enjoyed being around them. I never let my guard down though, always remembering that their culture had forsaken me; at the same time, however, I enjoyed the food and traditions I had been forced to leave behind.

According to my job title, I was a Public Relations Specialist. I accompanied my Korean bosses to all of their business meetings with Americans, and my job was to break the ice and bridge the cultural gap. The company even made me over, buying me expensive tailored designer suits so that I looked chic and professional, as if I belonged in the boardroom with powerful business men. At night, I worked at a boutique clothing store in Greenwich Village a few nights a week while Sonya tended to my boys' homework and even their dinner. She truly became a second mother to them, but in a few months, I decided to send them to a math institution in Korea. I wanted them to be with my mother, who would raise them in a moral environment and send them to a respectable school until I could save enough money to bring them home.

The Bronx wasn't where my boys needed to be. I was constantly worried about their well-being while I was at work, even though Sonya went out of her way to take care of them. The environment was unsafe, no matter whom they were with.

Sending the boys to Korea also allowed me to move into a one-room occupancy in a Korean home in Flushing, paying much less rent and saving more money each month than I would have thought possible.

Life propelled me forward, and I had a hard time remembering the shrinking, scared woman I'd been back in Baton Rouge with Hamid. I finally had a sense of direction and purpose, even if I wasn't sure I loved New York just yet—though the bagels and coffee made my knees weak each morning.

Without the boys to take up my evenings, I even dated a couple of guys. The first guy I went out with, John Durant who was an aspiring actor I eventually had to drop. He was a sex maniac, and that wore me out every single time. Yet I was attracted to his crazy sense of humor.. One night, before I cut things off, he said, "Hey, Jeanhee, you want to know something about me?"

"Sure," I said, and I rolled my eyes, expecting some off-the-wall secret. "Now what?"

He reached into his mouth and pulled out his top teeth, then popped them back in, smiling.

"What the hell?" I said, my mouth hanging open.

John just laughed. "My real teeth were crooked," he said, "and I can't have braces in auditions. So I got these perfect ones. I was already good looking, and they made me even better."

Still shocked, I stared at him.

"I've gotten small parts in *As the World Turns* and *Equalizers* since I got these," he said, expecting my impressed reply, but he didn't get any. I didn't care if he *was* nearly a movie star. I actually wished he wasn't looking for his big break. Unsure of what to say, I finally said, "That's determination, John."

The other man I dated at the time was an Italian businessman Ariante Tiani, who lived on Long Island but worked in Manhattan. He was a good-looking man, tall, and muscular. He was even more handsome than John. His office was in the same building as mine, so we kept running into each other in the elevator, and one day he followed me to find out where I worked. The next day he came by with one red rose to ask me out.

I said yes, reluctantly, but soon grew excited whenever I picked up the phone and heard his voice. Our dates were always amazing experiences. We would go to Yankee games and sit in reserved box seats, watching Darryl Strawberry from only a few feet away. Sometimes, Ariante would bring me to his home and prepare me delicious Italian meals, cooking completely naked to show off his nearly perfect muscular body. I remember thinking, "I have got to have this man. How can I not? He cooks for me, feeds me spaghetti, sucks my toe after serving me dessert… I can do this. I can enjoy life, but still do what I want. I can pick my destiny."

But my heart just wasn't in it. I couldn't fall in love again no matter how persistent those men were. I was still hung up on Hamid, making it easy for me to play without getting too attached.

On my nights off from my second job, if I wasn't seeing John or Ariante, I simply enjoyed the nightlife that really didn't get rolling until at least eleven o'clock. My favorite place was the LimeLight Club, where I flirted shamelessly with the guard so he'd let me in. Eventually, he even knew my name.

"No need to sweet talk me tonight, Jeanhee," he would say, opening the door while others in line waited their turn for his signal to get in. "Just go on in. Save a dance for me later."

Lee and I would dance all night to Madonna, me never even intending to take home a man. I knew they were looking for a one-night stand, and I was just looking for a good time on the dance floor. Or at least that's what I thought until one night, when a good-looking, curly-haired blond guy spent half of the night staring at me.

Finally, he came up to talk to me. "Hi!" he yelled in my ear over the music. "I'm Joseph, and this is Luke."

He led me and Lee into the VIP room where it was quieter and we could talk. They tried to impress us by claiming they were movie producers, but Lee and I didn't care. Neither of us was looking to become famous anytime soon.

We sat in that room and drank for hours—Lee and the men had rum and coke, and I had Coca Cola—until the club closed for the night.

"Let's go to my place," Joseph said, slamming his drink down excitedly. "We can keep partying. We'll watch the sun rise from my balcony."

I looked at Lee, and she shrugged. "Why not? It's the weekend."

The four of us went to his high rise overlooking Central Park, and the place was like a condo right out of a movie—with beautiful décor, expensive lamps, creamy marble floors, and glass windows from floor to ceiling. I flirted heavily with Joseph and could tell by Lee's body language that she would have taken Luke right there on the floor. She was always of the philosophy that what Choi didn't know wouldn't hurt him—and besides, he had a wife. He couldn't exactly complain about fidelity.

Soon, I felt pressured. I wasn't sure I wanted to have sex with Joseph. But he kept telling me how beautiful I was and how attracted he had always been to Asian women, and I let him lead me to his bedroom with his strong hand. Instead of laying me on the bed, he pulled a briefcase from his closet, popped the clasps, and took out a baggie of white powder. The briefcase was full of them, neatly stacked.

I had seen those bags on *Miami Vice* and knew what they were. It was cocaine. But how had he gotten so much of it? He tapped some out onto the counter, dividing it into straight little lines with a collar stay, and snorted them. When he had finished each neat line, he brushed his index finger into the bag and rubbed some on his gums. I was too shocked to say a word. I knew that drug deals went on in my neighborhood, but I had never actually seen anyone do drugs.

My good sense told me to get out of there immediately, that maybe he was a drug dealer. What if the cops showed up?

He recognized my panic. "It's okay, baby," he said. "Here, try some. You'll feel better in no time. On top of the world."

"No," I almost yelled. "I don't do drugs."

"Are you kidding?" he asked. "Isn't this what you wanted?"

I shook my head. "I'll be right back," I said. "I have to go to the bathroom."

I backed out of his room butt first, closed his bedroom door, and found Lee on the couch, half-naked with Luke's hands running all over her body.

"Get dressed!" I said. "You can do that later with Choi. We have to leave."

She looked embarrassed, clamping her arm over her breasts as she shoved Luke off and reached for her shirt. "Did he try to hurt you? What's wrong?"

"I'll explain later," I said. "Let's go."

Joseph and Luke tried to talk us out of leaving, but we were out in under two minutes, taking a cab to the nearest subway station.

"Those guys must have been drug dealers," I said. "Not movie producers. Joseph had a whole briefcase full of cocaine."

"Luke had a little bag, too," she said.

"Did you snort it?" I asked, curious.

She didn't answer my question. I guessed she had.

That was the only time at the Limelight Club I ever went home with a man, and after that I just focused on dancing. If I wanted to meet someone, it didn't have to be in a club, anyway. Men in New York were very forward, coming after me and professing their love in a heartbeat. I grew sick of those empty, insincere encounters. I was a country girl at heart, no matter how much I liked my new job and the New York nightlife, and I missed my boys. A void grew inside my heart.

I wondered what Hamid was doing. I missed his silly, stupid jokes and the passion we'd shared in bed. I hadn't felt that kind of raw lust and the subsequent animal satisfaction with any man since. I had forgotten all about that sad, long bus ride with my boys; and I made myself forget the physical and verbal abuse and just focused on what we'd had that was good. If Forrest Gump had been created at that time, his most famous phrase would have summed up my next step: "Stupid is as stupid does."

I couldn't stand to just enjoy my life in New York. I had to ruin it. I made that one sick phone call, and I should not have. I picked up the phone, initially just to talk, but ended up telling Hamid where I was.

"Hi, Hamid, it's Jeanhee," I said almost shyly. "How are you?"

He was quiet for a few moments, mumbling to himself like he always did when he was either overjoyed or irate, but then he pulled himself together.

"Jeanhee! I've missed you so much. I've been waiting to hear from you. Where are you?"

I started to cry. I wanted so badly to be needed and loved by someone whose touch was familiar.

When he asked if he could come visit me, I didn't even hesitate.

Hamid came to New York within just a few days, and by the time he went home, he had convinced me he was a changed man. We went to the top of the Empire State Building, visited the Statue of Liberty, and walked around Times Square, all the things I'd been too busy working to do. Our relationship felt as fresh and exciting as it had when we had first started dating. Though when he'd first arrived, we had been hesitant with each other, polite, by the end we were holding hands, laughing.

"I miss you, Jeanhee," he said. "I've been a bad person, and an idiot. And I've changed—I've been working on my temper, and I see how I treated you was wrong. I'll never lay a hand on you again if you'll just come home with me. We can attend the same university, and you can finish your four-year degree."

I wanted to believe him, and my need was so strong that it overrode all the bad memories; he melted my heart all over again. I agreed to move back to his new home in Mississippi. I gave notice to my bosses, telling them I was going back to finish my degree and leaving out that I was returning to Hamid. They were disappointed, but wished me the best.

When I arrived, it was a scorching day, the humidity hitting me like a hot brick, and fleetingly I thought, "I've come back to hell." But I pushed that thought aside. This time would be different. Things felt right now. I enrolled at Jackson State University, where he went to school, and this time I chose to major in secondary *education* since that degree didn't require zoology at Jackson State. A few months after we were settled, I brought my boys back from Korea, optimistic about being a family once again. Things went well for a while, but our happiness didn't last long. I studied hard to pass my first semester at Jackson State in the fall of 1986, but found out I was pregnant not long after. I tried to finish my second semester but was too big and tired, and Hamid and I were fighting again. Those fights really weighed me down. He was after me day and night to marry him so he could extend his stay in America permanently.

"I just found you again, Jeanhee," he said. "I don't want to lose you or my son. If we get married, I can get my green card and stay here forever. We can be a family—for real this time. I can get a job somewhere and support us both. Will you marry me, Jeanhee? Please?"

I sighed. "I don't want to marry you, Hamid. But I will do it for you so you can stay in the U.S., and if you ever are mean to me, I will divorce you in a heartbeat."

We didn't have a wedding, and he never put a ring on my finger; neither was expected. Our exchange of "I dos" in front of a Justice of the Peace in the Hinds County Courthouse in Jackson, Mississippi, was simple and cold. Then we returned home. Peace reigned between us for the time being, and that was good. My pregnancy allowed Hamid to pass the red flag of suspicion that often arises in marriages such as ours, and soon he had his green card. He could stay in the country. Even though I had helped him with the process, I wasn't sure if I regretted it or if I was relieved.

Not long after Hamid and I married, things became worse than before. Now that I was the wife of a Muslim man, I couldn't leave our bedroom when his friends came to visit, couldn't wear sheer fabric or make-up. The can't-do list grew daily. He cut up all my custom designer clothes the investment firm had paid for and slashed my swimsuit into pieces. I had to be modest, soft-spoken, and always submissive—and that was the most important thing of all.

Even going to the grocery store held potential tragedy. If a man looked at me too long in the freezer aisle, Hamid's fingers would dig into my arm, he'd shove me forward, and whisper in my ear. "He'd just like to have you. Keep moving, Jeanhee. Don't you dare smile at anyone else in this store."

Under this strain, my third pregnancy became a nightmare. Sorrow radiated through every bone in my body. Hamid continued to physically and emotionally abuse me, calling me old and ugly, fat and worthless, and he went out every night to gamble with his friends at poker games and smoke dope. I often wondered if he had another woman somewhere, maybe one he had started seeing while I was in New York. He denied it every time. I was again reduced to a ghost of my mama, except instead of being able to throw myself into farm work, I had to pace through the apartment, my heart ripped apart with grief and regret.

He would become irate if he thought one of my outfits showed too much skin, or if I were talking on the phone, he was sure I was whispering to a secret lover, not sharing gossip with a girlfriend.

"I'm pregnant for god's sake!" I yelled back sometimes. "I'm not having an affair. No one wants to sleep with a fat pregnant woman."

If I came out of the bedroom before his friends left, I embarrassed him by not acting like a proper submissive wife. My girlfriends were affronts to him, and he denounced them and me for spending time with them. I couldn't do anything right. Even the way I slept offended him.

Some days I wanted to hang myself. This pregnancy that

bound me inescapably to a man I hated more each day was my fault. I had come back to Hamid of my own accord and then forgotten to take my birth control pills. Hamid wouldn't listen to my pleas for divorce. He either ignored me or flew into a rage.

"Where you gonna go? Huh? You can't leave me when you're carrying my baby!"

Every time I brought it up, he got a little bit meaner. "You'll die as my wife, Jeanhee," he said one time. "That can be now or later, your choice."

I couldn't bear to think my life would end this way, with me afraid and lonely, the wife of a cruel man. I was so sure I wanted to end the pregnancy, and we got in a terrible fight about it before I made him drive me to an abortion clinic in New Orleans. He was against it, but he must have seen something in my eyes that made him back down. I told him if he didn't take me, I would do it myself, either by throwing myself down some stairs or smoking his dope until I miscarried. I looked up from the sterile metal table when the doctor came in. Seeing him and the nurses filled with me with waves of nausea, and I started crying hysterically.

"Stop," I sobbed. "You can't. I'm so sorry. I can't go through with this, I'm keeping the baby."

Hamid was overjoyed. He hadn't seemed too interested in having a child before, but now he knew he had me. I'd be stuck with him if I had his child. I had to drop out of Jackson State after that. I was too big, too tired and so filled with sorrow I couldn't concentrate even on boiling water, much less studying.

I spent most of my days crying in my room, trying to come up with a new *Run Away* plan, always reassuring myself my life wouldn't end in misery.

I reminded myself every chance I had, *I will find a way.* I had to stay calm and not be scared of him. I couldn't see any brightness in my future, but he hadn't destroyed my childhood dream yet. I had that to look back on and to hold on to.

What had I done to trap myself like this? I examined my face in the mirror, looking to see if I was too old, if I had ugly wrinkles like Hamid preached every time we fought.

When I craved simple things, like a can of 7-Up or mint ice cream in the middle of night, he yelled at me for disturbing his sleep. He never bought what I craved even when he did go to the store. He bought what *he* wanted to eat. So I didn't expect him to be kind during labor.

And sure enough, the pain I endured during contractions annoyed him; he was not even remotely sympathetic. He didn't lift a finger to help me to feed the baby or change diapers in the middle of the night, and yet he constantly demanded things he wanted. Life was all about him. He stayed away most days, hanging out with his friends, smoking dope, and gambling. I guessed he was seeing his old flame when he came home in the wee hours of the morning. I suddenly understood why my own mother had become desperate enough to drink rat poison and leave her own children.

I struggled with overwhelming waves of emotion after our son Ahmad was born. My mistakes were piling on top of one another. I often questioned myself. How would I live my American dream? Eating Hershey bars every day wasn't enough. That had been my first dream, but now I wanted more. I wondered how to get it, if I really was too old. I felt desperately unhappy, like an ugly failure. I searched for my strength so I could find a way to make decisions, and different scenarios slid through my head. Most of them sizzled away whenever I thought of Ahmad. He needed a mother.

Then one day I heard a song on the radio, my only company and, more often than not, my solace. The song was Gloria *Gaynor's "I Will Survive."* I couldn't wait to buy the tape, the first American song I had ever bought. I listened to it over and over on my mini tape player using my earphones, learning every word, every note. At first, I couldn't catch all the phrases, but I heard the punch words over and over that I would say one day to Hamid. The song became my religion. Somehow, every word of that particular song felt as if it were written just for me. The lyrics energized me every time I listened to them. Whenever Hamid wasn't around, I would blast it over and over again, dancing around the house with Ahmad and singing in front of the mirror, imitating how I would tell him one day to walk out that door and never to come back. I had given him five precious years of my life and had almost lost my childhood dream in the midst of it.

Wake up, Jeanhee, I told myself. This man isn't going to change. He's a disease in your life. He'll only hold you back and drag you down.

One night, when Hamid failed to come home on time, I nailed the front door shut so he couldn't get in. Eventually, however, he climbed in through the balcony. He was too shocked to be mad.

"What the hell is the matter with you?" he asked. "Why'd you nail the door shut?"

I smiled. "So you couldn't come in."

"Are you crazy?"

"Yes, I am," I answered. "And you made me that way."

I told myself every day that I wasn't old or ugly or useless; I was strong and beautiful and would get out of this. I started running again, back to five kilometers every morning, listening to that one song the whole way. I didn't need a nice track suit or fancy jogging shoes. I just ran in an old T-shirt and some sweat pants, each step taking me closer to my future and my dream. As my body healed from Ahmad's birth, my soul slowly recovered from Hamid's abuse.

First and foremost, I had to get rid of enemy number one: Hamid. I didn't want to worry anymore about every action I took or every word I said. Never again would I allow anyone to take over my life. I promised myself I would never marry. I would never let a man that close.

But how would I get rid of him? I couldn't kill him because I didn't want to spend the rest of my life in prison. I didn't necessarily feel bad about eliminating him from the earth. If I somehow managed to leave him, I was sure he would just do this to another woman, maybe one who wasn't as strong as I and who would be trapped with his terror forever. I had to do something that would not only show him he hadn't broken me, but also allow me to declare my independence.

I toyed with the idea of shooting him, maybe the knee cap,

in honor of Lee's mafia boyfriend, or better yet, in his balls, just to pay him back for the pain he'd put me through. But that would be too mean. I just needed to scare him enough that he would be forever reminded not to mess with me ever again. Besides, I didn't know how to shoot a gun. If I missed his balls and killed him, I'd probably go to jail forever. To become who I had always wanted to be, I had to let him go and find myself again. The answer was to respond to violence with violence, even if I didn't kill him. I just wasn't quite sure how.

Then one day, at a flea market, I spotted several small hand guns inside a glass case, their silver barrels gleaming with the promise of freedom. Just looking at them made my heart race. I imagined the solid, reassuring weight of one in my hand. *That's it,* I thought.

Another day soon after that, while Hamid was out drinking, I slipped out of the apartment and returned to the flea market. I browsed through the stalls until I found the one with the handguns and picked out a .22. The seller, a fat, grizzled old man, sat up and took notice. "Why are you buying a gun?"

"To kill my husband," I said grimly.

He thought I was joking. "He can't be that bad, honey. Just make him sleep on the couch for a few nights until you two make up." He chuckled at his own joke. "Do you even know how to shoot?"

"No," I answered. "Can you give me any tips?"

He gave me a quick two-minute drill about safety and loading and using the gun. "Here's the safety lock," he said, pointing it out, "and eight bullets fit here in the barrel. Don't point it at someone unless you're ready to hurt them. And don't leave the gun where your kids can get it. If you do, be sure to take out the bullets and put them up where the little ones can't reach. That'll be forty-five dollars."

I paid him in cash and waited for my next argument with Hamid. Our fights usually lasted for hours, raging and falling like a storm. The baby would cry the whole time, but Hamid didn't care. He'd never let me go to Ahmad. I would beg Hamid to give me just a few minutes to change the baby's diaper or feed him, but he always had to finish the fight before he would let me out of his sight even to care for this tiny new life.

One sweltering day in June, he finally picked the fight that would set me free. He walked in the door a few minutes after a few of my gay friends had stopped by to ask me about ordering a pair of eel skin boots from Korea, and he went crazy.

"You let gays come to our home? What if they brought a disease to my baby?" His screams of rage, half in Arabic and half in English, had my friends out the door in under a minute, but while they could escape, I couldn't.

"I'll kill you!" he yelled, completely mad and lunging for my throat, his hands like claws. "You'll burn in hell!"

His first punch swung toward my ear, but I was faster than he was. I dove toward the mattress where I had hidden the gun. He stopped yelling as soon as I pulled it out, a look of disbelief falling over his face.

"What the fuck is that?" His gaze flicked to the gun, and he seemed even more surprised that I pointed it at him with an emotionless, deadly calm look on my face.

"I bought this just for you," I said. "Get the fuck out of my life."

"You're acting crazy." He swallowed. "Just put down the gun. I'm not going anywhere."

"Oh yes, you are, you motherfucker." I smiled. "I'll plead insanity in court. All they have to do to know the truth is to pull the files, see all the pictures, and listen to the phone calls I made to 911."

I had been anticipating this moment for weeks. I had no other way to get rid of him. If I didn't take such a drastic step, he would suck the rest of my life away from me. I had planned to just scare him, maybe shoot into the wall. My heart beat a thousand times faster than normal, but I didn't show fear. I wanted to end his abuse *my* way, and the cops couldn't help me out this time. I had made too many calls and taken Hamid back too many times. The officers had told me I was on my own after the last episode, and I knew they meant it.

"I bought this gun to kill you with," I said calmly, thankful I had rehearsed this scenario for two whole weeks. "And I will shoot you if you don't leave right now. Don't push me."

Threatening to shoot him probably wasn't the best way to get him out of my life, but it was the only way I had. His eyes had gone wide in shock. He couldn't comprehend what he was seeing. I continued to point the gun at him without a shred of fear.

"I'll tell the police and the judge how much you hate Americans and Christians, and they'll bury you alive. I'll get off Scott-free, and I'll get to live a new life with my boys. And sooner or later, you'll be dead in jail. I'll raise your son to hate you. I'm not putting up with your shit anymore. Do you hear me?"

I strengthened my stand, got a better grip on the handle, and waved the gun back and forth between him and the door.

"If you don't want to die," I continued, "leave here now, and never ever come back. I'm done with you, you piece of shit."

He could tell by my eyes and the steadiness of my hands that I meant every word. I kept the gun trained on him as he hurriedly packed his belongings, stomping around to grab everything important to him. Then as he went out the door, he glared at me and picked up three-month-old Ahmad.

"I'm taking my son," he said. "And if you try to come after me and get him back, I will cut both Josh and Jason's throats."

I was so ready for my relationship with him to be over, to be rid of him and away from all the misery, and angry with myself for wasting so many years of life, that I gave in.

"Just leave if you don't want to die today," I said. "I don't want the baby."

I knew that if I tried to keep Ahmad, I really would have had to shoot Hamid. He would never let me have his son, and I wanted to end our marriage without bloodshed.

The slam of the apartment door swept away all my years of sorrow, unhappiness, and broken sobbing. Everything went silent; all the noise in the world disappeared, and I went numb.

The end, I thought as that door swung shut; *the end of*

the terror, I said to myself as his car door slammed; *the end of the misery,* I thought at the sound of his car screeching out of the parking lot. I hurried to peek out the window, to make sure that really was his car speeding away.

Hamid's sudden exit didn't seem real even though I had been waiting for that moment my whole life. Everything around me fell into a state of complete suspension as if even the clock had stopped ticking and maybe my heart stopped beating, too.

I went into the bathroom, washed my face with cold water, and wiped away my slippery tears. Then I looked in the mirror. Jeanhee stared right back at me. I was alive! I put my right palm over my heart and found that it pumped harder than ever. I was definitely alive, and I was alone. I had finally gotten rid of the demon.

I recalled the look of fear on Hamid's face when I pointed my shiny .22 at him and he knew he was about to be shot. He'd seen a Jeanhee he didn't know, and his time was up. I had been hoping he would put up a fight, to give me a reason to shoot him and pay him back for all the terror and hurt he had put me through. But just aiming the gun between his eyes had been enough. Like most men who hit their wives or girlfriends, he was a coward at heart.

I shook the memory of his fear from my head and listened, trying to hear something beyond my own heartbeat and the hum of joy running through my body. I had gone to hell and back, all one hundred pounds and five-foot-two inches of me, and I had come out alive. But my head was still blank—I had no questions, no answers, just millions of tiny stars and their dust revolving in my head.

Eventually, sounds trickled back in. A bird chirped on a branch right outside the window, as if reminding me to wake up. And I realized what I had lost as well as what I had gained. I stared in despair at Ahmad's baby swing, his diapers, and his half-empty bottle on the counter. I gave the swing a wind to hear it grind back and forth, imaging his warmth there. How I would miss him! My heart burst with tears. Finally, I could feel again. I knew letting go of my little baby was the price I had to pay to get Hamid out of my life. It was a trade I had to make, one that scarred my soul. If this was my punishment for that abortion back in Korea, for killing that helpless little baby inside of me, that punishment was well-served.

A woman can know no heartache like losing a child; it leaves an empty space in her heart that nothing and no one can fill. My freedom and my worst nightmare had come to me hand-in-hand, and the emotions overwhelmed me. They still do, sometimes, late at night—such an experience is not one from which one ever fully heals.

Chapter Eight

A High Price for Holding the Baby

Kicking Hamid out and losing Ahmad took a while to register with me. I couldn't believe it—I *wouldn't* believe it. My heart still pounded with relief that I hadn't shot Hamid, and a calm voice deep inside told me firmly that this day marked my last ever in an abusive relationship. I had to put myself and my boys first now, so I could finally reach my dream. I knew exactly what kind of man to stay the hell away from, or better yet, I should just stay away from all men. They were poison of the worst kind. This one had drained five years from my life. If I ever repeated that mistake again, then shame on me.

As I walked about the apartment, mindlessly straightening up and trying to ignore Ahmad's baby swing sitting forlornly in the living room, I muttered to myself, "I will be strong, I won't look back, I will not look back, no matter how much I miss my baby. I will not go back to Hamid."

I not only mourned Ahmad in those brief moments after Hamid fled, but my own self, the seventeen-year-old girl who thirteen years earlier had strode boldly onto a bus after throwing her wig into a dumpster, filled with the dream of going to high school in America. My goal had been so clear. I had shed my shame and embraced my strength, and now I needed to do that again, this time without relying on a man to save me or to see me through. But my dreams had to transform in order for me to survive. I had to face the reality that I would never experience college life or chase an *education* at the University of Oklahoma. My junior college degree would have to be enough for me now.

Still, I was sure I could succeed somehow, and I would do so without holding a grudge against Hamid. I could have left him or denied him, but I didn't. I would accept responsibility for my mistakes and move forward without regret.

Only then would I be free.

It seemed like I had all these thoughts in the blink of an eye, and when I looked at the clock, barely five minutes had passed. My gaze landed on a bill posted to the fridge, and that turned my mind to survival. I could figure out how to be rich and fulfilled later. Right now, I must find my way. A new range of thoughts clamored for my attention. *How am I going to live? How am I going to feed my boys? I can't afford this apartment by myself.*

I felt like a fish out of water, gasping and struggling in unaccustomed sunlight, but I never wanted to go back into the same small pond I had just left. I wanted to jump into the ocean and search for bigger challenges and better things.

As I considered my financial situation, my breath came in short, sharp bursts, and I grew dizzy. I needed to calm down before my boys got home from school. So I would make a list. I would figure it out. I grabbed a pen and a yellow notepad from beside the phone, but all that came out of my pen were helpless, hopeless doodles. I crumpled the page into a ball, tossed it to the floor, and started over, first making a list of what we did and did not have.

On one side, I had welfare benefits; on the other, I had no money, no car, no job, and no one to help me. Under this list, I wrote:

I am a thirty-year-old Korean girl—No. I scratched out girl, *and replaced it with* woman—*living in America. I have three failed marriages, and I am flat broke. I have two boys from my first marriage; the second time, I married for security. The third time, I did it to give Hamid a green card. I have just let him take my three-month-old baby away.*

Under that, I wrote:

What I've got to work with:

My education—my proudest possession, something no one can take away from me.
My health.
My working mind. I am not legally stupid.
My winning smile—the one I learned from Woojung.

What I want:
A divorce.
To be rich!

What I don't want:
A man.
Another relationship.
Another Marriage.
To be poor.

How will I become rich?
I don't know.

In that moment, if a machine had tried to analyze my life it would have asked:

"What the hell have you been doing with your life?"
"Why did you waste all those years with such a loser?"
"Why did you allow such a loser to ruin your life?"

And my answer? *"I was stupid."*

If that machine had arms, it probably would have thrown something at me, maybe an old text book from that failed zoology class.

Once I contemplated what I had done, I said to myself, "You are thirty-years-old. If you live to be ninety, you will have wasted one-third of your life, flushed it down the toilet. Wake the hell up, Jeanhee Kang!"

I needed to make money—but how? And where would I go to get a job? I could return to New York to ask for my one job back since I had left on good terms, but I loved Mississippi. My neighbor, Mary Ann, was as kind to me as a sister would be, and everyone in Jackson was friendly and goodhearted, the complete opposite of so many of the hard-faced, hardhearted people I had met in New York. Besides, I didn't have the money to move back there, and I had never gotten used to big city life. I was a country girl from Jolla Do at heart, just like Mama Sang had said, no matter how she meant it, and I felt more at home in Mississippi than anywhere else I'd lived. I also wanted a safe, clean place to raise my boys with no drug deals on the corner, no perverts on the bus.

I just didn't want to *run away* anymore. In this Southern state, I finally felt as if I had found a home. How could I not like a place where everyone called me "Hon" or "Sweetie" and said "howdy" with a good-natured smile that reached all the way to their eyes? My kids had good friends here, and so did I. We were all sick of being nomads, and it was time to end it.

Maybe Mary Ann could help me, not with money, of course, but with emotional support during the hard time I was about to face. We were the same age and height and had the same figure. She was half Japanese; her mother had married an American GI just as I had. But unlike me, Mary Ann had graduated from Ole

Miss and had a degree in criminal justice. She was divorced, with a beautiful six-year-old daughter, Jessica, whom she was raising alone, and she worked as a polygraph examiner.

MaryAnn and I had met as soon as I moved into the apartment complex, and we had bonded instantly. Her daughter, Jessica, had gotten her father's coloring. She was a beautiful blond with bright blue eyes, and I felt as if she were the little girl I never had. I cuddled her and babysat her every chance I got, and she loved me as her second mama. My boys weren't quite sure what to do with this makeshift little sister, especially since she was a master tattler whenever they stepped out of line. She always won them back over after getting them in trouble by bringing them candy from the jar that always overflowed on their coffee table, smiling and wrapping them around her delicate finger. She loved every minute of their suffering.

Thinking of MaryAnn and how much it would hurt my boys to leave Jackson helped me make up my mind. I would stay in Mississippi. I knew at least one family who would care for us as their own, and that was a start.

I looked at the clock again as I paced back and forth clutching my to-do list. Still, not even an hour had passed, and I fought to keep Ahmad's face out of my heart. I knew I would break down if I let myself think about that devastating loss for too long at a time. To calm myself, I sang softly to myself, hearing my favorite song inside my head:

"Go! Walk out the door."

I smiled. Hamid had *run* out the door because of what I had done. I had made him leave. The energy of Gloria Gaynor's anthem flooded my body as I looked forward to a life of peace, with no more fights, no more abuse, and no more Hamid.

I suddenly wondered if he had cleaned out our bank account on his way out of town. We had never had much, and most of what we did have had come from his father, but despite my feelings that checking the bank account balance would be futile, I thought, *What if he didn't?*

I got the phone number from the yellow pages under the

letter "B" for banks, skimmed down to find the number for the Deposit Guaranty National Bank branch on County Line Road, across from Northpark Mall. A male teller answered, and I told him what had happened, leaving out the gun part.

I asked him if any money was left in our account. He said there was fifty dollars—a paltry sum—but a few seconds later, he said, "Ma'am, there is another account in your name, as guardian for a Jason Burch. Who is he?"

I answered, "My son."

And literally, a light went on in my head—he was talking about the settlement money from Jason's accident a few years earlier. He had been five-years-old at the time and had wandered off one night during one of Josh's school plays. Even though the night was pitch black, he had thought he could find his way home without letting me know he had slipped away. The whole school helped me look for him, and when we didn't find him right away, I called the police and learned he had been hit by a car. He had broken his pelvic bone, and the frantic driver had called 911. The insurance company had paid his medical bills and given us a small settlement, and since I was Jason's guardian, they had put the money in my name. I had always thought of it as my son's money, so I had put it out of my mind.

"You can withdraw cash from that account as his guardian, ma'am," the teller said.

"How much is in there?" I asked breathlessly. "Please tell me. I need to know."

"Twenty-two hundred dollars," he answered.

I could not believe what he had said. I made him repeat the amount three times before I was satisfied. "Are you sure I can touch it? I don't want to get in trouble with the law."

"You're his guardian," he said patiently. "Of course, you can withdraw it."

"Okay," I said, my mind racing. "What time do you close?"

"Three-thirty."

"I'll be right there," I promised. "What's your name? You're sure you'll be there?"

"My name is James," he said. "And yes, I'll be here, Ms. Kang."

"Oh, my God. Thank you so much. I will be right there."

I wasn't sure if I said that thank you to the teller, or to God because I was sure God had sent me that bank teller to be my guardian angel. How else could this have happened? He must have looked down from heaven and felt sorry for me and my boys. That one simple phone call—one I had almost been too hopeless to make—would now change our lives.

I searched frantically for the car keys before I remembered that Hamid had taken the car. So instead, I put on my running shoes, lacing them sloppily in my haste, and grabbed my apartment key and my ID. I ran to the bank, afraid the whole time that the bank teller might have given me the wrong information or gotten my account mixed up with someone else's. I had to get there fast before he discovered his mistake. In minutes I was bathed in sweat and breathing heavily, but my years of daily jogging three to five miles to Gloria Gaynor's anthem had served me well. I quickly found my stride and sang the lyrics to myself in my head again to distract me from my worry.

I ran behind Northpark Mall on Northpark Drive to avoid County Line Road traffic, the same road I jogged along every morning. And when I reached the bank's double glass doors, I straightened my posture, breathing heavily as I wiped sweat from my brow.

I went up to the teller's window and asked for the man I had spoken with on the phone just a few minutes before. "I'm looking for James," I said. "I just spoke with him on the phone, and I got here as fast as I could." My words were thick and choppy because I was gasping for air from running so fast.

Having overheard my request, a tall, young black man walked out from behind the teller windows and held out his hand, obviously surprised by how quickly I had made it.

I shook his hand and got to the point. "I just spoke with you about my son's money. I need to withdraw it right now."

"Certainly. Have a seat, Ms. Kang," he answered. "I'll be

right with you. I just have to get the forms ready. Do you have your ID with you?"

"Yes, I do."

"Do you want to leave anything in the account?"

"No!" I almost yelled, and then I told myself to calm down and try to soften my voice. "No, I do not."

"So you want to close the account?"

"Yes," I said. "Empty it and close it."

"Okay, then sign here and put down today's date," he answered. I did everything he told me without reading the forms.

"How do you want it?" he asked.

"In cash."

"No, what size bills do you want? Twenties, hundreds…"

"Hundreds," I said. Big bills would be easier to count and also easier to hide if Hamid came back. I counted the money twice to make sure it was all there, and then folded the wad of bills into fourths. I ran back to the apartment as fast as I could, clutching the cash, the hope for my and my sons' lives, in one hand, my apartment key and my ID in the other hand.

This twenty-two hundred dollars was the biggest wad of money I had ever held. That my fate would be changed by a handful of cash I hadn't even known I had, after using my shiny new gun to get rid of the demon who had plagued my life, was too much to grasp in one short afternoon. To me it was more than just a second chance; it was a reward from God for getting rid of a monster who hated Him, who hated all Christians. Had He helped me make that call to bank? Had He guided me by saying, "Go, Jeanhee, get your money so you can survive?"

When I finally returned to our apartment, I entered it carefully, looking behind every door to make sure Hamid hadn't come back and hid somewhere inside. I threw my wad of cash behind the washer in case he did come back. He'd never look there. I checked to make sure it had landed safely and then took a deep breath.

Now that the *how* of getting money had been answered, I needed to finish my plan. Keeping up with every last penny was crucial. I tore off another piece of yellow paper and wrote with a hand still shaking with emotion:

Total money on hand: $2,200.00
Rent: $320
Electric: $65
Gas: $20
Phone: $35
Groceries not covered by food stamps: $150
Unexpected expenses: $200

That left me $1,410 after this month's expenses. It seemed like a small fortune, but I knew how quickly it would slip through my fingers. Perhaps I could rent a booth at the flea market where I had bought my shiny gun and then work my way up to having a store. The people at the flea market sold anything and everything, including their kitchen sinks. I thought, *What the heck? I can sell something, and anything and everything, too.*

Where would I get my merchandise, though? I frowned, and almost immediately the smells and sights of Chinatown came to me. I had walked through there once while living in New York— the fake purses and watches, the throngs of tourists. I could sell those things in Jackson, and I could make a profit.

I added to my list: *Round trip ticket to New York $460.* That left me $950 to make an investment, minus the taxi to and from the airport as long as I got an honest cabbie who didn't pretend not to speak English so he could take me on a scenic ride and then gouge me on the fare. I figured I'd have about $800 left to buy merchandise. That would either make me or break me.

I went over my list one more time. With such limited resources, I couldn't afford to make an accounting mistake, but the $800 truly appeared to be free and clear—giving me just enough cash to start my business. I was sure others had become successful on much less.

I glanced at the clock again. I had about thirty minutes before the boys arrived home. I called my friend Kim in New York, who owned a boutique on the corner of Third and McDougal in

Greenwich Village, the same one where I had worked nights. My good nature and sunny smile had made me quite the saleswoman. I hadn't spoken with her since I'd left New York, mainly because she had made it no secret that she thought I was a fool to leave.

"New York is where all Koreans get rich," she had lectured me. "Don't be an idiot over a man, Jeanhee."

Kim was single-mindedly devoted to making money. She had no girlfriends to chat with because she had no time for anyone who wasn't going to help her turn a profit, but she did seem genuinely pleased to hear from me.

"Jeanhee ya!" she cried in her fast, breathless voice. "Long time no see. How are you?"

"I'm great," I said, and in a way, that was the truth. I might have lost my baby, but at least that devil was gone, too. "I'm coming to New York in a week. Can I stay with you for just one night? I have to come right back here to watch my boys."

"You can stay as long as you want, Jeanhee," she answered. "What brings you up for a day? That doesn't even seem worth it."

"I want to start my own business," I said. "I need to buy merchandise in Chinatown. Can you help me get some of those fake watches you sell?"

"Of course," she crowed. "Finally, you're making a good decision. It's about time you started getting rich."

As I talked with her, I realized how much I missed her friendship. She was about four feet tall and weighed only about eighty pounds, a tiny slip of a woman, but she was mean as a snake. Her small, pear-shaped face was all slanted, sharp eyes, and her smile was as sweet as pie, but she was the smartest, most cut-throat person I knew when it came to business. She saved all of her cash under her mattress, and when she was ready to buy a condo in New York, she flew to Japan with the money tucked under her mink coat, deposited it in the nearest Japanese bank, wired it back to New York, and then flew back.

She loved retelling that story. "I never knew a hundred thousand dollars could be so heavy," she would say dramatically. "I swayed with exhaustion by the time I got off that plane."

She asked about Hamid in a suspicious voice, and though I kept the story brief and emotionless, an amazing feat considering what I had just gone through, she soon yelled across the phone line, "Ya! Babbo! Algo! Ya!" *Babbo* means *stupid* in Korean. I was not offended because I knew I deserved her chastisement. Kim had no patience for men in general, much less for demons like Hamid. If a man had ever hit her, he probably wouldn't have lived long enough to watch the bruise rise on her face.

She ranted on, "I told you those curly haired sandbags are no good bastards, but you had to go back to him and ruin your life. Didn't I tell you leaving New York was a mistake?"

By then, a groan passed my lips. Talking to Kim was like being on the phone with my mother; she didn't even need my answers.

"And everyone knows those sons of bitches take their kids when they go. At least you finally decided to wake up. You should have stayed with John. He came around asking for you a few times."

No way could I have stayed with John—the 24/7 sex would have killed me. But I didn't feel comfortable saying that over the phone.

"Well, I have his number if you want it. I told him you were on vacation in Hawaii with some other movie star just to make him jealous. I'm sure he'd love to see you again."

"No more men," I said. "I'm done with them. I have eight hundred dollars to spend on purses and watches, and then I'll put all of my energy into my business and my children."

"Eight hundred dollars?" That set her off even worse. "Algo! That is not even money, Jeanhee Ya. That is pocket change for Koreans in New York. When were you born?"

"1957," I answered hesitantly. I knew where she was going with the year of my birth.

I could almost see her tiny, short fingers adding up the years from 1957 to 1987, counting both forward and backward. Then she said, "You're thirty-years-old? Thirty-one, in Korean calendar; you're getting old. I bet you are the poorest thirty-year-old Korean in America. Most Koreans are well off by your age and already have their businesses. Delis, dry cleaners, shops—"

She ranted on for a few more minutes. and I didn't interrupt her. She was right. I needed a lecture about how I had wasted so many years of my life; it would help my motivation. I only wished someone had given it to me earlier.

Finally, since I knew my phone bill would be huge if I didn't hang up soon, I cut in. "Okay, Kim. You are right, and I hear every word you're saying. I was wrong for not listening to you. I should have stayed in New York. But better now than never, right? I'm ready to start fresh. Will you help me?"

"Hold on," she said, her voice softening. Maybe she felt bad for letting me have it, but I knew her frustration came from a good place. She was dissatisfied that her smart Jeanhee, who had gone to college in America, had let a man ruin her life. Kim's tone changed as she haggled with a customer. "No, fifty dollars is a good price. Other stores sell this for seventy-five. Take it or leave it."

The ka-ching of the cash register carried over the line, and then she came back.

"You can buy watches for eight dollars wholesale and mark them up to twelve, Jeanhee," she said. "Some can be sold for fifty to seventy-five, and you can sell really good knock-offs for a hundred and fifty. You can find vendors at Canal and Broadway. I'll see you in a week." She hung up. When Kim was done having a conversation, it was over.

I did the math on my scratch pad. Eight hundred dollars meant one hundred watches, with $8,000 in sales. Minus the airplane ticket, I could net $6,710. With that kind of profit margin, I really could turn my life around. I had to believe it was going to work. Those cheap watches were the ticket to my future. Failure had no room in my plan. As my heart filled with excitement about making a better life for myself and my sons, Josh and Jason came home from school.

"Mama!" they called from downstairs. "We're home!"

Josh looked for his baby brother to cuddle, the first thing he did after school every day. "Where is Hamada (Ahmad's nick name), Mama? Where is he?"

I came downstairs, my face grim. Time for me to break their hearts.

Josh lifted a brow at me and asked, "Why are you all sweaty? Did you go running?"

"Yes, son," I said, thankful I was calm by then. "Mama had to go for a very special run." I gathered them into my arms. "Come on boys, sit down next to mommy. We need to talk."

Once they were settled, I looked at them.

"Hamid moved out today. Because we fight all the time, we decided it was best not to be together anymore. He took Hamada with him. He wanted me to tell you because he had to leave in a hurry. He said he's sorry he couldn't say goodbye in person, and that he had to take Ahmad."

Josh looked confused. "What if we miss Hamada, Mama?" he said.

"We will miss him day and night," I answered. "But we had to make a trade. To have a better life, we had to lose Hamada to Hamid. I get to keep you two; he gets to keep Hamada. And from now on, I'm going to be your mama and dad all in one until you grow up. I'm done with men, period. No man is coming into our lives to terrorize us ever again. I promise. I will not get married ever again."

They both just looked at me solemnly, their dark eyes wide.

"Do you believe me?" I prompted them.

The both nodded quickly, still grasping what I had told them. Jason stared at the empty swing he used to push Hamada to sleep in the middle of the living room, but I cast my eyes away from it. Now was a time for moving on, not looking back. I had no time to spare to be sad. Everything I did from this point on must be worth the trade I had made with the demon. That way, I could minimize my heartbreak and regrets. And if I one day Hamada accomplished something great, he would understand why I hadn't been there to change his diapers, feed him, hug him tightly, and tuck him into bed every night. I wanted to show him my success had been for him, too, that I thought of him every day and longed to hear him call me Mama again.

Once I had made up my mind about what must take place in my life, I felt liberated from guilt. My heartbreak lessened and was replaced by personal ambition and a need for survival. No more heavy boots would sit in the hallway, no more doors would slam, no more shouts would ring off the walls… and I would no longer cry.

Our lives would be peaceful, but with a hole in the center where Hamada should have been.

*****

I spent the seven days as I waited to leave for New York filled with expectation and anticipation for my big break. I wanted a better life for me and my boys. Every day during that week, I drilled them about their responsibilities while I was away on business.

"Don't go outside to play when you get home," I said, looking first at Jason and then at Josh. "Make sure to leave the apartment key on the necklace, Josh, so it doesn't get lost. Get up when your alarm goes off. Eat all of your breakfast, and be sure to take your lunch from the fridge."

They both nodded.

"Don't miss the bus to school," I continued, "and if you do, call Mary Ann. Don't try to cook anything because you might forget to turn off the oven. And be sure to drink a Coca Cola. They loved soda, but I never bought it except for special occasions, and this was one. My instructions sounded like a lot for two little boys to remember, but I said it to them so often they could sing it back on command.

"You must be responsible boys while I am gone," I told them once I was done. "When I come back, I'll have things to sell that will make us rich, and I will bring you each a present."

Their eyes brightened at that last promise, and I believed they finally sensed the urgency in my words and understood just how important this trip was.

"Don't forget to do your homework," I said again. "And

don't forget to lock the door before you go to sleep. Don't tell anyone you're home alone, and only bother Mary Ann if you really need her. It's only one night, okay?"

"We can do it, Mama," they answered, no impatience in their voices even though I had lectured them endlessly. I hugged them and sent them to the bus stop, telling them again that I loved them.

As I made one last walk through the apartment, making sure the windows were closed and the stove was off, MaryAnn's car pulled up and her heels clacked on the pavement. I opened the door with my small carry-on in my hand just as she raised her fist to knock.

We didn't talk a lot on the way to the airport. We had already discussed my plan over and over again, and my sense of urgency filled the car, making words uncomfortable. She didn't speak until she dropped me off at the terminal.

"Be careful, Jeanhee," she said. "I'll be here tomorrow night to pick you up."

"Thank you," I said gratefully. Then I squared my shoulders and carried my small bag into the airport. The carry-on was almost empty because I was only staying a short time and wanted to be able to bring some merchandise back in it rather than having to mail it all.

Despite my excitement and anxiety, I fell asleep as soon as the plane took off and didn't wake until the transfer in Dallas. After that, I promptly fell asleep again. The grinding of the plane's wheels descending over Queens jolted me awake, and the view from the window seemed so desolate, with few trees, tiny homes squeezed back to back like match boxes, and cars bumper-to-bumper on every road.

As soon as I walked out the automatic doors to the curb, the blare of horns and the smell of grime and people moving in every direction assaulted my senses. I already missed Mississippi with its trees, fresh air, and friendly people who stopped to acknowledge each other's smile unlike the strangers in this bustling, busy city where everyone hustled hurriedly while staring at the ground. My turn finally came, and the whistle blower signaled me up to the cab line. I told the cabbie firmly that I needed to go to Third and McDougal.

"Up town or downtown?" he asked with a heavy accent worse than mine. He was testing my knowledge of the city to see if he could cheat me.

"I used to live here until just two years ago," I said. "I remember exactly how to get there. Let's see if your way is better."

"Really?" he answered in a dry tone before pulling out into traffic.

I was relieved when he didn't force me to tour the city before he brought me to Third and McDougal. I tipped him for being honest.

I walked a bit to reach Kim's store.

She hugged me warmly and then became all business. "You better hurry if you want to beat rush hour," she said. "The Chinatown vendors close at four."

"Okay, I'll be back." I dropped my bag at her feet and rushed back out, yelling over my shoulder, "Thanks, Kim!"

She rolled her eyes and pulled my bag behind the counter. I took another cab, tapping my foot in the back the whole way and got out at the corner of Canal and Broadway, where the counterfeiters hawk their wares proudly in the open for about three blocks side by side with hardly any fear of police interference. I walked the block around once, sizing up each vendor as I strolled. I didn't want a small-timer who might vanish on me; I needed a big fish, someone who would be able to send a continuous supply of wares to me in Mississippi. Eventually, I wandered back to the corner of Canal and Broadway. The Vietnamese man there seemed to be the busiest, and he certainly had the widest variety of goods. I waited my turn, looking at his watches while I waited for the tourists to pay and move on.

As soon as they cleared out, I strode up to him. "Hi! I just came to New York from Mississippi a few hours ago. I flew up here to make a business connection with someone just like you, someone successful who can send me goods to sell back home in

Mississippi."

I pulled out my carefully rolled up $800 and fanned it out before him. "I want to spend all of this with you today. But I can't afford to fly up here every time I need more merchandise, so you'll have to send it to me every week, and I'll send you money in return."

His small eyes widened, but his face stayed blank; his expression, inscrutable.

I kept talking before he had a chance to say "no" right away. "There's no place like Chinatown in Jackson, Mississippi, where I live; I will be the only one selling these things there, and I can sell a lot of watches and purses. You'll make more money. If you will trust me and send me merchandise, I promise to send you money every week. You are my only hope. My husband left me two weeks ago, and this is what I want to do to start my life over with my two sons. I have no family to help me, so this is it. This is all my money."

I patted the money out on the counter. He was probably thinking, *what the hell? A chick I have never met in my life asks me to trust her and send her merchandise all the way down to Mississippi? What if she doesn't pay me back? Where the heck is Mississippi, anyway?*

I looked him straight in the eyes, hoping to earn his trust. Perhaps he could find that place of trust in his heart, leftover from his home country, where people made deals with a handshake and a word of honor.

He thought for the longest two minutes of my life, and then pulled out a piece of crinkled paper. "Here. Give me your address. I will send them."

"Thank you." I quickly wrote down my name and address before he changed his mind.

Shaking his head at himself, he said, "You promise you will send me money back?"

"I promise," I said, and I meant it. "What's your name?"

"Call me Tony," he answered, writing on another piece of paper. "Here's my phone number. Call me every week with what you need, and I'll send it by the U.S. Postal Service."

I chose some watches and a few knock-off Louis Vuitton's he recommended as being good sellers.

"I have plenty, so let me know which ones sell best, and I'll send you more of those. You promise you will send money to me each week?" he asked again. He needed more assurance. "Tell me the truth."

"Yes, I will," I answered. "You can trust me."

"Make sure you call me before eight in the morning, so I have enough time to go to the post office before I open my business."

Those were the magic words. I knew now that miracles do happen. This Vietnamese man I had never met until a few minutes ago had just agreed to give me a chance. My heart sang. Finally, something had gone my way.

I had a few samples already to take back with me, and in a few days, Tony's merchandise would arrive at my home for me to sell. I was in such a good mood that I helped Kim in her shop until ten that night.

As she locked up, she said, "You decided to wake up and smell the roses? Huh. It's about time."

I took her words as a sign that she was somewhat satisfied with the direction I had chosen, even though I had only a little money.

That night we ate Korean food—kimchi, goggitang, and steamy rice—and it was so good, reminding me of my home in Korea I missed so much—a home I could never reclaim. We watched Korean soap operas, yelling at the characters on the TV for the crazy things they did. Her husband—whom I jokingly called *Tulbbo*, or *hairy man,* because of his beard, a rarity for a Korean man—kept shushing us, but didn't really seem to mind.

I had called my boys earlier in the evening before they went to sleep to make sure they were following my drills.

"I'm going to call in the morning in case you don't hear the alarm clock, and I'll be home tomorrow. Sweet dreams, my sons. I love you, and I am so proud of you for not worrying Mama. I have presents for you. Did you lock the door?"

I fell asleep as Kim stuffed cash under her mattress. Sleeping among other Koreans made me feel at home just a while longer. I slept like a baby.

*****

When I returned to Mississippi, MaryAnn was waiting to pick me up at the airport. She was almost as excited as I was. She knew how unhappy I had been with Hamid and wanted to help me make a fresh start. I told her about everything I had bought and how excited I was to see if the men and women of Jackson would love the items as much as I thought they would.

"Jeanhee, you should use my car during the day to help with your business," she said. "You can drop me off every morning at work, use it all day, and then pick me up at five o'clock."

"Really, MaryAnn?" I asked, ecstatic that she would offer such a thing. "You are my guardian angel. You know that, don't you?"

"Oh, Jeanhee, I just know you need help. That's all."

"I will fill up the tank for you."

"Please." Apparently satisfied by being able to help me and by seeing me so happy, she smiled and said, "Just promise me one thing."

"Okay," I said, curious about what she had in mind. "What is that?"

"Please bring my car back without wrecking it. That's all I ask."

I was so grateful to have friend like Mary Ann. Honestly, I hadn't thought about how I was going to get to the flea market and back. Transportation was the only thing on my list I had not worked out—and here she was, already covering it for me.

When I walked back into my apartment door, my boys were doing their homework, and their eyes lit up with excitement as they asked what presents I had brought them.

"Hi, Mama!" Josh yelled. "We missed you!"

He enclosed my waist with his arms in a fierce hug as I pulled out two I love New York T-shirts with apple emblems; a black one for Josh, and a grey one for Jason. I also gave them two digital waterproof sports watches with neon lights so they could see the time in the dark. They were so happy as they tried them on and figured out how to set the time and date. They couldn't wait to shower with them on to see if they really were waterproof.

"Mama, thank you!" they said. "We did everything you told us to do. We were good boys, weren't we?" They were always so eager to please me.

I smiled and said, "Yes, boys. I am so proud of you."

Jason ran to his backpack and pulled out a test with a *100* written on it in bold red numbers. He pressed the paper into my hand. "Look how smart I am, Mama."

"I beat all the other kids in a race," Josh interrupted, not to be outdone by his little brother, who was as smart as a whiz. Even though Josh was older, he couldn't beat Jason's exceptional IQ.

"I know… Jason will be a doctor, and Josh will be a football player," I said to settle the brewing fight. "I'll be so proud of both of you!"

"Will you make money soon?" they asked as they pulled on their new shirts.

"Yes," I said, eager to get started. "We'll have money to buy good food and maybe even enough to buy you some new clothes. How about that?"

I could see they wondered how this *rich mama* thing was going to happen, but I would just have to show them in time.

I threw myself into my business with the same passion I used to pursue my studies. I made a new plan every day after dropping Mary Ann off at work, mapping out what shops and new locations to visit. To save gas, I stayed within a ten-mile radius of the north Jackson area. I ignored businesses' *No Solicitors* signs and waltzed right in, inviting the owners and their customers to visit the trunk of my borrowed blue Cavalier. Salesmen at car dealerships proved to be the easiest prey. They paid premium prices for fake Rolexes, as much as $150, even though I had only paid $15 for each one of them. The solid gold ones rimmed in rhinestones sold the best. Beauty salons were also selling meccas. Entering one was like walking onto a movie set, with all the ladies wearing heavy make-up and red lipstick with perfectly styled hair and flawless nails. They loved having me stop by, so they could run out to the trunk of my car and rummage through the purses. My next stops were always at managers' offices at the many apartment complexes, where I also did well. I was a born saleswoman.

Within one week, I had sold every purse Tony had sent, and half of the watches. I couldn't wait to call Tony.

As soon as he answered, I burst out excitedly, "Hi, Tony, this is Jeanhee from Mississippi. I sold all the purses and watches in only one week."

I lied about the watches. It seemed like a good idea to impress him and show him just how profitable a partnership with me would be.

Wanting to press him, I continued, "So I need more stuff. Can you send it today?"

He was surprised but happy he had made the choice to believe in me, and so he agreed to send more. After all… when I made money, he did, too. I placed about $500 worth of merchandise in a word of honor credit account with him and repaid him every week as he sent more goods with sometimes larger orders.

From there my business took off. Soon, I was selling enough to pay my bills *and* Tony. Through a combination of my smile, my born salesmanship, and a healthy dose of persistence, even people from out of town started looking for me at the flea market, and if I didn't have what they wanted, they would sketch what they were looking for and I would send the drawing to Tony so he could find it.

*****

About two months after I flew to New York, my heart no longer raced when a man's heavy footsteps walked past my door, and I no longer feared Hamid would come back. The dust had settled, my heart had hardened, and I dealt with the loss of Ahmad in my own way. I pressed my heartache deep inside, hiding my pain behind constant work. Of course, as soon as I started feeling at ease, I heard from Hamid again. When the phone rang that day, its shrill jangle shattered the peaceful silence of a Sunday afternoon. Hearing his familiar, hated voice on the other end of the line did not surprise me.

"Hi, Jeanhee," he said shortly. "Do you miss our son yet?"

"Yes. Of course, I do," I said. My heart spasmed within my chest, the meanness in his voice turning my body to ice all the way down to my toes. "What kind of mother do you think I am?"

"This is your fault," he said. "You ran me off with a gun, you bitch. You're lucky I haven't come back and killed you all while you were asleep. I've been thinking that I brought you here to Mississippi, and now it's time for you to leave. I can't stand you being in this town with other men around you."

"Leave?" I spat the question. "No, I don't think so. If you can't stand me being here, *you* can leave."

I tried to be rational and keep my voice down, not wanting to antagonize him, but he still had great emotional power over me because of our shared son. One thing I knew for certain, however, was that I would never take him back. The crazy feelings I had experienced when I had made that fateful call from New York and agreed to give him a second chance were gone.

"Jeanhee," he wheedled. "Don't you want to come back to me?"

"No," I said again. "If you hadn't left that day, I would have shot you. And I still have that gun in case you come back."

He drew in a breath with a sharp hiss. I knew he wished he could slap me around and close his fingers tightly around my neck. But those days were over.

"I'll kill you one day, you bitch."

"You dare try, and I'll shoot you in the balls. What do you want, Hamid? I don't have any more time to waste with you. Tell me, or I'm hanging up."

"If you want to see your son," he snarled back, "I will let

you see him tomorrow. Here is my number." I could tell by the first three digits he was somewhere in south Jackson.

"I'll call you tomorrow," I said, about to hang up.

"I'm not going to take a son away from his mother, no matter how terrible you think I am. But you have to come here," he said. Either he wanted to get on my good side, or he had something up his sleeve, but I couldn't resist seeing my baby.

I wanted to hold Ahmad desperately, longed to see his dark almond eyes gazing up at mine with trust, his delicate baby fingers gripping my hand still scarred from the hardship of my childhood. Several weeks passed before I could get up the courage to go to Hamid's apartment. I became unsettled when I realized how close he lived to us. He still shopped at the same grocery store and drove down the same roads. I wondered if he had seen us and maybe even passed by the house, unnoticed. I suddenly felt less safe.

I didn't want to go back to him. I would rather die, but I had to see my son. I hadn't even gotten to say goodbye to him. The morning I decided to go see Ahmad, I put the gun into my purse and took it out again at least ten times. Should I take it? Should I leave it behind? If he managed to take it away from me, he might kill me with it. In the end, I tucked it under the mattress. Then I called Mary Ann to let her know where I was going, so if I disappeared, at least someone would know why.

"Jeanhee, no," she said angrily. "Make him meet you somewhere public; don't go to his apartment."

She always looked out for me. She was especially aware of how dangerous men like Hamid could be, and I was touched by her sisterly concern for my well-being. Still, I had to see Ahmad, so I went to visit Hamid in his south Jackson rental home against her wishes.

The place was small and shabby, but his smile when he opened the door was as warm as it had been when I had first met him. I found it hard to believe this was the same man who had raised his fist in anger at me so often. He tried to fold me into a hug, but I stepped back, wary.

"No hug for your husband?" he asked, trying to revive the

good old days.

His charm used to work on me, but not anymore. "You won't be my husband for long," I said, punctuating every word. "The divorce papers should go through any day now. Where is Ahmad?"

"What? Are you really going to divorce me?" Hamid asked with a hiss.

I replied, "Yep."

He tried his hardest to look genuinely hurt, but I didn't buy it. He wanted to know how I was making it without his money. He had been certain I would crawl back to him, but he now he realized he wasn't getting anywhere with me in the financial department.

"Don't worry. I'll pay the attorney's fees," I said. "You just sign on the dotted line."

I brushed past my shocked husband, who had never seen a Jeanhee like this, cold and harsh with every word coming out of her mouth like the gun pointed at him two weeks ago.

Behind Hamid, Hamada pulled himself up in his crib and tried to crawl, his chubby baby legs barely holding him up with his big Buddha belly. I was glad he hadn't lost any weight. His hair had grown longer and thicker, and he grabbed his blanket with his little fat little fingers as I scooped him up into my arms.

"Hi, my sweet baby," I murmured to him, hugging him tightly and smelling his sweet baby breath. I had missed his milky baby smell, and I rolled my nose over his cheeks. I wanted to let him know how much I had missed him. "I missed you, my pumpkin. Your brothers Josh and Jason miss you, too."

I kissed him all over his face, tickling his belly with my nose as he giggled. He still liked belly tickles. I wished I could turn my cheek and put up with his daddy for his sake. I hated myself for not being able to compromise. I started to cry. "Here are kisses from Josh and Jason."

I kissed his tiny fists and feet, and he gurgled happily. I wasn't sure if he remembered me or was just naturally affectionate. If it was the latter, he certainly hadn't gotten his father's disposition. I hated that in the span of just two short months, I didn't even know my own child.

Hamid left me alone, busying himself in the kitchen while I sat in the floor rocking and singing to Ahmad. But I knew I had to go soon. There was no sense in tempting the devil.

After a little while longer, I changed the baby's diaper, then kissed his forehead and settled him back into his crib. A strong arm snaked around my waist as I straightened, and I looked down in surprise.

Hamid's tanned skin and curls of black hair sent fear skittering through me, and my breath came out in a hard gasp. I flashed back to that moment on the bus in Korea, my nose full of the smell of kimchi and sweat, when the monster had groped me. Hamid's big hand inched toward my thigh, and I twisted around angrily.

"What are you doing?" I yelled. "Don't touch me! Don't you dare touch me."

He pulled my hair back with one hand and ground his lips into mine.

"Jeanhee, we can be a family," he panted when he lifted his head. "You can see your son all the time if you just come back to me. He needs his mama. Can't you see he missed you?"

"I'll never come back to you!" I shouted, trying to shove him away as terror and disgust filled my stomach. I swore at him in Korean, my whole body trembling. I had to get out.

But it was too late. My nightmare with Hamid was not yet over. Within only seconds, he had me cornered in the bedroom. He pinned me to the bed and fumbled with my pants, popping a button off in his haste. I didn't even think to scream. If this was the price I had to pay to see my baby, I would pay it.

After a few minutes of labored thrusting, he gave a grunt of satisfaction and rolled off me, pulled his pants back up, and walked out of the room. I slipped off the bed and tried to straighten my hair, then tugged the front of my shirt over my pants to hide the missing button. His warmth ran down my thigh.

Then he walked back in. "Don't even think about calling the police," he said. "We're still married. It's not rape when I'm still your husband."

I don't remember driving home, but I got back before the boys returned from school. I felt horribly violated, but I had gotten my tubes tied after Ahmad, so at least I didn't have to worry about having another baby with that devil. When Hamid called me a few weeks later, begging me to forgive him and promising not to touch me if I came back to visit the baby, my mother's heart overcame my good sense, and I went again. The rapes went on until the baby was almost a year old, and by then I knew I had to stop. I couldn't face that pain anymore, not even to see my beloved child.

"I won't see my baby again if I have to be raped to do it," I told him over the phone the next time he called. "I am not doing it."

"What do you mean, you won't see your baby?" he asked incredulously. "You can't mean that."

"I do. I won't see him," I answered. "You will not ever rape me again."

Eventually, he agreed to meet me in the park by the reservoir so I could see the baby. I knew the place would be filled with people even on a weekday morning, so I felt safe. Ahmad was growing fast, and I missed my baby so much. I cherished every hour I spent getting to know him again. As I sat in the front seat of the car bouncing Ahmad on my knee and singing him a Korean lullaby, I tried to ignore Hamid's dark presence.

Finally, he reached across the seat and grabbed my elbow. "Jeanhee, I've changed."

Oh God, I thought, refusing to look at him. *I've heard that before.*

"I know I've made lot of mistakes," he said, "But I'd like to start over. I will change. I'll do anything; we can even go to counseling. We can keep our own places for a while, but I want you to be Ahmad's mother. Babies need a mother. I want us to be in love again. I'll find a job; I'll even work for Americans."

"No, Hamid," I said without hesitation. "I'm never coming back to you. I'll hate you until the day I die."

Almost before the words were out of my mouth, he pulled a knife on me. Its edge glinted dully in the sun as he pressed it against my inner thigh.

"There's an artery right there," he hissed, smiling so no one walking by would think we were having an argument. "If I cut you, you'll bleed out. No one will be able to save you."

"No." I shook my head. I would not let him terrorize me into going back to him.

He cried like a baby, one more plea in his fight to convince me to change my mind. Hamada blinked at him, chattering to himself in his baby language, then wailing for milk and squirming. He needed to be changed.

Hamid, to hurt me more, made me ignore my baby's cries.

"Why won't you just let us be happy, Jeanhee?" he snapped. "I swear to God I've changed. We can be a family. Why won't you fucking listen?"

Hamada's sobs increased in volume. People walking by the car turned to look, their attention caught by his wails and my swollen, tear-stained face.

"Let me change Ahmad," I begged. "He's wet, and he's going to get a rash. He's also hungry."

Hamid kept me in that car for nearly four hours, running the knife over my thigh and alternating between threats and proclamations of love. When he finally ordered me to get out and popped open the child-proof lock he had used to keep me inside, I didn't have to be told twice.

I went straight to justice court to file a complaint. The officer on duty at the desk was short, about my height, and middle-aged, with curly light brown hair. Her name was Fay Peterson. I could tell she was trying to look tougher than she was. When she entered my name into the system, she stopped typing.

"How many times have you dropped charges against your ex-husband, ma'am?" she said.

"I don't remember," I answered, figuring that because she'd asked, she didn't know I'd refused to press charges before. "I just want a peace bond against him."

"Okay." She took my report, but said, "I don't know if the judge is going to give you one since you've changed your mind about it so many times already."

Well, she did know. I never heard another word from justice court.

I got an answering machine to screen Hamid's calls and decided never to see him again. I couldn't bear his threats or his heavy weight on top me. The hour's worth of joy I received from holding Ahmad in my arms wasn't worth being raped.

Another few months passed before I came home to a message from Hamid that was different from all the others he had left. His voice was calm, very business-like, and he measured his words as if they were precious gold.

"If you ever want to see your baby again," he said on the tape, "or if you want Josh and Jason to see him, this is it. "Your last chance," he snarled, and you'll never see him again after this, "so take it or leave it."

I called him back within minutes. "What do you mean, Hamid?" I asked. "Where are you going?"

"None of your business," he said. "You abandoned him. You're lucky I'm letting him see you again. You can come by my apartment this afternoon."

After a few minutes of pleading, he instead agreed to let us meet him in the Wal-Mart parking lot on County Line Road. Josh and Jason talked excitedly the whole way there.

"Mama, I thought you said Hamada was gone?" Jason asked. "Is he coming back? Can he live with us again?"

"Hamada is going move with Hamid," "We don't know when we are going to be able to see him again," he said.

When the time came for us to meet Hamid, he managed to say "Hi" to my boys and handed me Ahmad, saying brusquely that he expected him back in three hours. I gathered Hamada into my arms, showered his face with kisses, went to lunch to Burger King on County Line Road, where we could all sit in a booth together Josh and Jason holding Hamada, me laughing as he gnawed fiercely on chicken nuggets and French fries, the four of us squeezed into one side of the booth together. After lunch, we decided to take our first family photo at the JC Penny at North Park Mall.

If I could have looked into the future and known it would be our only family picture, I might have lain down under the table and never gotten up.

"The first and the last picture with all three of my sons"

As it was, I gave Ahmad back to Hamid with hope in my heart that I would see my baby again. I knew Hamid was full of bullshit lies. I thought we would probably go through the same scene in a few weeks. But another two months went by, and I didn't hear anything. No messages, no phone calls.

Finally I couldn't stand it anymore, so I broke down and called Hamid. I just wanted to hear how Ahmad was doing, even if I couldn't see him.

"He's with my father in Kuwait," Hamid said. His words knocked the breath out of me, and I struggled to comprehend what he was telling me. "I told you to come back to me. I told you he needs a mother, and you didn't listen. You didn't want us to be together. You were selfish, and now he's gone. It's your loss."

He laughed at me, knowing his derisive chuckle would hurt me even more, his joy a knife digging into my heart. I hung up without saying another word. The next time Josh and Jason asked about Ahmad, I told them he was gone forever, and we all cried together in my big bed, mourning a brother and a son and a life that could have been.

I justified my decision to cut Hamid— and therefore, Ahmad— out of my life by my need to go forward. Letting go of my baby hurt me immensely, but going back to Hamid would mean taking a terrible step backward into a life of unhappiness, pain, and suffering.

I had no one to help lessen my pain. The only fix for it was to see my baby again someday, and I decided right then and there that I would find him one day and bring him home, home to a beautiful house and a life of ease enabled by my success.

Despite my pain, now that I was no longer able to see Ahmad at all, I didn't feel as guilty as I had when he had lived so close, though my heartache never eased. Maybe one day he would grow up and look for his mama, or maybe I would go after him, but either way we would see each other again. When he was grown, he would understand why his mama couldn't accept being raped to see him smile or to see his first steps or to hear his first word.

I remember watching *The Oprah Winfrey Show* one day during one of my few free hours confirmed my decision. The topic was why women stay in abusive relationships. The two women being interviewed had suffered broken limbs, cracked teeth, and worse beatings than I had ever gotten. Oprah's sensitively asked them why they had stayed with their abusers, and why they had gone back after escaping, but the women couldn't answer. They didn't know— until the show's psychologist finally revealed the answer to the audience. A guest speaker whose name I can't recall, "Each of the women had witnessed abusive relationships between their parents, and upon adulthood had fallen into their mothers' familiar roles."

I remembered that theory from the counseling I'd received during my time in the battered women's shelter, but hearing it spoken so openly on a show that reached an audience of millions made me even more determined not to be a statistic. I had survived, and I would never go back. This was my new beginning. The time had come for me to reinvent myself and define who I was positively, not in relation to any man. Now I would be rich, with plenty of white steamy rice, a maid to clean up after me, beautiful silky clothes, and a bank account full of cash to buy whatever I wanted.

Chapter Nine

Reinventing Myself

I had to believe it was not too late. I had to believe that I still have it in me to finally pursue my dream. The odds were against me, but the new Jeanhee Kang could do anything. I decided I was pretty. I decided I deserved better, and I decided I was worth every bit of what life had to offer. Enough time had passed me by. I counted the years I had been in the land of opportunity: America, the country I used to call *Meegook* or *beautiful nation.* That coming October, I would have been here for twelve years, and my number one priority now was to be able to say *no* to marrying a man for financial security, to get off welfare, and to have enough money to be independent and financially stable without leaning on a man or getting any kind of government assistance. I must make as much money as I can so I could stand on my own two feet.

I had married all three men for the wrong reasons. I won't make that mistake ever again. I will make money first, enough money to live, then more than enough, and I will think of ways to spend it. Once I had a clear goal, talent I never knew I possessed— talent as a saleswoman— came out in me. But I had to be a likable person. The only sales experience I'd gotten before I'd gotten the merchandise from Tony was working that second job for Kim in Greenwich Village a few nights a week while I was in New York. Of course, I had sold my body for $20 in Osan, but that didn't count since it didn't require intelligence or a special skill, just acting sexy.

To be a great saleswoman, I had to smile a lot. My friendship with Woojung had taught me that a smile wouldn't kill anybody and that if nothing else, it would leave a good, friendly impression. So I brought out my best smile, the one she had taught me years before. Whenever I felt as if my English wasn't strong enough to communicate with a customer, I just smiled harder to bridge the gap. I became a quick thinker, a mover, and a fast talker. If I could have painted my face like an Indian going to war, I would have. For the past five years, I'd been weak… and now, to fight off that demon within myself, I had to be a warrior. My street peddler phase was in full swing. As time went on, I got better, using the skills I had taught myself to become a successful, fast- talking saleswoman. I always smiled first, because like Woojung taught me, a smile won't hurt me.

I had one friend in Jackson, Mississippi: my neighbor MaryAnn. I had forgotten how to socialize. Over the next few months, I found the outgoing Jeanhee I had been back in high school again by watching TV, mostly comedies, and mimicking the most charming characters. Soon, I could speak Ebonics, ghetto English, redneck English, and Southern English, always with the accent I can't replace. I knew all the slang and decided some of my customers had to be amused to hear my accent develop a distinct Southern drawl. That made me laugh, too. How many other Koreans out there could boast a Southern drawl?

One day, I drove MaryAnn's car up I-55, took the Northside

Drive exit, and drove one block to Old Canton Road, where I summoned all my courage and looked for a place to stop. Finally, I pulled into a strip mall called Colonial Mart and parked in front MC's Beauty Salon. I had to start somewhere and decided this was it. So I pumped myself up a bit and went inside. They initially thought I was customer, but I quickly set them straight.

"Hi," I said. "I'm Jeanhee, a street peddler. Would any of you like to buy something?" They looked at me; I was smiling. They couldn't turn me away.

One of them said, "What are you selling, honey?"

"Earrings, watches, and bracelets. I got 'em all." My enthusiasm got them interested.

Mary Catherine, the owner of the beauty box said, "Bring 'em in, Honey, and we'll see if you have anything we can't live without."

I instantly got Tami, Nichole, and Mandy's attention, too. They became lifelong friends from that moment to this day.

"Okay. I'll be right back." So far, so good. They had accepted me even though I had expected them to turn me away. Not giving them time to change their minds, I hauled stuff in to display at the welcome desk. Earnings and bracelets were $4.99. I went on to give them the run down on the rest of my prices. Nothing was in order, and none of my goods were in pretty boxes. I'd dumped the jewelry into a plastic basket and kept the purses loose, grabbing what I could carry out from the trunk.

That was the beginning of my peddler business. At the time, and maybe even now, most hair salons were located in strip shopping centers or corner stores near housing areas, and they were easy to spot. Some of the names of the salons were funny, indicating the owners hadn't been in a normal state of mind when they had picked them. Many of them included a person's name on the shop. So whenever I walked into a new place, I looked for the person belonging to the name on the sign.

Each day, I became a better saleswoman. These were my kind of people, and I figured that if they could name their businesses such crazy names, I would fit right in. And I was right on the money.

They were easy to get to know. They couldn't believe I spent my days driving around in my girlfriend's car selling anything and everything out of the trunk.

"Welcome to my shop," I'd say, popping the trunk to reveal my merchandise. Stuff would be everywhere, and they would dig around as if looking for childhood treasures. Some of them would pull on the same item, and they would fight over it. Sometimes one would give in, and sometimes they wouldn't. They were crazy customers. *My* kind of customers… and they loved me even though what I did wasn't something they would ever want to do. They all knew they didn't have my guts, but I became one of their best friends.

Some days, they bought things they didn't even want. They liked my gutsy attitude and wanted to make sure I came back. Their professions and their happy personas eased my worries about my unpolished people skills. Some of them were lesbians. I had never met a lesbian before, but as long as none of them were men who would smother me and ruin my life, I liked them. Some may have even have had the hots for me. Who knows? But none of them ever actually made a move, so I didn't care what they did in their private lives.

I treated them like my girlfriends, and soon learned that most hair dressers are movie star wanna-bees. They wore thick heavy makeup, lipstick to match the blood red of their fingernails, and funny looking hair. One day it might be fiery red, and the next it would have purple streaks mixed in. They would do anything to stand out and be noticed. After all, they sold beauty products aimed at making women beautiful. So why not be flamboyant?

My new friends charged their clients a lot of money, but I never got a professional haircut. I simply gathered all of my hair in one hand and sliced it with scissors. I always had my hair in ponytail anyway, so I saw no sense in paying somebody else $35.00 to do it. I never would tell them how I cut my hair, though, because they would holler at me for mutilating it.

These girls were fun and crazy. They would talk about their customers as soon as they left the shop, beauty box rumors. And they knew everybody's business. I didn't have to speak perfect English with them either because they all knew what I meant. If they didn't, they eventually figured it out.

They knew who owned all the shops, who worked at which shops, and they were always eager to spill everything as soon as they had finished shopping. When I gave them each a *word of honor open credit line*, I had no problem tracking them down even if they quit one shop and moved on to another. They always went to other beauty shops, so I was in no danger of not getting paid. With the exception of the shop owners, the rest of them were always broke, so word of honor credit, so they could pay later, worked well. And many couldn't resist. I added fashion jewelry and clothes to my line, along with more fake purses and watches.

I became a walking mannequin. I always remembered to wear the outfit I wanted to sell that day, and I draped on all the jewelry, earrings, bracelets, rings, headbands, hairpins, scarves, necklaces, belts, and whatever else I had onto my body before I walked into their shops, and I sold just about everything. I hated wearing earrings because they always hurt my ears, so I was doubly glad whenever someone said they wanted the ones I had on. I sold a lot of outfits, too, since I always lied and told them it was the last one. I always carried other clothes with me so I could change.

I would walk in carrying my bag and say, "Honey, you can buy whatever I got on except my underwear and bra. I won't take those off."

And they would burst out laughing. Those women had finally met their match and couldn't help but wonder who was more crazy—me, or them. They knew little about my sales tactics, and they didn't want anyone walking around wearing the same thing they were, anyway.

I even sold eel skin cowboy boots to car salesmen once I learned how to measure feet. They would pay half down and half on delivery. I sent their sizes and a half of the cash they prepaid to a Korean shoemaker in Osan. Then at delivery, the other half of the money they owed me was my pure profit—$150. I gave away eel skin key rings as thanks for shopping with me, and they soon wanted to match their key rings with eel skin wallets, belts, and briefcases, all at a 300% markup. Car salesmen were easy prey; they liked to spend their money as soon as they received their commissions, and I was there to harvest it.

A few of them asked me for dates, but I always turned them down. One in particular, so full of himself, called me later in the day after buying a wallet and asked again. And again, I said *no*. He went off on me for hurting his typical car salesman's, testosterone-filled ego

"Who do you think you are?" he asked. "You're just a salesgirl, selling stuff out of the trunk of your girlfriend's car. You don't even own a car of your own."

I listened calmly. I had been there before and would not date a car salesman if he were the last man standing. I was turned off by their fast talk, slick hair, gleaming teeth, fake smiles, and handsome, dressed- to –kill- suits.

"Andy," I said once he was done. "That's just it, that's who I am. I'm nobody you want to know. I am just trying to survive with two boys, trying to pay my bills. You know?"

He calmed down; I had shut him up and accomplished two things in the process: I had salvaged his ego, and I could now go back to his dealership without a qualm. In addition, I would never be picked on again at that particular dealership. I was just like them, trying to make a sale, a profit, conducting business just as he was when he tried to sell a car.

I learned very quickly that every customer is different. To become their closest friend and get them to buy, I had to first get them to like me. I learned quickly that the rich bitches in North Jackson, the trophy wives, especially, didn't want to associate with just anyone—and I could tell they looked down on me. I watched how they acted, mimicking their carefully chosen words and taking stock of their manners for future reference. Their lifestyles were at the top of my list, with the exception of marrying a man with lots of money. That part, I didn't envy, but the rest—their composure, their rich living, the way they dressed to kill, and their nice cars—I did want.

They all gave me a fake "I just love your smile, Jeanhee!" and other false compliments, rolling their eyes as soon as they got into their cars, so sure they were above me. But I could deal with that, as long as they left with my purses on their arms and my watches on their wrists.

I finessed my sales skills as time went on, and I soon became a good judge of body language and tone, knowing just what to say to make my final successful sales pitch. My English may have been broken, but I calculated every word. Every customer was my best one, no matter how little they spent. And they were all my best friends, no matter how much or how little I liked them. I always remembered their names, what they bought, and which styles they preferred. If I knew any gossip about them, I remembered that, too.

Making money was my salvation, and it became my obsession, my pure joy. Money meant freedom. All I could think was, "How can I make more money?" If I had to sleep less and work more, making extra stops to sell the last few watches, a few more purses, I was willing to do it. I would stand on a corner near various festivals with bags of watches to sell without shame, my boys standing next to me. Sometimes, they would even find a grocery cart to help me display my wares, yelling out "Sale! Sale!" to passersby.

Around that time, I spotted an advertisement in the paper looking for food vendors for Jubilee Jam, a music and arts festival in downtown Jackson. The organizer wanted fresh food ideas, so I skimmed through other vendors' food lists to see what I could propose that was different. I told them I could do a tempura tent, and I beat out the others even though they were sponsored by restaurants. I signed up for two and half days and paid the $1,000 booth fee. Now, I just had to learn how to make tempura. "How hard can it be?" said to myself. All I could think of at that moment was making money with my bare hand, tumbling a few vegetables seemed like too easy prey.

I stopped by a local oriental grocery store on Highway 51 owned by Vietnamese and asked the owner for some tips. She never stopped bagging groceries as she answered. "Always use Japanese tempura mix and make sure you mix the batter with ice cold water and keep the batter super-super *codd- atthertimm...ess...*, okay? She meant *cold all the times, speaking* in her Vietnamese accent mixed up with a southern drawl.

I asked her why, and she told me so that the food would come out extra *crunchiii* and *yummiii*.

She said, "Heat the fryer to 350 degrees, and then pop in the vegetables, okay?"

I then went to Little Tokyo, a sushi restaurant I loved and asked the owner, Tommy Sang, for a favor. I figured since I was regular customer, he would oblige to order me six bags of tempura mix from his vendor at wholesale price. I even had two deep fryers I had bought cheaply at the flea market a while back. It was time for me to make more money.

My food booth had the longest line and was the busiest one at the festival. I cut vegetables nonstop, my knife flying and catching everyone's attention. I threw sweet potatoes, zucchini, broccoli, and four jumbo shrimp into a basket for five dollars. My boys stirred the batter, I dropped the food into the fryer, and my girlfriends fished it out, took the money, and handed out the steaming baskets. One night after the festival, a few of my friends called me, saying, "Jeanhee, I saw you on TV chopping vegetables at the festival. No man who saw you with that knife will ever mess with you."

I had been so absorbed I hadn't even noticed the camera pointed at me. I wished I had known so I could have taped the news that day, but the only thing I took with me from that tent besides money was a hellacious heat rash around the seams of my underwear and bra, everywhere my clothes pressed in. What a small price to pay for financial security. The rash eventually faded, but my sense of satisfaction at making enough money to support myself on my own terms lingered on, a fierce warm pride. I made $5,000 in those two and a half days, and I ended up frying tempura in scorching 100-plus degree heat for the next three summers. The same cameraman filmed me every year, too.

"She's back," he'd say, "the lady with the chopping block."

I hadn't even known I had a hidden tempura-cooking talent, but once I found it, I fried those vegetables with merciless intensity. I didn't even take a bathroom break all day. I had no time, and I didn't want the impatient crowd around my tent to wander off.

Each time a big box of purses and watches from New York arrived at my door, I slashed through the thick tape with trembling hands. Tony had kept his word, and I would keep mine—to him, to myself, and to my children. I was going to have a better life. The more money I made, the happier I was; I had earned it. What an amazing feeling to no longer have to wonder how I would pay all my bills in a given month. My second childhood dream besides an *education*, to be wealthy and live without worries, was slowly but surely becoming a reality. Knowing that I was in control of my own destiny, rather than having a man dictate my every move, helped me wake up each morning, happy, motivated and full of energy, even when I had to spend twelve hours a day on my feet. I even dropped my welfare benefits. I didn't need the government's assistance anymore.

My customer list grew longer, and they all looked forward to seeing me. I think they appreciated my gutsy attitude about making it on my own with my two young sons. They all knew about my hard life with Hamid and how I had lost Ahmad. I had no shame in telling anyone my story because I thought perhaps it would help someone else get through a hard time, and they admired how hard I hustled to make a buck.

They wanted to help me succeed even though some of them were barely making it too. It helped that they didn't feel ripped off by my merchandise. Even though it was counterfeit, it was good quality. Once everyone started telling their friends about my business, I even bought a beeper, and it went off almost constantly. When I called my clients back, they would say, "Jeanhee, where are you? Has anything new come in yet? Don't sell to someone else before you see me; I'll pay you extra if I get first pick." That summer, every woman in Jackson somehow found a way to mysteriously afford a new designer purse.

I had finally figured out how to keep selling to the same

people over and over again—not counting my sunny attitude—and that was by using the Korean way, based *on word of honor*, the same reason that Tony had trusted me. I never asked for money upfront; that made it easier to sell more at one time since they had no upfront commitment, and it also made the customer feel good that I trusted them.

Word of honor was the recipe for a strong relationship, and soon my *black book* was born, a notebook with all the names of my clients, where they worked, their phone numbers, their purchases, and how much they owed. I listed them in alphabetical order and meticulously kept up with not only what styles they preferred, but also little details about their personal lives that made us seem like best friends. I'm not sure where this business savvy came from. I had gotten my associate's degree in elementary *education*, after all, and that doesn't prepare a person for a life as a saleswoman. Perhaps I had inherited it from my mother, who had a natural knack for running a hotel even though she had never done anything but farm work before. Or perhaps it had been born of desperation and hunger for a better life.

If I discovered window of opportunities at all times, I dove through it. I even opened a little lunch deli off Fortification Street once. How hard could it be? I was only open for lunch, then I went back to work, trying to maximize my profits in any way I can, but I didn't realize a person had to be eighteen or older to serve beer. A kind customer whispered in my ear one day that Josh was too young to be delivering alcohol and that I could get in big trouble with the law. I needed a beer license to sell beer and such. I closed the deli within three months in fear of getting in trouble for breaking the law. I thought a sales license was all I needed, besides the place required too much work for too little return.

I also tried to date a little. I missed the companionship of a man, and I wasn't used to doing without it. The first guy turned out to be like Hamid, obsessive and violent, so I dropped him immediately. I had learned that lesson; I didn't need to be taught twice. On my second try, I fell in love with a married man. Apparently, I was incapable of making good choices with men. And because I was still a young woman, I struggled with sexual urges that were sometimes overwhelming. I didn't want to meet men just for one-night stands, but at the same time, I craved physical intimacy. I wished I didn't desire men at all. My whole life would have been different if I hadn't been pulled along by sex. I guess I could have bought one of those sex toys my girlfriends often talked about, but I thought it would just be a cheap thrill, and I didn't want to have to explain it to my boys should they come across it.

I decided upon a genius solution to this problem, but waited until I went to see my doctor, Dr. Russell, at the medical clinic on State Street for my annual check-up. When Dr. Russell asked me if I had any questions, I couldn't wait to ask him if he could remove my clitoris so that I didn't have to deal with wanting sex. I had read in a magazine that they do it all the time in Africa. His eyes widened. My question must have really been out of left field to surprise a doctor.

"Why would you even consider that?" he asked.

"Sex gets in my way," I said. "I don't have time for it. It always gets me in trouble with men. I had to poke myself in the leg with a knife last night so that I didn't run out and fall into bed with the first man I met."

"Mutilating yourself won't stop your desire, Jeanhee," he said, looking as if I'd just made the most peculiar request he'd ever had. "Removing your clitoris will just keep you from ever having any satisfaction. That's the worst of both worlds. You are a young woman; it's natural to want sex. Besides, that's a barbaric practice. It's not anything to take lightly."

My only other urge besides the sexual one was the need to let loose after I had worked so hard all week, so I went out with Laura some nights on weekends. She was single, with no kids, and I had met her at the beauty shop she owned. We had hit it off on our very first meeting, and she often loaned me her car whenever Mary Ann was out of town. But I just couldn't bring myself to have one-night stands like Laura often did. I was too afraid of catching diseases, especially since many of the same men went home with different women each week. Some of those girls were worse than the whores in Osan and took a man home every time they went out. I honestly believe they couldn't stand a night alone without man. I simply couldn't do it.

"What would I say to my boys if I did?" I asked myself. It was not going to happen, especially in my home. Maybe I would have found it easier to take a man home if I got drunk, but I never drank alcohol, so I couldn't lose that final inhibition. Laura smoked pot and popped pills, but she never once asked me to join her. She knew I would never touch drugs. I decided she had some sad stories in her life, too. I could see it in her eyes, but I didn't ask. Neither did I volunteer to tell mine. My secrets were mine to keep.

Except for my nights out with Laura or the occasional date, I buried myself in work, focusing on street peddling and the flea market on weekends. At night, I focused on my boys. I had little time to spare beyond that. And, of course, I spent a lot of time collecting what was owed me. Almost everyone paid the full amount on time. A few girls lost their jobs and had to choose to either pay me or the rent, and I didn't hold that against them. What I had made off them overall was more than what they owed me, and I figured they needed the money more than I did.

My flea market business boomed, and many of my customers who became my friends opened their beautiful homes to me and invited other friends over to buy my goods. One of them even ran an advertisement in the paper that read, *Jeanhee is setting up her fashion purses on Thursday night. Please come by.*

All of the North Jackson housewives talked about me. They even made trips to the flea market, a place they would never dare enter under other circumstances, to look for me on the weekends… wearing diamond rocks on their fingers and heavy make-up, their fake blond roots showing, their hair teased high off their foreheads. They had probably never worked a day in their lives, but they pretended I was their best friend. I smiled and sold those purses. I liked them for their money, and they liked me for the purses they got for so much less.

I didn't really get cheated until I tried to expand my business. Alvin was a tall, skinny black guy who was one of my best customers at the flea market. He came by four or five times a week, and I suspected he sold my stuff to his friends at a marked up price. But who was I to crush someone's entrepreneurial spirit? Instead, I gave him discounts for being such a good customer.

When he approached me one day and promised to sell my merchandise if I gave him a chance, I gave it some thought and agreed.

"Yes, I will give you a chance," I said. After all, someone had given me a chance once. I gave him $1,000 worth of merchandise. At that time, it might as well as have been $10,000. The sums were the same to me. He was supposed to pay me back with profit a week later, but he never showed up.

"What happened to *word of honor?*" I muttered under my breath.

I drove home after the flea market and dropped off my boys, looked his address up in the phone book, and headed toward his apartment on Robinson Road in South Jackson. It was in a rough neighborhood with sagging porches, rusted cars, and a general atmosphere of despair and poverty. A few black children played ball beneath a hoop nailed to the side of a shed. When I reached the complex on the edge of the neighborhood, I parked as close to Alvin's door as I could in case I had to run. Before I got out of the car, I tucked the .22 into my back pocket. I didn't want to use it again, but it might come in handy. I wanted to teach this guy a lesson. Plus, I hated liars. I would forgive a lot, but never lying.

"Alvin!" I yelled, angrily pounding on the door. "I know you're in there."

I could see him peering through the peephole, but I was so short he probably couldn't make out who was there.

"Open the door, Alvin! This is Jeanhee from the flea market, and you owe me money!"

He opened the door slowly, his eyes wild. He was twice my size, but he was still afraid of this tiny Korean woman on his doorstep.

"You are a liar and a thief!" I berated him in a loud voice. "I trusted you and gave you a chance, and you cheated me."

"Ms Jeanhee, please!" All the sudden, I am MS Jeanhee to him. He raised his hands. "I was going to pay you. Don't yell, the neighbors will call the cops. I really was going to come find you tomorrow, I swear."

"I came to you instead," I answered. "You better give me back those watches."

"I don't have them anymore," he said. "I can pay you tomorrow."

"Oh, no! I'm not leaving until you give me something to take back," I said, standing my ground.

He looked at me warily. "What do you want?"

"Let me in," I said, "and I'll look around. And don't try anything funny!"

As I walked past him into the apartment, he drew in a sharp breath. I figured he had seen the gun sticking out of my pocket.

The first thing I saw was a brand new Hitachi color TV, still in the box. I pointed at it and hissed, "Did you take that and not pay for it, either?"

"No, I paid for it," he answered.

"With the money you owed me?" I asked. Then, not waiting for an answer, I said, "I'll take the TV, and you are going to carry it to my car, please."

He did, without saying a word. His girlfriend didn't say anything, either, amazed at her big boyfriend being directed by a short Asian women yelling in broken English.

When I got home with the television, my boys were over the moon.

"Mommy, Mommy, for us? We can watch cartoons in color now? Thank you, Mama!" At first they thought I had bought it, but when I told them I took it from a big black man, I became their hero. "Wow, Mommy, you did that? Really?"

Twenty-five years later, I still have that TV in my garage, and the remote, too. I won't get rid of it. That was my prized possession for standing up to that big black man who owed me money, a reward for not backing down and for coming out of hiding after my nightmare with Hamid. It set the tone for my stand against injustice.

I had one bad check written to me the whole time from a lady in Forest, Mississippi, a $175 check. A big check. She had seemed so nice when she wrote it at the flea market. Her address was written on the check, so one afternoon I put my kids in the car and told them we were going for ride to Forest. I had never been there, but I was going to find that lady and get my money back. The town was about an hour's drive from home. I pulled into a gas station once I got there and found an old man having coffee in the little snack bar.

"Hello," I said to him. "I came all the way here from Jackson to find an old friend. Her name is Tina Story. She told me how to get to her house, but I got lost."

That old man showed me some old-fashioned southern hospitality and drew me a map. Fifteen minutes later, I pulled up and knocked on her door.

Tina just about shit in her pants.

"Hi! Tina," I said, kindly, pretending she had no idea the check was bad. "I went to the bank yesterday to deposit your check, but it came back as unpaid."

"I'll bring you the cash," she said. She nervously gnawed her lip. "I don't know what happened to my bank account. I'll go ask them about it tomorrow."

"Okay," I said. "When will you be able to give me my money?"

"I'll meet you at the Waffle House on Terry Road tomorrow at four-thirty."

"All right," I said. What else could I do? She knew I would drive back to Forest to find her again if she didn't show up. "You also owe me thirty dollars for the insufficient check fee. So you need to bring me two hundred and five dollars."

With a swift bob of her head, she agreed.

I couldn't believe it, but she met me the next day and gave me all my money. As I came to embrace my survival skills, how to communicate in diplomatic terms even with the people who wrote bad checks, Tina became one my favorite customers. I let her write me a check after that episode, too. She couldn't believe I trusted her. I figured she knew I knew where she lived. And besides, she had honored that first check and paid the extra fee.

*****

I changed my personal theme song from *I Will Survive* to the Pet Boys' *Let's Make Lots of Money*. I controlled my destiny, and money was going to help me to do everything I wanted. My dream was shaping up, transforming my life into one of financial security. Although I had spent over two decades single-mindedly pursuing an *education*, that diploma had been replaced in my thoughts by dollar signs. I had discovered other paths to success and was eating steamy white rice wrapped in toasted seaweed every day. So I tucked away my regret about not having attended a four-year college, of not cheering at football games and strolling along tree-lined sidewalks on campus. A new Jeanhee had been born, and she convinced herself to settle for a two-year degree; there was more to life than my childish dreams of college. Besides, with three sons and three husbands behind me, my experience could never have been the *normal* one I had hoped for when I first ran away from Korea.

My new reality was all about money. It helped me put a roof over my head, shower my remaining two boys with gifts, and keep men at arm's length. Never again would one hit me, rape me, or keep me from happiness. I would say "hell, no!" to all of them and enjoy doing it.

I continued peddling counterfeit purses and watches, putting all of my heart and soul into it. It was my only option. Unlike in New York, Mississippi had no good jobs for Koreans who spoke only broken English. I knew selling knock-off goods was wrong and that it was against the law. But I figured that if I told my customers my merchandise wasn't real, I wasn't cheating them. Besides, my life was on the line with my sons in this foreign country, with no family to ask for help. *Do or die* was my choice, and what was my little bit of dishonesty in comparison to the corporate greed of big companies making billions of dollars on overpriced merchandise in the mall? In my mind, I wasn't selling drugs. I wasn't robbing anybody, and I was off welfare and paying my bills on my own. Best of all, I hadn't taken my ex back and would never have to. My only regret was that I hadn't pulled that gun on him sooner so I could have been where I was today back then. I was happy street peddling, doing door-to-door and business-to-business sales.

My success allowed us to finally be comfortable and enjoy things others take for granted. I had needed a car of my own for a while since the wear and tear from my business on my girlfriends' cars was wearing on their kindness. I visited car dealerships so often to sell my goods that I already knew which car I wanted to buy. It took me a while to save up the $3,000 I needed for a down payment, but eventually, I did it. I finally went to Herrin-Gear Chevrolet on High Street as a customer and not a peddler, and marched right in, my shoulder bowed down by the money in my purse.

"Can I see Buck?" I asked the receptionist. She and the rest of the salesmen on the floor probably thought I was trying to sell him another fake Rolex watch. Buck overheard me and came into the office.

"Hi, Jeanhee," he said. "You get in some more watches?"

"Yes, but I'm here on different business today," I answered. "You said you would sell me a car for $3,000 cash, remember? I bet you thought I was kidding when I said I'd be back."

"No, no," he laughed. "You're one of the most determined people I've ever met. No, I didn't think you were kidding, no siree."

He took me out to see the brand-new red Z-28 I had been eyeing since the first day I had visited the dealership in MaryAnn's car.

"I have three-thousand dollars right here in my purse," I said, patting it. "I'll count it again, just to make sure."

"Do you want to test drive the car?" he asked.

"No, I'll drive it when it's mine," I said to him. I pulled out my cash and counted the money the Korean way, by holding the stack of bills in my left hand folded upward in half, with my second finger pointing down and my ring finger holding the other half, all the fingers of my right hand except my thumb pushing down all at once, rubbing every single. I counted money so fast and so often that I even had a callous on one of my fingers.

The other salesmen stopped what they were doing to stare at me and my fingers in action on that handful of cash, whispering, "Shit, did that Korean street peddler woman really come in to buy a car from Buck?"

"Jeanhee," Buck said, shaking his head at me and smiling. "You really shouldn't carry that much cash in your purse. It's not safe."

When he wrote the sticker price on my contract, I shook my head and jabbed the paper with my finger. "That's not a good enough price," I said. "I can either buy it from you today for two-thousand less than that, or I can leave and you might not sell it at all."

"You're a crazy lady, Ms. Kang." Buck shook his head but wrote in the lower price. "Good luck."

He gave me his business card. The fine print on the back read, *Bring a customer to me today or any day, and get $50 bucks cash on me.*

I drove my brand new car home that day to show my boys, bursting with pride that we finally wouldn't have to beg rides or borrow a car from my friends anymore.

That same year, as I was driving around peddling, I saw a sign that read, *Lease to purchase* in front of a beautiful condo on the reservoir. The asking price was $65,000. I stopped and wrote down the real estate agent's name and number. At that time, I wasn't sure what *lease to purchase* meant, but maybe I would qualify.

I was making good money by then and had some cash reserved, and the location of the condo was perfect. And with 1,200 square feet, all three of us would have plenty of room. The boys could even ride their bikes or take the bus to the nearest school.

Within a few days, I made an offer and called the bank to ask what I needed to do to apply for a loan. They told me to bring in a few qualifying documents: tax returns for the past three years, pay stubs, and asset information. I didn't have any credit history and had never had a credit card, but I had managed to buy a car, so how hard could it be?

I gathered what I had and hoped it would be enough. I also took in my green budget book, the record from day one of my business that included every expense down to the fifty cents I had spent for a Diet Coke, and my black book with my list of receivables from all of my customers as proof of income.

I walked into the banker's office just as confidently as I had walked into that car dealership. After I filled out the loan application, I met with the banker and his assistant.

I pulled out my green and black books, and a short, older man hurried in and looked at me over his gold wire-rimmed glasses. His assistant looked as if he were fresh out of college, with his dark hair and handsome, preppy vibe.

They both peered skeptically at my tattered books as I quickly explained. The older banker huffed and said, "This is the most peculiar loan process I've ever done."

"I'm a hard worker," I said. "I'll never miss a payment."

"Well, I'll say again, this is peculiar," he answered. "But I like how detailed and responsible you've been with your income and expense records, and I believe we can make it work, Ms. Kang."

That condo was our very first home. With the banker's approval, I signed a lease to purchase agreement, and in six months, if I didn't miss a payment, the condo would be mine for good. We moved in with just a few belongings. Our old beds and battered furniture looked shabby in such a clean, new condo, but we were so happy to have a home of our own on such beautiful waterfront property.

My life had been completely transformed. I had been roaming around Jackson as a street peddler for two years, running my flea market booth on the weekends, and had been off welfare for a year. I had my own home, my own car, and cash in the bank. I had crossed *worrying about money* off my daily to-do list. But as time passed, I became more nervous about making my living doing something I knew was illegal. Whenever a cop car drove by or an officer strolled past my booth in the flea market, my heart pounded. If I went to jail, who would look after my boys? Now was the time to at least start the process of becoming legitimate. I needed to have an exit plan, to slowly switch my merchandise to accessories that weren't knock-offs. I needed to stop selling counterfeits before I got into trouble.

I wasn't sure how to stop ordering goods from Tony when he had been brave enough and kind enough to take a chance on me, so I started making up excuses whenever he called to ask me if I needed more merchandise.

"It's just not selling as well right now," I would say. "My clients aren't as interested as they used to be." I didn't tell him I was afraid of getting into trouble with the law. I didn't want to offend him or make him angry in case later I did need to order from him again. I did tell Kim the truth, though, and she helped me contact various vendors in the Broadway wholesale district. If I had been in New York, I don't think she'd have been so generous with her time. She hated competition, and it had become a sore subject after her husband's friend opened a business right next door to her selling the exact same merchandise she did. But since I was in Mississippi, her profits were safe if she helped me.

At the time, inexpensive fashion watches were all the rage among women, bands in all colors, faces in different shapes and sizes. I could buy them for $5 and sell them for $20 and still make an excellent profit margin. Most of the vendors in the wholesale market were Korean, so we spoke the same universal discount language, and they helped me get rock-bottom prices and taught me how to mark up the earrings, sunglasses, and accessories 300 percent. The vendors were also eager to stay on Kim's good side. She had opened another store and now made over $20,000 a day, so she was one of their biggest catches.

With my contacts in New York, no one in Mississippi could beat my prices, and I made sure they didn't try. When I eventually hired employees I sent them out scoping stores around town and in the mall, so I could always sell my goods for less. Kim's help also meant I had the trends before they even hit the magazines. If something was hot in New York, I was selling it in Mississippi before anyone even realized they wanted to buy it.

Once I had received my new merchandise, I went to Northpark Mall in Ridgeland, the biggest mall in the state, and walked from one end to the other, taking in the beautiful wide glass doors, the marble columns, the bustling anchor stores, and the specialty stores with their high-priced, perfectly arranged merchandise. Tall, slim, size zero mannequins posed in nearly every window displaying the latest fashion. I could only imagine how expensive renting one of those stores would be, not to mention buying enough merchandise to fill it.

The marble floors looked too expensive for a peddler like me to walk on. I could only dream of what the store owners had done to allow them to own such beautiful stores. How did they get the money? Did they have rich parents? Or had they had a dream like me and worked their way up? It seemed like an impossible dream, but I couldn't help wishing that maybe one day, I would join them.

I looked at my reflection in the glass windows and saw only meager little me. How could I possibly think I could ever get a store like that? I shook my head and continued walking, and as I did, I kept noticing empty kiosks in the middle of the corridor. I had to start somewhere, so maybe I could start with one of those. I had passed at least seven empty kiosks before I finished my tour of the mall, each with a display sign that read, *This could be yours, see the mall manager today.*

All of a sudden, those little kiosk wagons looked very attractive—cute and quaint—and probably not beyond my budget. But which one was the best? I picked one near the main entrance, because it would receive more foot traffic. I wanted to get walk-ins as soon as they came into the mall. Though just moments before I had been feeling hopeless, now I was encouraged. The kiosk was small enough that I could work it myself, and I was sure that if I spread out my stock, I could fill all of the shelves. I scoped out the mall office before returning to my car, my feet almost flying as I got more and more excited. I grabbed the laundry basket half filled with jumbled fashion watches from my trunk and arranged them as nicely as I could before heading back into the mall with it, passing the heavy double doors into the leasing office.

A secretary sat typing at the front desk. I glanced at her nameplate and said, "Hi, Sharon. Can I talk to the manager?"

She stared at me as I sat my basket on the chair beside me, her eyes moving back and forth from the basket to me. She picked up the phone, pressed a few buttons, and said, "PJ, there's someone here to speak with you," as her eyes still zooming on my laundry basket.

He must have asked who, because she turned away and whispered, "An Asian lady with a basket full of watches," covering her mouth with her right hand.

I could tell she thought my basket was tacky, but I didn't care. Using it was easier than hauling them around in the cardboard box they'd come in. She kept looking at me strangely while I waited. I hadn't noticed I was so weird the last time I checked, but maybe she had never seen an Asian woman before. Jackson wasn't exactly a diverse city in those days.

As I thought about what I was doing, I got nervous. Here I was, trying to convince the mall manager of the newest, nicest mall in the state of Mississippi that my little watches would sell well in the main mall entry way—their best location.

When PJ came out of his office a few minutes later, I got up and shook his hand.

"Hi, PJ," I said. "I'm Jeanhee Kang. I'd like to sell watches at one of your carts."

"I see." He gave me the same peculiar look Sharon had given me, and he stared at my basket. His gaze was curious. Perhaps he wondered if he should pity me, or if he could actually get some money out of this crazy Asian lady.

While he was deep in thought, I anticipated his first question, looked him straight in the eye, and burst out with, "Yes, I can," using the same sincerity I had shown Tony at Canal and Broadway. "I can make the rent and still make myself a profit. I just need you to give me a chance."

"I can only rent it to you if you promise not to sell those watches out of that laundry basket," he said gruffly.

"I can buy a better basket," I said quickly.

"No baskets!" he barked. "This is too nice a mall for your baskets."

"Fine." I wasn't offended. I would toss that five dollar basket in the dumpster as long as I could have a kiosk. I had to jump on this opportunity now and show him how eager I was, how dedicated I would be, so I asked, "How much is the rent?"

"Eight-hundred a month for a six-month lease," he said, his tone growing amused as he picked up on my excitement. He had probably never had anyone so excited about the little wagons out in the mall, especially when the stores were so much nicer.

My face fell in disappointment. That was more than my mortgage. "Eight-hundred dollars?"

"Tell you what. I'll give you a short-term lease, so if you can't make it you can leave," he said. "But you gotta give me a thirty day notice before you move out. Can you do that?"

"Yes, sir," I said, grasping his hand and shaking it again. "Thank you."

"When do you want to start?" he asked, beckoning me into his office.

I followed him in and sat in the chair across from him. "Can you give me a few days? I need to call my mama's fortune teller for the best move in date."

Though I had embraced my life in America, I still held strong to some Korean traditions, one of which was consulting a fortune teller for large life decisions, like the best day to open a business to ensure its long-term success.

The secretary twirled around in her chair to look at me, and PJ's mouth fell open a little bit in shock before he responded. "I can wait for that," he said slowly. "but only if you ask your fortune teller about my future. Am I going to be rich one day?"

"I can ask her if you give me your time of birth and the date," I said, rummaging in my purse to find a scrap of paper so I could write down the information.

He chuckled. "I was just kidding, Jeanhee. You can have a few days. Just call me when you're ready to come in and sign the lease."

I couldn't wait to call my mama and tell her I was opening my very first business in the most beautiful mall in Mississippi. Despite all the bumps in our relationship, I still wanted her to be proud of me. I waited for her nighttime before she went to bed and then dialed her number, my hands trembling. I hadn't talked to her in months because my shame sat so strong within me. The last thing I had done worth bragging about was getting my associate's degree six years before.

This time, though, she could tell by the tone of my voice I was calling in excitement and had good news.

"My Jeanhee is finally going to be rich in America," she said with pride. She had no idea my store was actually just a little ten-by-three foot kiosk. To her, opening a business in America was a million-dollar dream. She must have been imagining a beautiful store, full of pretty fixtures, a full line of merchandise, and lots of employees to boss around.

I decided to let her dream on. In my mind, I would make that dream come true one day. Only time would tell.

I called her the next day to get the fortune teller's date recommendation and was soon ready to rise to the top of the retail food chain in North Park Mall. I opened my first business as a kiosk vendor on February 2, 1990, and I called it the *Time Machine*. Brenda, another staff worker in the office, had lectured me on making my display pretty, not like it belonged in a flea market, and so I spent hours arranging my watches until they were perfect. I couldn't afford risers like the other stores could, so I covered small cardboard boxes in pretty fabric I bought from the fabric store, and pinned the back to make it look as if the entire box were covered.

I opened an account at the same bank I had run to for my once-in-a-life time chance money from the same black guy who had helped me the day I ran Hamid out of my life. I installed a phone, applied for an MS sales tax number, and bought an inexpensive cash register from Sam's wholesale. I also made sure I had absolutely everything I needed to open shop that first day: change, bags, pens, paper clips, scissors, staplers, a receipt book, a budget book to record daily sales, and extra paper rolls to refill my register and credit card printer, in case I made more sales my first day than I expected. I was ready for business.

Every shop in the mall opened and closed at the same time, and I worked eleven hours a day Monday through Saturday and seven hours on Sunday. but that was no problem. I had the time and a burning desire to make money that fluttered like butterflies in my stomach. I dreamed of being rich one day, and a fear of failure was not in the equation.

My first few days were slow. I sold only a few watches, but soon business started to improve. I noticed that the colorful bands and sparkling rhinestones drew impulsive women who were eager to make a purchase but didn't want to pay three times more at an anchor store. I didn't mind telling them how much cheaper my watches were, either. I must have said, "McRae's is selling the same watch for sixty dollars" a hundred times a day, and they took the bait. My salesmanship skills from street vending came in handy. I even added services I had learned from a local jeweler, changing bands and batteries, shortening metal links, and changing pins. Soon, I was able to employ Kristine to run the kiosk, so I could continue street peddling and collecting payments. But it turned out, I did a little too well as a full-time street vendor. My luck was about to change, and not in the way I had dreamed.

One day when I returned from peddling, two U.S. Customs and Border Patrol officers stood waiting on me by my kiosk in the mall. My heart raced, and I flashed back to the police station in Osan, so long ago. I almost expected Mama Sang to be stomping along behind them, finally getting her revenge on me, but I couldn't quite picture her in this shiny American mall.

"Are you Ms. Jeanhee Kang?" one of the officers asked.

"Yes, I am," I answered, my voice quavering. Still, I held my head high.

"We have a search warrant for your home," one of the

officers said. "We have reason to believe you've been trafficking in counterfeit goods."

He named off a long list of things I'd never heard of and had certainly never sold, but I was too shocked to even try to correct him. I had just started my path to success. How could this be happening to me just when I was trying to be honest?

"We'd appreciate it if you'd come back to your condo with us," he said. "We'll need to go through your things."

The other agent asked for my car keys and said I should ride with the first agent and that he would follow us in my car. En route to my condo, we stopped at the Harbor Pine Storage on Spillway Road, where I had stored the leftover goods that were too damaged to sell.

The officers placed some of the goods on top of my car and took pictures of them. Cops were everywhere on the road in front of the storage facility, and I figured they were waiting to chase me with their lights flashing if I decided to run. Suddenly, I worried if this investigation might be much more serious than I had thought. What were they trying to pin on me? What were the penalties for breaking the law? I had never even checked.

The officers could tell by the tone of my voice that I was not going to answer their questions. I didn't want them to see my fear, so I stayed cold and reserved. They would later use the photo they took at the storage unit as an excuse to confiscate my vehicle for transporting illegal goods, leaving me once again without a car.

The boys were home when we got there, and I told them to stay close by me.

"Mommy is in trouble," I said. "These officers have to search our home."

Josh nervously looked over at the beloved San Francisco 49er memorabilia he kept lovingly displayed in a bookcase. Tears filled his eyes. I could tell that both of my boys were scared to death for me. They had no idea what I had done to cause these officers to dig through our home.

"Mommy, are they going to take away my Joe Montana and Jerry Rice cards?" Josh asked, crying.

One agent who was kinder than the others stopped his search and said, "No, son, we're not going to take your football cards."

"Thank you, sir," Josh quickly answered, swiping his eyes with his shirt sleeve. He ran over to his cards and clutched them to his chest, then returned to my side. We sat quietly at our kitchen table as the officers went through everything we owned, opening cabinets, rummaging in drawers, overturning the toy chest, even going through our trash cans. They didn't find a single thing, and they left with a black cloud of frustration over their heads.

But suddenly I was notorious. This went far beyond getting my picture in the high school newspaper or my face on the news chopping vegetables at Jubilee Jam, and it didn't bring with it a sense of pride. My face was on the primetime news and in the *Clarion Ledger*, the town's leading newspaper; it was surreal. People who walked by my kiosk in the mall gave me a second look, trying to see if I was that lady they had seen in the papers.

I got calls from all of my customers and friends, asking how I was doing and telling me I had been on the WBLT news as the biggest counterfeiter in the state. The agents had taken my black book and had everyone's phone numbers. My life was in a tailspin. I had just bought the car and given the bank the down payment on our condo, and I only had $3,300 left in the bank, yet those agents acted as if I were Donald Trump. I wanted to yell at them and tell them I had barely gotten off welfare, and that I had to hustle long hours seven days a week to afford the things we had. And when I found out I was facing five years in jail and a $250,000 fine, my terror increased exponentially.

I was terrified of what would happen to my boys. When would I see them again? I could send them to their dad in Mexico City, Missouri, but then I might not get them back. And how in the world would I afford a lawyer? MaryAnn's then boyfriend, Richard, was an attorney, so I tried him first. Richard told me that he didn't practice criminal law.

"Legal fees are steep, Jeanhee," he said. "You can try George Noon. He doesn't practice criminal law, but he takes cases for cheap. He might be your best bet."

I hired George shortly thereafter but then had second thoughts. What if George couldn't get me out of trouble? I hadn't exactly heard glowing praise about his services. I looked in the yellow pages and found James Bell's phone number. He was a former Hinds County judge, and his office was off Fortification Street downtown, near where my short-lived deli had been. I remember him paying special attention to me whenever he came to have lunch. Kristin told me he would ask for me at the kiosk whenever I was out peddling around town. He heard the desperation in my voice and agreed to set up a consultation with me. Since I didn't have a car to allow me to visit his office, he agreed to come to the mall. We met at Ruby Tuesday.

James could easily have passed as a preacher. He had a certain peace about him, and his kind, soft voice instantly invited confidence and trust. The more I told him about my situation, the more I felt he saw *me,* not just a case or a situation. In fact, he reminded me a lot of Robert, and that left me with certain sort of longing, but I pushed that thought away quickly. James was a married man. We agreed on a payment plan, and I left the restaurant with the first spark of hope I'd felt since the customs officers had first showed up at my kiosk.

Luckily, my cart business made enough for me to pay my mall rent and restock my merchandise, but I was forced to file Chapter 11 bankruptcy to protect my condo. I tried not to feel disheartened. Even though I felt as if I had ended up in the same place I had started, broke and alone in America, I didn't stay sad long. I didn't lose hope; I had to believe everything was going to be okay, and after meeting with James, having hope became easier.

I think this crisis was harder on my boys than on me. Every day I told them over and over that things would be okay and that we would get through the trial and all be together, but boys at school taunted them. Rumors flew, and when one of the boys in Josh's class told him I was a cocaine dealer, that kid went home with a bloody nose, a black eye, and more than a few bruises. Josh never told me about the fight because he didn't want to upset me, so I heard about it from another parent—but no one made fun of him after that.

I distracted myself from worry by working seven days a week. I didn't have much choice if I wanted to keep a roof over our heads and food on the table. I needed to make every penny I could, especially with the lawyers' fees piling up. My boys had started playing soccer, flag football, and baseball—any sport they could, really—but they never asked me to come to their games. Instead, they got rides with their teammates' parents. They knew it would hurt me if they asked and I had to say no. They understood I was working to make our life better, and their job was to support me by not interrupting me during working hours. In two months' time, I had saved enough for a down payment on another car.

This time I went to Blackwell Chevrolet on I-55. I couldn't go back to Herrin Gear since I assumed Buck was upset that I had stopped payments on the Z-28. I saw a red Geo Tracker in the front of the showroom, the least expensive brand-new car on the lot. It had a stick shift, and I had no earthly idea how to drive it, but I figured its price might be within my range after I negotiated and got the salesman to lower the price a few thousand dollars.

The first salesman had barely introduced himself before I pointed to the red Geo and said, "I want that car right there. I have fifteen-hundred dollars as a down payment, and I want two-thousand off the sticker price. Can we make that happen?"

"You came to the right man," he said. "Are you ready to take it home today?"

"On one condition," I answered. "You have to teach me how to drive a stick shift."

"Not a problem," he said, talking even faster than me now. I was probably the easiest sale he had ever made. "I used to run a driving school. You'll be a pro in no time."

I thought that sounded like a lie, but I decided to believe him. Ten minutes later, I had signed all the paperwork and we were out in the parking lot, with him sitting nervously in the seat beside me as I lurched the car frontward and backward. He showed me how to maneuver around the clutch and release the brakes while changing the gear with my right hand. I was sure I could get the hang of it.

"Ms. Kang!" he shouted at one point. "Watch out! Don't hit the new cars!"

"Okay." I just barely squeezed by one before slamming the gear back into park. "That's good enough," I said. "I bet I can make it home. I'll just stay off the highway and away from hills."

"You're a crazy lady, Ms. Kang," Thomas said, shaking his head. "Good luck."

We shook hands, and I drove my brand new car to the Beauty Box, where Tami who would become my best friend for life, worked. . Tami could pass for Nicole Kidman's sister; her skin is pure white, but her eye sight isn't good enough to read street signs to drive a car so everybody drives her round. I knew she'd love to make fun of me for buying a manual car on the spot when I didn't know how to drive a stick shift. She already thought I was crazy half the time anyway for all the things I did to make sales around town; this would top them all.

I veered into a parking spot and went inside, the sharp scent of dye filing my nose. "Hey Tami," I called, "Come outside for a minute! I have something to show you."

"I'll be right back," she said to the lady in her chair. "You've got another twenty minutes till the dye is done."

She followed me out the door, slipping on her black sun glasses to protect her eyes from the bright sun. "Oh, My Gosh, Is that your new car?"

"Yes. Get in," I answered. "I'm going to give you a ride. Better put on your seatbelt." I didn't want my inexperienced gear shifting to throw her into the floorboard.

"Are you ready, Tami?"

"I'm ready," she said. She still hadn't noticed the gear shift, and I smiled, knowing we were both about to have an adventure we'd talk about for years.

"Here we go," I said. Unfortunately, Thomas hadn't warned me about going uphill. I couldn't get out of the parking lot into the street. Shifting gears, pressing the gas, and pushing the clutch on after was different than driving on a flat road. After three or four tries, my car went dead. Tami hollered with laughter.

"You bought a car you can't even drive, Jeanhee?" she asked. "You're still going to be walking everywhere. If you wanted a lawn ornament for your condo, you could have gotten flowers."

"Shut up, Tami," I said good-naturedly. "I can drive this damn car if you give me a minute. Do you want to try instead?"

"Nope," she said, sitting back. "I'll wait for you to figure it out all yo'self, honey." She pushed up her glasses and wiped her eyes; she was in tears by then.

It took me ten tries to get up that two-foot hill, but I still gave Tami a drive around the block. She didn't stop laughing the whole time.

"I love your car, darling," she said as she got out. "See you later."

As I drove away, she called out, "Watch out for that hill on your way out!"

Moments of laughter such as that kept up my spirits during my legal troubles. All of my friends and customers received me with compassion and didn't look down on me the whole time. They wanted to help me by buying more things they didn't even need to help me pay my attorneys.

*****

I had waited six months for my trial, and I was determined not to settle or take a plea bargain. I wanted to argue that I wasn't hurting anyone that I was just trying to make a living for my two boys and me. I knew the law, though, and realized things did not look good.

But I wouldn't feel desolate and forsaken for long. I had passed a church called *Family Life* on Old Fannin Road many times on my way to the flea market on weekends. On Sundays, the church's parking lot spilled over with cars. I didn't know what kind of church it was; the sign hanging below a white wooden cross didn't say. One Sunday morning after a hard night out with my girlfriends, trying to forget my stress and worry for just a few hours, I jumped out of bed with a certain urgency, wanting to change my lifestyle and put my life in order. I needed more than a miracle this time. I needed a higher power. I was ready to initiate that process myself, and I needed to get to the nearest church to do so. I was tired of barhopping with my loose girlfriends who always took a strange man home. I stuck out like a sore, sober thumb among them, anyway.

I didn't even have time to shower or wash my hair, and it was still filled with smoke from the night before, but I was certain nobody at church would notice. I decided to open my booth late and pulled into the church's parking lot. I didn't know it then, but I was on my way to be saved—to be renewed as a person, leaving behind the sinful life I had lived. During the sermon, Pastor Mark spoke straight to my heart about being in trouble with the law and turning one's face away from sin. I felt as though he were talking directly to me. I knew then I needed help from Jesus, and my heart was ready to receive Him.

I had been to services before, of course. My participation in church was what had prompted my most vicious fight with Hamid, the one that had sent me running to New York, but never before had I been moved so deeply.

At the end of the sermon, a guest pastor, Kenneth Hogan, stepped up to the pulpit and said words I had heard before: "If any of you would like to be saved by the blood of Jesus Christ, please come forward."

By then I was in tears and ready to ask for my sin to be wiped out. I walked down that aisle, knelt in front of him, confessed my sins to God, and asked for forgiveness from Jesus.

Dear Jesus, I said in my head, *I will be a believer now and forever, but I'm here for a reason. Please be with me in court and don't let them send me to jail. Please give me peace in my heart, heal me from the hurt, and wash out my past, including my prostitution days back in Osan. And even though it may be wrong to want material things, I am greedy, Lord; I want money and lots of it.*

That might not have been a conventional prayer, but that day I was saved in front of that three-thousand member congregation. A great sense of relief poured over me as I unburdened my troubles to a higher power, and I slept peacefully for the first time in a long time that night. I dreamed of Pastor Kenneth, the man who had asked those who were lost to come forward, and he waved away the shadows in my home and replaced them with sparkling chandeliers and soft beams of light. By the time he had finished, my home didn't contain even a single spot filled with shadows. I felt light as a feather, floating around my house with absolute happiness. I had never been in a place that felt so right.

I went to services twice a week and was reminded each time to be good and stay away from temptation. Even though I still went out, I now knew where the line was, and I left the sinners to get drunk and get laid. I was proud to finally know what was right and what was wrong with such clarity. Never before had I received such glowing, wholesome guidance, and I reveled in it.

*****

November, 1990

The day had arrived, the day on which my faith, my future and my boys' futures hinged. Federal Judge Henry Wingate, known for his tough sentencing guidelines and emotionless verdicts, was to preside over my case in the United States District Court on Amite Street. I had never been in an America courtroom before and had only seen one on television. It looked smaller and sadder than I had imagined.

I was scared to death of what might happen that day. I didn't want to be a crybaby, but I felt like being one. I had nobody else to blame for what I had done. I knew there were consequences for breaking the law, but I had been left with little choice. I had taken on the job that made the most sense.

I had no one to call for moral support and no way to ease the situation. The only thing I could do was to wait for the verdict and face my wrongdoing on my own. For the first time, I was my glad my mama wasn't close to me. If I were found guilty, I would be ashamed to tell her that America had decided I was a criminal. I had called home not long ago to give her news of a better life, not to fill her days with more hardship.

The morning of the trial, I made my boys go to school just like normal; in my heart, I didn't think the authorities would take me to jail right away. Of course, they would let me say goodbye to my boys, wouldn't they? I dared not tell my sons about my court appearance. I didn't want them to know.

I got up at 2 a.m., got my thoughts together for the day, drank three cups of coffee, and checked the weather. It was cool, but not too cold for my morning run. So I jogged across the trestle bridge over the reservoir. As I ran, I tried to shake off my worries, but worst-case scenarios streamed through my head. What would happen to Josh and Jason? How would they live? What would they say to their friends?

"My mom is in jail."

The possibility that I might go to jail weighed down upon my feet and I sped up, running as if I were being chased by some unknown being. I had had no contact with Josh and Jason's dad for so many years; I didn't want to pick up the phone. I had no earthly idea what he might be doing, who he might have married, or what his financial situation might be. I didn't want my kids to grow up poor in Missouri and be unable to have a dream for an *education*. Instilling in my boys the motivation to be a success was my job, and I had to protect them from the poor lifestyle their dad lived. He hadn't gone to college, and I didn't recall any of his siblings ever going, either. He had no ambition.

My boys were my responsibility. I had brought them into this world, and I had to give them hope and dreams. I wanted to make sure they wouldn't have to struggle as much as I had. My boys would not repeat my mistakes. They were going to graduate from high school with their friends, and they were each going to graduate from a four- year college with the same friends, and they were going to go to football games, not necessarily cheering for the

OU Sooners, but somewhere within driving distance. My job was to give them guidance as to the importance of getting an *education*, finishing both high school and a four-year college. I wanted them to live the dream I had envisioned and hadn't been able to fulfill. If they were sent back to their dad, my failure to instill in them the desire and need to go to a four-year college would be my failure all over again.

"Please, God, I am all they have. Please allow me to stay free." My boys did not deserve to be elsewhere but with me. Their dad would have called to check on them if he cared. He didn't feel as if he deserved them anyway; he never called them on holidays or birthdays. He hadn't been in contact with me since they were three and four years old. Perhaps my friend Tami could take them for a while. She always had us over for Thanksgiving dinner and Christmas Eve, and she usually didn't want us to leave. Or perhaps even MaryAnn could pitch in—she loved the boys like her own.

No matter what happened, though, I wasn't ashamed of what I had done. If I hadn't, I would have still been on welfare, still enduring Hamid's abuse. I had no doubt he would have killed me in slow motion as he slowly sucked the life right out of me. Maybe the judge would have compassion for me if he understood the monster I had fled and how I had lost my youngest baby to a faraway Arab country. Perhaps he would also weigh the fact that I had been trying to quit selling counterfeits. I was only about a month away from dumping all of that merchandise and only selling legitimate, honest goods. But no matter his thoughts on my character or my crime, I was done getting in trouble with the law after this. The thought of possibly losing my children and my freedom were not worth it. I would be Jeanhee Kang, model citizen, and I wouldn't even get a speeding ticket.

As always, the 5K run cleared my head. As sweat washed away my tension, I felt renewed and hopeful from my endomorphic runner's high. I got into a luxuriating hot shower, then finished off with a quick, two seconds of cold water before jumping out of the shower to raise my body temperature.

"Okay, Jeanhee, Are you ready?" I asked myself in the

mirror. I slipped into the clothes James had recommended, a dark suit with a skirt that hit just below the knee; low heels, no jewelry, no nail polish. I needed to look conservative and respectable with no heavy makeup. I never did like makeup, so that was not a problem.. As I pulled my hair back into my trademark ponytail, taking extra care to make it neat and sleek, I said a silent prayer. God, this is the time I need you most. Please walk beside me this day. If you can't forgive my sins for my sake, can you please do it for my boys? They need me. I am all they have, as you know.

I prepared for the worst as I walked into the courthouse and found James and George waiting for me in the lobby. They both sensed my nervousness and could tell I wasn't in the mood for conversation, so they kept a respectful silence.

Before we walked into the courtroom, James tried to soothe my nerves. "You will have another hearing after today. Even if the judge decides to send you to jail, that won't happen right now." For the time being, that was a relief.

I expected to feel small, cold, and alone on the wooden bench before the judge, but as I walked through those doors, trying not to let the tremble in my knees show, I found the hard rows of benches filled with rows and rows of familiar faces. My friends and customers had come to support me. Some of them had told me they were going to come to court to protest my trial and be there for me, hoping to pressure the judge into a lighter sentence, but I didn't really believe them until that morning. Suddenly, I didn't feel like such a loner anymore. These people had shown up at the lowest point in my life to show how they cared about me. They had placed themselves in my shoes, knowing I had to work for a living and what being broke meant. They knew that if I were sent to jail, it would not only destroy my life, but also my boys' lives as well. I was so touched they had taken a day off from their jobs to show me their friendship that my eyes welled up with tears.

My friends had come to stand up for me. In America, making a mistake didn't mean one's friends turn away as had happened in my home country. It means they grab your hand and hold on until the hard part is over. I was so proud to be a Mississippian; I was so happy to live in America as one of them.

The bailiff said, "All rise."

Seconds later, the judge came in, and I stood up with everyone else. The judge was a tall black man, his heavy black robe flowing out around him as he walked to his seat and settled in, adjusting the microphone and shuffling the case files before him. He was even more surprised than I by the turnout at the trial.

After we were again seated, Judge Wingate peered over his glasses and cleared his throat. "Who are all these people?" he asked. "Is this a trial or a block party?"

James stood up. "They're the defendant's friends, Your Honor," he said. "The community holds her in high regard."

"It doesn't matter what the community thinks," the judge answered. "Right and wrong are what matters. If anyone disrupts this trial, they will be thrown out or charged with contempt. Is that clear?"

He then nodded at the government's side. "Counsel, you may proceed."

My dearest customer, Sandra, who either must not have heard or cared about the judge's instruction, stood without fear before the prosecutor began his opening argument.

"Your honor," she nearly yelled, "Jeanhee was just trying to survive and take care of her little boys. She never said those bags and watches were real. We all knew they were fakes when we bought them."

I could tell by her face my situation had agonized her, and she was ready to plead my case before the judge.

Of all my customers, Sandra had always believed in me the most. She was beautiful, with thick silver hair she always pulled into a ponytail, flawless makeup, and long fake eyelashes. She always bought something from me whether she needed it or not. She helped me get new customers whenever she could and even let me come into the nursing home where she worked to sell to all of her employees. She also gave me the encouragement I so craved. She told me she admired me for working so hard and being brave, that she believed one day I would be a millionaire. She would say," I have no doubt in my mind you will be, Jeanhee." She never saw me without wrapping me in a big hug filled with warmth and genuine pleasure at seeing me.

Maybe because she was beautiful, the judge didn't seem as annoyed by her interruption as I had thought he would be.

"Sit down!" he said tiredly. "We'll have none of that."

I was so proud to have her—and everyone else who had showed up—as my friends. That part of me that had been broken when everyone in Korea had turned away finally started to heal. I felt as if I had found a home there in the state of Mississippi. I was so happy I hadn't moved away after leaving Hamid, even though staying had landed me in this position.

In James's opening statement, he pleaded with the judge, "Jeanhee Kang is a good person and a good mom. She got off welfare two years ago and has been paying her bills all on her own. She has never been in trouble with the law, not even a speeding ticket. In her mind, if she could make enough to survive and not go back to an abusive husband, she was doing the right thing. She was trying to make a life in this country with no family to help her. She doesn't receive child support from her ex-husband, she has no family in this country, and she's raised her boys by herself since they were two."

The prosecutors did everything they could to build a case to send me to jail. The government had a long list of brands I had supposedly sold, as well as the amounts I'd made, but they didn't have any proof except what they'd found in the storage room, and they couldn't find a single person to testify against me. In the end, Judge Wingate gave me three years' probation and no fine, sparing me from having to serve a jail term. Still, I was now a convicted felon, adding another layer to my shamed past as a prostitute, to be shamed as a felon forever. I was so glad neither of the shameful deeds in my life would be written on my forehead; however, I could always pretend I wasn't either one by being a success in life. I had a lot to make up for. It might take me my entire lifetime to do it, but I wasn't discouraged. I wasn't going to be locked up; I was going to go home and be a mama to my boys.

The entire courtroom went crazy. My friends jumped up and down, hugged one another, and celebrated the outcome with me. Some of them said loudly, "Thank you, Judge Wingate. Thank you, you're a good judge."

I silently thanked God for staying with me during the trial, and then I hugged James and George and thanked them with tears of joy in my eyes.

When the atmosphere in the courtroom calmed, the judge reminded me I couldn't carry a firearm and I could no longer vote. I became a felon forever, but at least I had my freedom and I hadn't lost my boys.

After the trial, I dropped by the mall to tell my part-time kiosk worker, Kristin that I didn't have to go to jail; she was happy both for me and for her secured employment. I needed time to calm down. All the worries I had lived with for the last six months came with emotions I had never felt before. I took the afternoon off to go home and cook my sons' favorite meal: tuna casserole with no onions. On the way, I stopped to get a Coca-Cola and a Hershey's bar to celebrate. Those small bars, so plentiful in America, still held great meaning for me.

My boys were so surprised to see me. I usually didn't get home until hours after they got off the bus. I hugged them and told them how much I loved them, laughing when Josh asked if I was sick.

"No," I said. "I'm not sick. I'm just so happy to be your mama."

My nerves were too frazzled for me to work for the next few days, so I took a rare break and spent the time visiting all of my old customers and friends, thanking each and every one personally for supporting me in my time of need. My eyes welled up at almost every stop. Occasionally, theirs did, too. They all gave me a tight long hug and said, "Jeanhee, go and make lots of money. You did it once, and you can do it again."

I was ready to be a success for both myself and for those who had stood by my side, and I hustled more than ever after the trial. From time to time, my mean-eyed parole officer would stop by without notice to check on me, making sure none of my goods were counterfeit, and once a month, I had to take a urine test and jump through other hoops I didn't quite understand. But in my determination to be a model citizen, I never complained. I was just grateful not to be behind bars, and I was eager to meet any demands they made of me.

Chapter Ten

In Memory of Joshua Burch
April 27, 1977 – August 16, 1994

On August 15, 1994, I received the phone call I hope other mothers never receive. The call came from Jason.

"Mama," he cried, "please sit down."

Startled by the urgency in his voice, I quickly sank into a chair.

"Mama, Josh is hurt bad. You need to get to the hospital—UMC, Mama, right now."

I headed out, dropping everything, running out to my car. Even as I rushed mindlessly to the hospital, the reality of what had happened was lost on me. I expected to see Josh when I got there, that he would be okay, ignoring what Jason had told me, how badly he was hurt. As I drove, all I could focus on was Josh and what it would mean to lose my beautiful, loving son.

Just like his mother, Josh had a dream plan, even as young boy. He wanted to be a quarterback on a pro football team one day and make a lot of money. He used to tell me, "Mama, I am going to take care of you one day, buy you a beautiful home and give you so much money,you will never have to work another day."

His wanting to be the best quarterback began at home. All he ever wanted was to make me happy. He wanted to thank me for taking care of him and his brother alone. Staying out of trouble was the very first thing on his agenda.

He would get his brother up as soon as he woke up every day, and he got ready for school on his own. Jason would not get up at his first call, and Josh would badger his brother until he got up. They took turns showering, tiptoeing their way past my bedroom to slip into the kitchen and eat breakfast. If Jason dropped something on the floor, Josh would reprimand him in a whisper, "Quiet! You gonna wake mama up."

I would eventually get up to give each boy lunch money for the day. I usually hadn't seen them the night before after I got home, so I wasn't sure what they managed to eat for dinner. I didn't have change for $1.25 for lunch, so I would pull out a $20 bill. Jason would take it quickly, promising to bring change, but Josh would not take his.

"No mama," he would say. "I don't need it today. I am not taking twenty dollars. You had to work so hard to get that money. I may lose the change in the locker room at football practice." Later, I learned he would ask his friends who didn't eat all their food for what they had left in order to save his mama money. He hated to ask me to buy him anything. He would wear tennis shoes with his big toe coming out. When I told him he needed a new pair of shoes, he would assure me he could wear them for another month, that only the left shoe had a hole in it.

After days of hard work at the mall, by the time I got home, I was exhausted. The house would be clean and my bed made. One day, Josh placed all the stuffed toys I had given him over the years against my headboard in rows, from the smallest to the largest. As soon as I walked in, if he was awake, he would hug me and lift me into the air.

"How was your day, Mama?" he would ask. "Did you have a good day?"

If he hadn't eaten yet, a can of tuna, a package of macaroni noodles, and a can of cream of mushroom would be on the counter while he salivated for his favorite dish: tuna noodle casserole. I would cook it for him, and he would eat all of it.

After all I had been through, just as our life was coming together and we were established as family, I finally was able to afford to buy Josh a brand new truck. I wrapped it in the biggest red bow I could find and had it delivered to his school while he practiced football.

How surprised he was and so happy. His proud eyes welled up with tears. His joy was priceless to me. I had seen a movie years before about a rich girl's birthday, and her parents bought her a brand new car with red bow wrapped around it as a surprise. I knew I never would have gotten that from my parents, but I wanted to replicate it for my son and see him jumping around touching every detail of his very own brand new car.

"Mama, am I dreaming?" he said. "Or is it for real?"

I wanted to spoil my boys, to give them what I didn't have as child growing up so poor and destitute, starting with a car. I had to let them know their mama was on their side, even if I was unable to attend their football games. While other moms, dads, and grandparents came to watch their friends, I worked to better our lives, to give them what they couldn't have unless I worked long hours.

Josh knew where I was during all his football games. He didn't expect me to come watch them; instead, he came home to tell me about the awesome pass he had thrown to so and so for a touchdown. I would listen to his joy and say, "I am so proud of you, son!"

My words of praise were good enough to last him until the

report about his next game. If he didn't have good night, he would say, "Mama, I have got to grow fast. I need to be strong and tall, Mama."

Practically useless in helping in that department, I would sneak a raw egg, a banana, and a cup of orange juice into his daily protein mix drink.

His friends' parents often begged for my secret to raising good kids, ones who minded their mother and showed her respect. They would beg to have my kids come over, wishing some of my boys' goodness would rub off on their children.

I didn't have an answer, really, but I appreciated my boys for being good, loving kids. All I had said when Hamid left was that this was the time for us, for the three of us, and that I would work 24/7 if I had to give the boys everything they needed. The only thing I wanted in return was for them to "be good boys." That is all I wanted.

But Josh had his own dream. Rain or shine, he was outside throwing the football with no one else out there to throw to him. He often begged me to find him a daddy who could practice drills with him. His football idol was Joe Montana of the San Francisco's 49ers, with Jerry Rice as his winning wide receiver. He knew every winning throw Joe Montana had made, every route and catch Jerry Rice made during every game. He lived and breathed his dream of being a pro football player like Joe Montana. His life was built around his dream. His wall was filled with posters, newspaper articles about the 49ers, and his drawings of 49ers who had won their games.

Whenever the 49ers played on TV, he would display all of his beloved 49ers memorabilia on the coffee table. Everything he had collected—including a blanket, several posters, and the beloved 49ers jacket he had gotten for Christmas he would only wear after he had showered to make sure he wouldn't get it dirty. Oh, boy, oh, boy, was Jason mouthy, ever the motor mouth brother, during those games. However, Jason learned quickly that he'd better not bother Josh while one was on. If he did, he was awarded with a knuckle sandwich. Josh took notes on Joe Montana's and Jerry Rice's every move. No one could deter him.

When Josh was only four-months-old, he was already rocking back and forth with the urge to crawl, and by eight months, he was walking. He was never a cry baby. He slept all night from the time he was only ten days old. I sometimes wondered why other babies cried so much. Josh never did unless he was hurt. I could almost see his physique, the definition of his muscled thighs when he began walking. I didn't know most babies don't walk until they are about a year old. Josh was running everywhere by the time he was that age.

"Mama," he said, one day, "I was invited to try out for the Junior Olympics in Singapore, but I turned it down. I was afraid that I would miss football practice."

He had developed a burning desire to be the best quarterback ever, just as I had the burning desire to make more money. Josh's dream, to be a quarterback on his high school football team, became an obsession when he was in the seventh grade.

I remember when Jerry Rice, the man with the golden hands, #80 for the San Francisco 49ers and a native Mississippian, came to Jackson to visit his brother Tom, a football coach at one of the high schools in Jackson, whom I had befriended. He called me—the call Josh had been waiting for—one day and told me that Josh could come and get an autograph from Jerry; he told me what day and time. Josh was so excited he forgot to eat, pacing himself all day for the time to go and meet the greatest wide receiver. Josh was in heaven, and his best friends Wes Bell and Kevin Hammond were right next to him in the back seat as he kept saying, "Hurry up, Mama!"

They each had a handful of cards for Jerry to sign.

We got there, and Jerry's brother met us at the door and took us to meet Jerry right away. Josh screamed with joy.

"Mama, I am so nervous," he said. "Do you think he will shake my hand? Do think he will sign these cards for me?"

When we met Jerry, I introduced myself, shook his hand, and immediately turned to Josh, saying to Jerry, "This is my son. He worships you."

Jerry shook my son's hand. Josh was in shock and shook with joy to actually shake Jerry Rice's hand. "Mama, oh, my God. I just shook Jerry Rice's hand."

Well aware of their excitement, Jerry shook Wes's and Kevin's hands as well. Then I took their picture. Josh had made sure he brought his gold 49ers jacket. He beamed standing next to Jerry as I took the photo.

Jerry told them, "If you all wait and watch this basketball game, I will sign all of your cards," and so the boys and I watched Jerry play basketball with his old friends from way back when. After the game, Jerry patiently signed every one of those cards for them. He shook my hand and asked for my number. Of course, I gave it to him.

That night, he called me to meet with him at Zoli's, a nightclub on Lakeland. I refused nicely and told him I was very tired. I thought that was the end of it. He called again the next day. He said he was somewhere in Greenwood and that he would send a plane to pick me up so I could meet him at some hotel. Josh was ecstatic to answer, he quickly pushed the record button to record him chatting away with Jerry Rice, and the greatest receiver ever, "the man with golden fingers." Josh yelled, "Mama, it is Jerry Rice!" so excited, he is jumping around in the living room with the taped voice of Jerry Rice on his hand. Again, I refused. Josh was so disappointed. I couldn't tell Josh what *meeting him* tonight would mean.

*****

Josh prayed every single night before he went to sleep. He would kneel down by his bed, lights off, palms together, his head bowed, and his forehead touching the end of both index fingers and say, "Dear Lord, remember me? I'm Josh. You remember me, don't you? I have been good all day, and I practiced my routes really hard. I didn't do so well on my midterm test, but I think I passed. My mama is still working; please help her to get home safe. Dear Lord, I know I ask every night but I am going to ask you again. Will you please make me taller and stronger? In return, I promise to be a good son to my mama and work hard to be the best quarterback my school has ever had. Thank you, God!"

Then he would tuck himself between his 49ers logo sheets without getting them out of order, center himself in the middle of the bed, checking to make sure he was completely surrounded by his 49ers posters, the notes he had made, and his drawings of memorable throws Joe Montana made to Jerry Rice, his idols. He would cover himself to perfection, grab his football, and place it in the center of his belly, on top of his navel, to be exact, and hold it with both hands as he went to sleep, dreaming of the pro football team he wanted to play for when he grew up. He would often wake up from his nightly dreams, a lot of them with throws he would make the next day at football games or running fast to get away from big linebackers or finding a way to throw the ball to Terry Wray, the fastest running back on his team, the Northwest Rankin Attendance Center Cougars in Brandon, Mississippi.

His salvation, by his keeping his prayer to God, his promise to be good to his mama every single day and not do anything that might even remotely upset her, meant he stayed away from friends who drank or did drugs. He selectively chose good friends, good boys, preferably those who played football so he could practice throwing to them after practice, especially on weekends. He needed them since he didn't have a daddy to help him like the other kids did. He had begged for a dad once, but I explained why he didn't want one in such a way that he never asked again. He sure didn't want another Hamid to haunt his mama.

Josh knew he needed to be bigger and taller to play pro football, but looking at his mother who was a mere 5'2" and only weighed a hundred pounds, he knew he needed divine intervention to get the extra twenty pounds and four inches in extra height. So he chose to go to God for help. He attended Sunday services, Wednesday services, and prayed to God whenever possible to hang on to his dream of one day being a pro quarterback like Joe Montana. He knew exactly how tall Joe Montana was and how much he weighed. He knew he needed to be stronger and taller soon to beat out another boy in the running for first string quarterback in August of 1993.

The new school year had begun and soon the boys would find out who would be the first string quarterback for the varsity team. Josh had not missed one single practice, and he had worked out all summer to impress Coach Coats, the head coach for the football team. After practice every day, he would practice some more in an open field near where we lived. Even on rainy days, he was still out there, looking for someone to catch his passes. Often, he would throw the football just far enough so he could chase it since no one was around to practice with him. Almost daily he begged his best friend, Wes Bell, to come catch the ball. He had filled up his black book with daily squat and pushup counts, lists of detailed workouts, including how many times he ran wind sprints, dreaming that one day he, too, would play like Joe Montana.

My son was en-route to football practice with his girlfriend Christie White in her dad's navy blue Mercedes the day I got that call. His best friend Wes Bell was in the back seat. Christie ran the red light at the intersection of Old Canton Road and County Line Road and slammed into the back of a school bus. The side where Josh sat slid underneath the back of the bus, and his head hit the bumper.

He was the only person hurt in the accident. I feared he wouldn't be able to play football anymore, the game he loved so much. Being quarterback meant so much to him. If he had to stand on the sidelines and watch, I could only imagine how awful that would be for him. *Please God, don't make him suffer,* I prayed. *That will kill him.*

When I arrived at the hospital, the waiting area of the emergency room was already filled with his friends, football teammates, and teachers. Ms. Jan Hughes and Coach White hugged me before I got to see the doctor. They told the nurse I was there and asked for the doctors to come talk to me. The doctors told me their titles, but I couldn't remember their names. They said, "Ms. Kang, we're doing everything we can while we wait for Dr. Das, the plastic surgeon."

Josh had received a serious head injury and was unconscious. I wanted to see him, but the doctor told me I couldn't, that Dr. Das must do emergency surgery first to repair his jaw.

In tears, I screamed, "Oh, no! Not my son! Please... I beg you. Please bring him back to me. Please."

I cried for my baby, my son, my Josh. The doctor told me they would keep me posted. Frantic with worry, I couldn't hear much of anything. The doctor ordered the nurse to give me a shot for my nerves. Shock and disbelief overwhelmed me, part of me saying this wasn't happening, it was *not,* it couldn't be. I looked at what was going on in third person.

I lost him in less than twelve hours. His head trauma was too severe. During the last stretch, I grabbed Coach Coats and demanded he tell Josh he was to be named Northwest Rankin's first string quarterback.

"Please let him hear you," I said. "Please tell him he made first string."

"Josh, did you hear me?" he said to my son. "This is Coach Coats. You're my first string quarterback. You made it, boy."

By that very word from his coach, Josh would have gotten up if only he could. He would have jumped up, but he couldn't.

Looking at his injuries, I knew he didn't want to come back like that, unable to play football, unable to fulfill his dream. Knowing what was in his heart, if coming back meant living as a paraplegic, as a damaged boy who would never play the game he loved again, I knew the misery he would have suffered would be worse than death. Knowing and loving my son as I did, I knew that dying would be the route he would have chosen. There was no doubt in my mind.

I lost him. I lost my Josh without ever having a chance to say goodbye, without ever hearing him say, "I love you, Mama," to me ever again. My heart broke into a million pieces. It was shattered and left bloody with bruises that would never heal. At first, I thought someone else's son must have died. It couldn't be mine. But as the days drifted by, my emptiness grew. His bed and all the 49ers memorabilia remained untouched. My heart ached with a wide open wound that couldn't be closed.

Then I remembered him sharing a dream he'd had three months earlier, in May of 1994, when he had dreamed of his own death.

Early on that Sunday morning, I was having coffee at the breakfast table. The mall opened at noon, and that was the only morning I was able to see my boys in time for breakfast. Josh came out of the shower wearing his favorite black gym shorts, showing off the buff muscles and tightly packed six-pack abs he'd gotten from working out. He didn't have an ounce of fat on his body. Water dripped from his hair. I could tell something was bothering him; his pouting lips always indicated when something was wrong.

"Mama, I got to tell you something."

"What about?" I asked.

He looked at me. "I had dream last night; this one had nothing to do with football."

"Okay, I am listening."

He then said that dream was about his own death.

On a few previous occasions Josh had shared dreams that actually came true. These were mostly about football. In one of his dreams, he had thrown a touchdown pass, and that dream came true the very next day, exactly as he saw it in his dream, in a game against their cross-county rivals.

Josh said to me that morning in May, "Mama, this one was so real. I felt the pain of dying from a wound. I think I am going to die before the end of the summer in a car accident."

"Wait, Josh." I had trouble grasping what my darling son had said. "Let's call that dream a nightmare, son. Don't worry. We dream things like that sometimes. It's a nightmare. You must be worried about something."

If I had believed his dream might come true, I could have prepared myself, but I didn't see his death coming. I didn't believe he or anyone else could dream about their own death. Had he— or God—tried to warn me that Josh's short stay on this earth was near its end? Had God, who loved Josh so much and had seen us struggle so much, tried to prepare me? Had Josh, who loved his mama so much, unconsciously asked God to show him a sign to lessen his mother's pain? I would never know why I lost my son that day. If I could just have one minute to say goodbye to my sweet boy, to tell him I will see him in heaven one day, I would trade everything I have. Just to give him a tight hug and assure him I will see him again.

If I had chance to write to my son who is in heaven, this would be my letter:

My Dear Josh,

I hope your life in heaven is a happy one. I hope you are playing football every single day. I hope you've also had the chance to find the makeshift dad you so wanted to play football with you, to catch your passes and throw the ball back even on rainy and snowy days. I am so sorry for being unable to give you a daddy like all your friends had.

Rich or poor, famous or not, no matter what the circumstances each parent may be under, especially mothers all over the world, the last thing on our list to mourn is to mourn the baby we carried in our womb and birthed, the one we hugged to welcome into this world. The death of that same baby, no matter how old they might be, isn't supposed to come before our own.

No mother expects to bury her child.

As hurt and empty as I was, however, I knew I had to meet with Josh's girlfriend Christie and forgive her. That was the only way I could go on. Christie had been under suicide watch since the accident. She had cried for days, unable to eat or get up and go to school, refusing to come out of her room.

Jason and I talked about poor Christie. We wanted to stop by her home in North Jackson to comfort her. On our way, we stopped by Greenbrook Floral Shop on Old Canton Road and bought two dozen yellow roses.

Her mom came to the door in tears, surprised to find us on her doorstep. Apologizing to us for Josh's death, she told us Christie wasn't feeling well enough to see us. We asked Christie's mom if we could take Christie to dinner at Amerigo's when she felt better. She agreed.

Christie's mother called us the next day to say Christie wanted to see us, so Jason and I met her at the restaurant that night. As we sat down, I could tell Christie was in a fragile state and was scared to death of us. She was a skinny girl of about 5'3", with long blonde hair, a freckled face, and blue eyes that were bloodshot from crying over Josh. The poor thing was unable to cope with the sadness and guilt of causing the death of her boyfriend—my son, and Jason's brother.

She told me she wished she had stopped at that red light at the corner of Old Canton and Country Line Roads, instead of hurrying to beat it. She couldn't quite find the words to express her sorrow. We hugged each other through our pain. Jason and I both knew how much Christie loved Josh. She would drive her mom's Mercedes to take him around, hanging out with him every chance she got. I had not met her officially, but I knew of her from when she'd stopped by to pick up my boy.

We ordered cheese fritters as an appetizer, and pasta with shrimp for me, a salad for Christie, and a steak for Jason. Christie had trouble maintaining her composure in front of us. She finally managed to say, "Thank you for the yellow roses. I liked them a lot."

"We both know you feel remorseful for our Josh's death," I told her on behalf of Jason and me, but we want to let you know we forgive you right here, right now. Josh would want you to live happily; he wouldn't want you to be sad. We want you to go on, too. Will you do that for us? We all know you didn't mean to kill him."

"I'm so sorry, Ms. Jeanhee," Christie said, crying profusely, "I'm so sorry, Jason. I am so sorry. I didn't mean to run that red light and cause that wreck. I promise. I didn't mean to kill Josh."

"We know, Christie. We know, we know… Let's have dinner together and call this a celebration of the new life ahead of us. Josh is in heaven, looking down on us, happy we have gone on with our lives instead of crying all the time."

Christie finally calmed down. She had accepted our forgiveness, and that had put her at ease. She couldn't believe we had extended our love to her at a time when some people would seek revenge.

After our somber dinner, we consoled each other. Then Jason and I gave her one final hug before her mom came to pick her up. My son and I cried together on the way home, our hearts aching from missing Josh. How we wished he was with us still. But we were also happy we were able to help patch up Christie's soul.

We had buried Josh only three days before.

When a mother loses a child, she feels as if someone has ripped her heart out of her body while she was fully awake. And that pain never goes away. Nothing will ever undo that pain.

My Josh was meant to die *after me*, not *before me*.

Looking back on all I had achieved by working non-stop since I kicked Hamid out of our lives, I wished I had stopped working long enough to enjoy Josh, to spend more time with him and tell him that I loved him more often.

Jason once asked me if I could be a *Brady's Bunch* mom. He'd seen that mom on TV as the mom he wished he had. How could I be like that, though? I didn't know how. I hadn't had a chance to learn, nor had I experienced such a home environment. I was too busy making money doing anything and everything possible so we could survive.

But money isn't everything, no matter how it softens life. All of the hardships in my life paled in comparison to the death of my firstborn son, Joshua Wayne. When he was born in 1977 in Glendale, Arizona, I was not sure I wanted to be a mother—my heart said *yes* when he was placed in my arms, but my head said *no*—how could I finish my *education* with a child in tow? At the time I was still in love with John, still happy just to be in America, and so I tried to be a good mother. Being affectionate was hard for me—my own mother had only touched me a handful of times—but I decided I could give Josh gifts greater than hugs and kisses. I could give him an *education*, the drive to succeed, and the appreciation of what it meant to be born in America rather than on some desolate rice paddy where hope didn't exist.

Josh gave me a note he had found at the flea market not long before he passed away. It was titled, *"Climb 'till Your Dream Comes True"* by Helen S. Rice. He said to me, "Mama, You must keep this note and read it when you are sad, Okay? Mama? "

Did he know he was going to die? I think he did. But if he didn't, God did. Just as He had tried to tell Josh in his dream so he could to warn me, he gave me this note out of the blue to help me understand life without my son.

Josh QB #11

After Josh died, I understood that life wasn't going to be perfect. In fact, my life was never perfect. I looked at the life I had lived and was somehow able to forgive the human being who had taken my son away from me. Christie was same age I was when I had made one of my worst mistakes, when I had cried out begging for a second chance but no one would give it to me. I wanted to give that girl a second chance. Heartbreak helped me become a better human being, to have empathy for others, to feel their heartbreaks through my heart. Losing Josh was a turning point in my life as a whole person. Life became all the more precious.

I learned to love life as it is, no matter what it brings me. I also learned that I can't force anything because life can't be forced. Every precious breath I took in from that point on was a blessing, and I vowed to live my life more fully.

I wrote a note I would never mail on August 16, 1995, on the one year anniversary of Josh's death, and I felt as if Josh were standing behind me while I wrote it.

To Josh, #11,

My heart has been at my feet since you've been gone. If I could only turn back the clock and say goodbye. Just hug you and say, "I love you." That would be okay. I wish I'd listened to you seriously when you told me that time you were going to die at the end of the summer. Then we would still have had three months.

The hardest thing I've ever done was kiss your cold lips and tell you goodbye, then bury you underneath the dirt. I know how much you like to be neat and clean. I see you in my dreams often, in heaven playing. I know you are happy being with the Lord, but it seems so unfair to a mortal like me to not be near you, watching you throw the football in your favorite torn up clothes and drinking Gatorade.

Miss you ever more with Jason and Ahmad.
Love, Mom

Chapter Eleven

Bringing Ahmad Back to America

For years, I had thought Hamid was out of my life forever, and I believed my separation from Ahmad, my beloved son, to be a necessary sacrifice to keep Josh, Jason, and me safe from that vicious, abusive monster. But sometimes the past doesn't stay where you put it, and on May 30, 1995, my cell phone rang—and it was Hamid. I'd had the same number for years, never changing it, for the sole reason that I hoped to see Ahmad again somehow. The only way, of course, would be because Hamid contacted me, and now he had finally reached out. I knew immediately something was up. He wouldn't call unless he needed something.

"Hello?" I asked suspiciously.

"Hi, Jeanhee. How are you?" Hamid asked, his voice falsely cheerful. "How are Josh and Jason?"

"Jason is fine," I said shortly. Hearing Josh's name broke my heart all over again. "Josh isn't. He's dead. What do you want?"

Hamid was silent for a few seconds. "What do you mean, Josh is dead?" he finally asked, shocked at my words.

"There's only one way to be dead, Hamid," I answered. "He died in a car accident."

I didn't want to give him any more details. I couldn't stand to share my pain with him.

"I'm sorry, Jeanhee. I really am," he said, true emotion cracking his voice. Even monsters have hearts sometimes, I guess. His condolences seemed genuinely sorrowful, but I didn't let down my guard.

"Cut the bullshit," I said. "What do you want?"

"Well, Jeanhee, I've been working hard ever since you loaned me the money to be a truck driver." Even though my friends had warned me against it, I had given him $3,500 a few years before to get his commercial driver's license, in hopes he would one day tell me where I could find Ahmad. He never paid me back, but I wanted to stay on his good side, so that was okay. I had grown enough as a person by then to realize hate wasn't productive—that keeping a connection to my baby, however tenuous, was more important.

"I finished truck driving school, and I've been working for Warner ever since. But if I had my own truck, I could make double or triple my salary now. So I need eleven thousand dollars. I'll pay you back in six months… a year, tops."

"Do what?" I said. "Why should I loan you that kind of money? You never paid me back the last time."

"I know, I know," he said. "I got married and we have a son now—Joseph—and times have been tight."

"Do you beat and rape her, too?" I asked, forgetting I needed to stay on his good side. "Are you going to steal her baby?"

"I still love you, Jeanhee." He paused, then started trying to sweeten me up again. No matter how much he disliked it, I was the only hope he had to borrow some money. "I do."

"I just bet you do," I said, waiting him out. I could sense he was desperate. Otherwise, he would have cursed at me and slammed down the phone.

As he kept talking, I wondered what I could get out of loaning him the cash. He had refused to tell me where Ahmad was for $3,500, but maybe he would do it for $11,000.

"Why should I loan you money you won't pay back?" I asked. "What do I get out of this? I'm a businesswoman now, you know, and this isn't a good deal for me."

"Jeanhee, please," he said. "I just want to start a new life."

Had he just said *please* to me? I think the earth stopped turning for a minute when he used that word, but I knew I had him by the balls.

"Since you have a new baby now," I started, "maybe you can give me back mine. If you have any heart left, give me my son. I've lost one forever. I don't want to lose Ahmad, too."

Instead of yelling, he again became silent. I continued on, "If you give me Ahmad, I will give you the money. And you don't have to pay me back."

"Jeanhee," he finally said. "It's not up to me. And I can tell you my father will never let you have him. Never mind about the money."

Then he hung up, but by the sound of his voice, I could tell he was going to call again.

Sure enough, he called back the next day and wanted to negotiate, but I stood firm.

"I have one condition, Hamid. Give me back my baby. I'll go get him and never ask you for a dime, and I won't let him call anyone else his dad." I talked so fast the words probably made him dizzy, but I'm sure he heard *no child support* and *no new dad* loud and clear.

Then I appealed to his soft spot again. If nothing else worked, maybe that would. "I lost Josh. Please, please let me have Ahmad."

"Jeanhee…" he said, letting my name trail away. Then he

said the magic words, "You can have him back, but it's for Josh, not for you. I will call you tomorrow after I talk to my father."

The next day I paced by the phone, breathless. I would have paid anything to get my baby back; $11,000 was nothing in the face of seeing Ahmad again. I wondered who he looked like now. Did he have my smile or Hamid's eyebrows? Was he a sunny, happy child, or was he shy? I couldn't wait to meet my son again.

When Hamid finally called, he gave me the phone number of his father's neighbor..

"My father doesn't have a phone," he said. "You can call him at ten o'clock tonight. He'll be waiting for you."

This was going better than I had expected. My heart was about to jump out of my chest. "Where do they live now?" I asked.

"They're in Jordan. They moved from Kuwait when the Palestinians got kicked out after Saddam's invasion. My father lost everything."

I didn't care about his father. I only cared about Ahmad. "Did you tell your father why I'm coming?"

"Yes, and he said he'll decide if you can have Ahmad after he meets you face to face."

"I'll call him myself, and then I'll loan you the money," I said. "You can call me back tomorrow." I didn't want to get taken in by one of Hamid's lies. I had met his father before Ahmad's birth, and I knew he spoke English; if there was no hope of my getting Ahmad, I wouldn't give Hamid a penny.

My conversation with the elder Ahmad—Hamid's father was my baby's namesake—was surprisingly congenial. I knew a little Arabic, so we switched back and forth between the two languages to better understand each other.

"How is my son?" I asked after we had exchanged the usual pleasantries. I was so eager for news of him.

"He is good, a grandson to be proud of," Ahmad answered. "He is so smart."

"Did Hamid tell you I'd like to bring him back to the States to live with me? That I am coming to Jordan?"

"He told me," Ahmad answered, his voice guarded.

"I am rich now. I have six stores and a beautiful home. Ahmad will have his own room and the best *education.*" Then I mentioned what I knew would be his biggest worry. "I am not married, and I will not marry as long as Ahmad lives with me. I won't bring another man into his life as his father. He will always know Hamid is his dad. I can promise you that. May I meet you in Jordan to discuss Hamada's future? He will have so many opportunities in America."

"You can come," he said. "And we can talk about it, face to face. I want the best for young Ahmad, too."

I was shocked by how easy it was. If only Hamid had been this reasonable, things might have turned out differently for us. I wasn't sure what to expect when I reached Jordan, but I knew I would bring my baby home. I hadn't seen him in six and a half years, and now that part of my heart could finally mend.

Even though it was late, I called James Bell, my attorney, to ask him for help. He instantly wrote a letter to Senator Cochran and researched international law, telling me that under the Hague Convention on the Civil Aspects of International Child Abduction, I could get Ahmad back whether or not either Hamid or his grandfather agreed.

However, I still wouldn't wire Hamid the money until I had permission from him, in writing, to take our son and raise him in America. When his promise finally arrived, sealed in a letter, I carried it with me everywhere. I couldn't risk losing it.

With James's help, I received an order granting me temporary custody of Ahmad, and the United States Embassy in Jordan not only offered to help me get Ahmad to America, but they also found out where he was living. Now I could find him even without Hamid's help. I wished desperately I had known about that law before because I could have spent more years with my son. The American Embassy made me promise to report to them once a week while I was in Jordan to let them know I was okay. If they didn't hear from me, they would initiate action and start searching. I still didn't feel safe traveling to that country, but I was reassured knowing I had support there, especially since the embassy had paid a visit to Ahmad's grandfather to let him know they would oversee my visit.

Two weeks later, on June 28, 1995, I flew to Amman, Jordan, to see my son in hopes of bringing him back home with me. The entire flight, I practiced what I would say to my baby boy. How could I explain why I had let his father take him and then abandoned him to life in an Arab country? I wondered if he spoke any English. If not, I would not be able to share my feelings and heartaches or make him understand how I loved and missed him. But then I decided he was my blood. We must have a connection that would allow me to show him the depth of my affection and the longing I had to have him in my life.

As the plane descended at Queen Noor's International Airport, all that stretched around Amman was endless desert—flat sandy plains, red mountains, and no trees. The waiting area was muggy and humid, with no air conditioning, but I barely noticed. I only saw Hamid's father waving at me, and beside him stood a little Jeanhee lookalike—my son, the little boy I hadn't seen since he was sixteen-months-old.

I ran to him and knelt beside him. I had no doubt in my heart that he was my long-lost son. He looked just like Josh, with a slightly larger nose; his skin was lightly tanned, and he had short-cut curly hair, and my eyes. I pointed at my heart and said, "I am your mama!"

"Mama?" he asked, as I started crying. He wiped tears from my cheek, saying "stop" in Arabic. He looked a little scared. Perhaps they had told him I was dead, and he never even knew he had a mother.

He didn't know any other English, but he held my hand tightly as we walked from the airport, and I knew he had forgiven me. Maybe he had never even been angry. Ahmad didn't let go of my hand the entire ride back to the little village, primarily a Palestinians camp, on the outskirts of Amman.

Ahmad Sr. drove a red, four-door, stick shift Toyota that had seen better days. As he changed gears and bumped long the road to get away from the busy airport, he looked at me in the rearview mirror.

"Jeanhee," he said in broken English, "I am sorry about your son Josh's death. I was sad to hear it. Losing a son is a terrible thing."

"Thank you," I said, feeling his condolence was genuine and that, as a parent, he could easily share my pain and sorrow. "I think about him every day. Ahmad looks so much like him."

Perhaps playing on his sympathies would make him give up his grandson more easily. Only, I didn't want to get my hopes up. I primed myself to fight if I had to.

The little community outside of Amman reminded me in a sad way of my Korean hometown. It was impoverished and hopeless—rundown houses covered with sagging tin roofs all built side by side, skewed TV antennas pointing toward the sky; unpaved roads; leaning outhouses; a small country store selling only the basic necessities.

When we reached Ahmad's house, just as sad as all of the others, the entire family awaited our arrival. All of them greeted me, Ahmad's grandmother, his Uncle Tariq, his Aunt Hanna, with a hug and a kiss on each cheek, but I could still read the mistrust in their eyes. All of us understood why I was in Jordan—to take Ahmad— but we all also wanted to act in his best interest, meaning either I or they would be left with a broken heart. And I was determined that this time, it would not be me.

That night, Ahmad's grandmother cooked a dish Hamid called *upside-down*—chicken cooked with rice and potatoes, stirred and then dumped from the pot into a large tray. After it had cooled a bit, we all sat on the floor around the tray, scooping it up with small slices of pita bread and salad. We drank hot tea, heavily sugared, with the meal.

I tried not to feel heartbroken that my son had grown up in a house such as this. I hated that he had spent his early years in poverty almost as terrible as my own in Korea. The whole family lived here in three small rooms, sharing one toilet they had to pull to flush. The wall was concrete without wallpaper; their beds were thick blankets they rolled out at night. They had no shower, only a small sink, but water, like electricity, was rationed, so they only had access to it for a few hours a day. And the water that did flow weakly through the taps was brown and had to be boiled to drink. They had no air conditioner or heater or even a refrigerator.

I slept with Ahmad in one room while the rest of the family shared the others out of respect for my attempt to build a relationship with my son. I was with my son again. He had grown so much in those years that he was away from me.. In my heart, he was still my little baby son just as I had last held him in my arm. As I caressed his short, curly hair, he fell asleep, finally lying next to me. How I wished Josh could have seen him. My heart was filled with realization of the dreams of what it would be like to hold my son next to me again, letting him know how I would make up for his missed childhood. I made silent promise to his heart that I would never let him go again. I kept waking up to touch my son next to me, feeling his little shoulder, his face, hearing him breathing next to me.

The next morning, I rolled out of bed gently, so as not to wake Ahmad, and put on my jogging shoes and running clothes. Even on vacation, I couldn't go without my run though I made sure I was fully covered. No skimpy jogging tights here, so as not to offend any of Ahmad's Arab neighbors. People still stared, however. I doubt the women, covered as they were from head to toe, ever worked out.

When I returned, Ahmad's family had put out quite a spread for breakfast—hummus, homemade pita bread, eggs, and hot tea, all delicious. I helped Ahmad's grandmother clean up, and then Ahmad went to school, turning around on the road until he couldn't see me anymore. I waved at him the whole time, wondering how far he had to walk and if he knew how very important an *education* is.

Tariq, Ahmad, Sr.'s youngest son, was a taxi driver, and he took the day off to show me around Amman. Markets filled with everything from vegetables to shampoo to discounted cases of water, all in disarray, sat on every corner, but sprinkled in every few blocks were also Western clothing stores and restaurants. We ate lunch at Pizza Hut as my treat. Tariq's excitement made my heart sing. I didn't see anyone in this family as the one who had stolen my child. Hamid had done that, and so I held no ill-will toward them.

"This is so good, Jeanhee," Tariq kept saying in his broken English. "I have always wanted to come here. I like pizza."

"We can come here every day I'm here," I said. "Let's bring Ahmad. We'll have a feast."

After that, Tariq and I went to the grocery store and came home with a trunk full of food. Tariq had picked out most of it, so I wasn't even sure what some of the packages and cans contained, but the family seemed pleased.

Over the next few days, I met the family's neighbors— the women, anyway. We weren't allowed to socialize with men who weren't relatives. The older women dressed in conservative Arab style, with head scarves to cover their hair, while the younger generation wore Western clothes, though still with long skirts— never pants. They spoke Arabic; I spoke English. Somehow we communicated with my broken Arabic I spoke to connect in between. I couldn't read what they thought since everyone was trying their best to be cordial, but somehow I felt better among the older women. I felt they understood my pain as a mother. They all checked me out from head to toe, and I wondered what kinds of stories had been passed around about me. Did they think I had abandoned Ahmad? Did they think that I was an unfit mother? I didn't let it bother me. I had long since stopped caring what anyone else thought.

However, that didn't mean I refused to respect their culture. I soon bought some full-length dresses and long-sleeved shirts to cover my arms; luckily, the summer wasn't too warm. At night, the temperature hovered around 60 degrees, which at first surprised me, I had always imagined the desert to be sweltering and miserable. My religion did come up a few times. Ahmad Senior was ready to grill me about the Koran and how I would raise Ahmad, but I refused to discuss it. My response was always the same: "I don't know anything about the Bible or the Koran. My mama always told me to believe in God above all, and that's what I do."

"Will Ahmad have to go to church?" Ahmad Senior asked suspiciously when I tried to change the subject.

"No," I said immediately. "He will always get to choose what he believes."

Ahmad's grandmother watched me silently, her sad eyes full of emotion, during these conversations. She spoke no English, but she knew why I was there and didn't want to lose her grandson to me. I found out later from Ahmad that he had been told I was a whore and a drug addict. I'm not sure if the entire family believed it, but I hoped they could tell by looking at me that it wasn't true. I knew I had to show them I would be the best mom, able to give Ahmad a good home and a comfortable life. I showed them my photo album whenever I could—pictures of my beautiful home at the country club; my white baby grand piano sitting on my gleaming wood floors; my fireplace, the deck in the back, the view of the golf course. I showed them pictures of Josh and Jason, including the last one I'd taken of them with Ahmad, and my Mercedes. I wanted them to see I truly was rich and could provide for my youngest son. Ahmad was especially impressed by my boat and the jet skis, but the last page of the album truly captured his attention—our family picture taken at JC Penny that could never be replicated.

I also tried to show the family how generous I was by taking them to the grocery store every day, letting Ahmad put anything in the cart he wanted. On one trip, I noticed he paid special attention to the toothbrushes and toothpaste. I found out that he, like me growing up, had never had his own toothpaste. Our lives were so parallel. I vowed to take Ahmad away from this and give him the childhood I had longed for. After all, he was the same age I had been when I had first tasted the sweet heaven of a Hershey's bar. It wasn't too late for him to have a good childhood.

About a week after I arrived, Ahmad's school let out for the summer, and I decided to take the family traveling. We went to the Dead Sea, spending half a day there. The water was so salty and nearly black. As I had heard before, nothing would ever live there. People floated in it like little buoys. No one wore a swimsuit;

they were all fully dressed, even in the water. Ahmad filled his belly with popsicles and cookies from the beach merchants, always calling out, "Mama! Mama!" to show me something new he would like to try rather than the Dead Sea, not realizing he may never see it again.

The next day, we went to the city of Jerash, where we viewed centuries-old Roman ruins, and on to Petra next, where they had filmed the original Indiana Jones movie. The place was truly wondrous; they didn't allow cars, and we all stared in awe at the famous waterway, filled with marbled caves carved in the limestone. Hala, Ahmad's oldest aunt, and her family, who had come to Amman from Jerusalem for Hanna's upcoming wedding, went with us to Petra. I was glad to get to know her. Hala spoke English, and she said to me, "Mother needs son; son needs mother to raise." She felt my pain for all those years, and she also told me what the others said about me. I was supposedly a crack head and a whore. After making daily trips to various historic sites with Hala and her family, I felt more encouraged as each day passed.

Hanna's wedding day arrived. Ahmad Sr.'s youngest daughter was about to marry a doctor, the son of a distant uncle. They had been engaged since she was five years old. Everyone was in a festive mood, and the family was warmer toward me than usual. Before we left for the nearby restaurant where the ceremony was to be held, I found Ahmad sitting by the side of the house, trying to paste together his torn-up black shoes for the wedding.

I pulled him to his feet.

"Come on, Ahmad!" I said. "We have time to get some new shoes."

I asked Tariq to speed all the way to Amman in the car I had rented a day before, and Ahmad picked out a brand new pair of shoes. He held my hand tightly as we walked from that store, the bag clutched in his other hand.

"Thank you, Mama!" he said, his eyes ever so proud of his brand new shoes. My own eyes welled up to hear his first full sentence in English, and a few tears spilled down my cheek that he had forgiven me so easily for giving him up.

That night, everyone danced and enjoyed all kinds of Arabic food—goat, lamb, figs, piles of exotic fruits, and wedding cakes. Hanna wore a white wedding dress, and her husband-to-be had on a suit. They didn't wear traditional Arabic dress. At the end, we all joined hands to dance in a circle, celebrating the new life for the bride and groom.

That night, Hala held my hand to her heart before she left. "You are Ahmad's mother, and you should raise him," she said. "Don't let them keep him. I asked my mother to tell my father about it for you. Okay, Jeanhee?"

"Thank you so much, Hala. You are my angel. I promise to give him the best life," I said, "and I will write to you and send pictures."

I had now been in Jordan for ten days, and I needed to go home. I had my businesses to run, and I missed Jason. The next day, I sat down with Ahmad Senior for a heart to heart.

"Ahmad," I said, "You know I must go home soon, and it is best for Ahmad to go with me. A child should always be with his mother. It is not fair that he stay in this country where he cannot blossom or have a future. I have worked hard to be rich and I am going to stay rich, and I will give Ahmad everything he needs. I will send him to the best schools. Whatever Hamid told you about me is not true. Please don't believe him. I promise you again Ahmad will never forget you or call another man his father."

Ahmad Sr. shook his head. "Ahmad should be raised in his culture. American values will ruin him."

"Would you like to come with us?" I asked. "To see where he will live, his school, where he will play? I will take you and your wife to America with me and pay for everything." I spoke truthfully then. I knew as long as I could get Ahmad onto American shores, his grandfather could not take him back. "You can even visit Hamid while you are there."

That sealed the deal. They were eager to visit America and see their long-absent son, whom they still cherished even though in my eyes he was lower than nothing.

After that, Ahmad Sr. went with me to the Jordanian

officials to help me negotiate custody. I refused to pay any bribes, and even after I finally got custody of Ahmad, getting passport clearance wasn't easy. They claimed my son was in their country illegally and wanted a hefty fine for every day that he had been in the country.

"No!" I said hotly. "My son is an American citizen. He was born in Jackson, Mississippi, and was stolen from me. I will not pay when he was here without my permission."

Finally, I mentioned the American Embassy, and those were the magic words. They waived the fine and gave me the document that would allow Ahmad to leave the country. Within thirty minutes of arriving at the Embassy the next day, I had a passport for my son, even though the only photo we had was from when he was two years old. The passport even had a special stamp marking it *red-tape status,* meaning that customs wouldn't ask me any questions.

That night I called Jason, telling him excitedly, "I have Ahmad. I'm bringing your brother home."

"You did it, Mama," he answered, real warmth in his voice. Though he had been young when Hamid had taken Ahmad away, Jason still remembered how he and Josh had loved their little brother. I also soon received a note from James, my dear friend and my attorney who had tirelessly helped me, , saying he would be waiting at the Miami Airport with law enforcement, in case Hamid showed up and tried to make a scene or take Ahmad. Knowing I had James' support, especially after he had been my rock through the customs trial, comforted me greatly.

Early on July 16, we flew out of Amman, stopping overnight in Rome. I took everyone sightseeing the next morning, making quick visits to the Vatican and the Sistine Chapel. Seeing Leonardo da Vinci's painting on the ceiling, Adam's finger reaching for God's, I felt God's presence in my heart. I knew he would help me take Ahmad home safely. At the same time, however, I sensed a growing unease in Ahmad's grandparents. Their faces had become drawn; their eyes, hollow. I hoped they wouldn't make a scene. I would fight for Ahmad, but I didn't want him to see his family torn apart over his future.

When we finally arrived in America, our clothes wrinkled and our eyes bleary from the long flight, Hamid was there to greet us; his presence distracted his parents from their impending loss.

"My son, my son!" Ahmad Sr. cried, hugging Hamid. If only he knew what a monster his son was, but then, parents love their children no matter what.

Ahmad was shy around Hamid, not warming to him immediately as he had to me, but Hamid didn't notice. He was too excited to take us to his apartment and introduce us to his new wife and baby. He hung back as his parents entered the apartment, holding my elbow and whispering in my ear, "Let's be a family again, Jeanhee. I love you more than anything. We can raise our son together."

Those words had worked before, but that was then.

"So you're going to leave your wife and take her baby like you took mine?" I said, shaking his hand off my arm. I brushed past him and went inside. Now that I had Ahmad, I didn't care if Hamid was happy, sad, or dead. It truly didn't matter.

When we finally reached my home, Ahmad was in heaven. Jason ran toward him and swung Ahmad around in the air.

"Hey, brother, welcome home," he said. "We're a family again. Do you remember me? Can you say *brother?* Or *Jason?*"

Ahmad just laughed. He didn't understand a word Jason had said, but he knew he was home and that he was going to be. Jason couldn't wait to show his little brother his own room, with brand-new furniture and a TV and stereo I had prepared. He didn't want to sleep by himself for the first few months, so he slept in my bed with me until he got used to his own room. I don't think he had ever slept by himself before.

I took him shopping almost every day for brand new clothes and school supplies for August, and we would stop at Burger King, his favorite fast food restaurant in America. A double whopper and large French fries and a Pepsi were his standard order. He loved it and asked for it every day, but soon I had to slow him down. His little tummy had already doubled in size.

I felt that I had to make up for lost time. I bought him all the simple electronic items and a new bicycle to ride around the block. He was absorbing everything anew. He slowly spoke in English, enjoying a life he had only dreamt of, just as I once had as a child back home in a rice paddy, so long before. His grandparents stayed two weeks before they left for Jordan. They had a change of heart as the time came for them to leave grew closer. One day, Ahmad Sr. asked for Ahmad's passport, and I asked him why he needed it. He told me that Hamid would like to keep it. I told him there was no way that I was giving Hamid Ahmad's passport. Besides, I'd given it to my lawyer for safekeeping. They cried all the way to the airport, heartbroken at giving up a child they had raised and may never see again. All I could say to them was, "I will take good care of our Ahmad."

Even though they had seen that the life I could give Ahmad was better than anything he could have in Amman, they were not ready to say goodbye.

I told them as they boarded, "I am sorry. He is *my* son, and he is staying with me. Please, don't worry. I will send you lots of pictures."

While Ahmad got to know his older brother and adjusted to life at his new home in America, I registered him at Vine Street Elementary School as a third-grader. Since he spoke no English, I sat next to him for the first two weeks so he wouldn't feel alone. Luckily, kids are kids, and they make friends even with a language barrier. On the very first day, he played basketball with a group of other boys, and within three months he had become thoroughly Americanized with the help of his teacher, Mrs. Livingston. Eventually, he even forgot most of the Arabic he had known, leaving me to send messages to his grandparents.

But as Jason, Ahmad, and I worked on becoming a family again, Hamid once more tried to tear us apart. Once he realized I truly wanted nothing to do with him, he threatened to snatch Ahmad and take him away from me again. That was the last straw, the last time I would ever let him threaten or affect my life. I called Mr. Cane, a sweet man in his 60s who worked as a security guard for my store on weekends and as chief investigator for the assistant DA on weekdays. When I told him what Hamid had said to me, he became very agitated and indignant.

"What's his full name and social security number?" he asked. "Write it down and give it to me. I'll take care of this."

He knew a bit of my story because I'd gone to Jordan to save my son, but mainly he respected my work ethic and sunny attitude, and I knew he would help me if he could.

About a week later, he called and said, "Jeanhee, you never have to worry about your ex-husband again."

"Thank you so much," I said. "What have you done to him? He's stubborn as hell and scaring him off won't be easy."

"Like I said, don't worry," Mr. Cane said. "I'll tell you the whole story this weekend." The instant he showed up for work, I bombarded him with questions.

"Tell me what you did. Please, Mr. Cane," I demanded. "I'm dying of curiosity."

"I ran a check on him and found his address," Mr. Cane said. "I sent three officers to pay him a special visit and tell him that if he ever came around your home, your son, or your son's school again, or even thought about it, they would hunt him down and send him to jail for a long time on kidnapping charges. They said he turned white as a sheet and slammed the door. Men like your ex-husband are cowards; they can't handle jail time. He'll leave you alone now."

Mr. Cane was right. Hamid never bothered us again. Ahmad stayed on the National Kidnapped Network List until he was eighteen and wasn't allowed to leave the United States as a minor unless I accompanied him.

He went on to graduate from high school with all his friends at Northwest Rankin Attendance center in Brandon and he recently graduated from the University of Mississippi in Oxford, Mississippi, becoming a die-hard rebel fan following his brother Jason. He's now twenty-five years old and says, "I love you Mom!" every chance he gets. I never tire of saying it back to him. He keeps in touch with his aunts and uncles, as well as Hamid through Facebook, though their relationship is not a close one.

When I sent pictures to Hanna in Jerusalem a few years

after Ahmad came to America with me, she wrote back, "Jeanhee, you don't know this, but you almost didn't make it out of Jordan with Ahmad. The day you flew out, his uncle was trying to have you arrested on a kidnapping charge. I'm so glad he didn't catch you. I can see how happy Ahmad is in America, and I wish you nothing but love."

I may have come close to losing my son then, but even had I known about Ahmad's uncle, I would not have believed God would have broken my heart like that twice. I put my faith in him, and he reunited me with my beloved son.

Ahmad in room he was sharing with the rest of his family

**Ahmad was living in Palestinian camp in the outskirts
of Amman, Jordan**

Ahmad's Recent Photo

Chapter Twelve

Rags to Riches

One of the luckiest days of my life happened four months after my trial. As I was working at my kiosk, a commotion two stores away, at Accessory Accent, caught my attention. The store was going out of business, and people walked out with bags full of deeply discounted merchandise. I saw a clear chance, the opportunity of a lifetime, perhaps, and instantly started planning in my head. How amazing would it be to have my own store in such a good location? I wasted no time. Feeling an urgency to make a move, I put a sign that read, *Will return in 5 minutes* on my register and literally ran to the mall office to see PJ.

"Hi, PJ, how are you?" I bounced in without even knocking,

filled with the buoyant possibility of owning that beautiful glass-front store. I had dreamt about that store since the first day I came to the mall.

PJ was always too busy for a small fish like me, and he didn't stop flipping through his files. I hadn't noticed until that day that he was missing half of his right index finger, but I tried not to stare. I knew this wasn't the best time to ask what had happened.

"I'm fine. What do you want?" he answered.

He was a short man, only about five-foot-four, but he still managed to intimidate me. Perhaps it was his icy blue eyes or his brisk, business-like northern accent. Or perhaps it was because he held all the power to say *yes* or *no* to my future business, but I knew he had been on my side throughout my trial. When I had briefly brought up my situation to him at the time, all he had said was, "As long as you pay your rent on time and don't sell fake watches on my property, you're okay with us." I hoped he still wanted to help me succeed.

"Is Accessory Accent available to rent?" I asked.

"Who wants to know?" he said absentmindedly, not even thinking the person might be me.

"Me," I said. "I want to rent it."

You? He must have been thinking, the lady with the laundry basket half full of watches who had struck a deal to rent a measly kiosk less than a year ago. Now she wants store space, forty yards from center court? He had to make sure he had heard me right, so he asked, "You?"

"Yes, me!" I said, smiling my most winning smile as I awaited his response.

"I don't have a tenant for it yet, so you can have it. But it's temporary," he said. "We don't usually rent such a prime location to locals. We save them for national businesses. But you've done so well with your kiosk, I'm willing to risk it."

"I'll move if you tell me to," I answered. "How much is the space?"

"Eight-hundred dollars a month," he said.

I blinked. Eight-hundred dollars was what it had cost me

to start my business with Tony from Chinatown, to rent my own kiosk, and now to rent my dream store. I decided that eight-hundred must be my lucky number. I didn't even think about the possibility that he was giving me a special price, though looking back he must have been. "I'll take it."

"If a national chain wants it, you'll have to move within a week."

"Okay," I said, backing out of the office before he changed his mind. "Less than a week. Three days."

I didn't mind that I was only renting the space for a short term. In fact, that was even better. If the business didn't work out, I wouldn't be committed to a long-term lease that would drain my savings account.

"You know if you don't pay the rent, I'll keep all your merchandise and kick you out. You remember that, right?" he called out the door as I left.

I grinned and hollered back. "Thank you, PJ!"

The space was about 900 square feet, in the center of the mall, and—the best part—the old renter had left behind the glass display cases and racks. I wouldn't have to buy any new fixtures. My only problem was that I didn't have enough merchandise to fill the store. I wasn't even sure what to put in there. I couldn't fill a whole store with hair clips and watches.

For the time being, I stretched my merchandise around, spacing it as far apart as I could to make it look purposeful. To fill the blank walls, I called a friend in New York to sell me cheap printed T-shirts, as well as sunglasses and popular costume jewelry. I scattered the sunglasses and jewelry on the counters and hung the T-shirts on the walls. I hired two teenagers to help me in the store, and they were amazed at what I could remember, every shirt, every watch in inventory, even down to the color and size.

I also memorized every customer's name who bought something and what they bought, so that when they came back I could act like their best friend, asking them how they had liked their purchase and recommending new goods. My black book customers came back, too, and bought merchandise each week. They were proud of my progress. Even if they didn't buy anything, they would always stop by to say hello. My heart felt so good when I realized how many friends I had in Mississippi.

The T-shirts proved more popular than I could have imagined, so I ventured out to add to my inventory after listening to the teenagers who worked for me and the teens who came in to look for things. I always remembered to ask what they were looking for, what they hoped to see in my store, and they were more than happy to supply me with information. Even more cool, I developed a list of people to call when I got in new merchandise. They couldn't believe I had them. Those sales were guaranteed simply because I had picked up the phone.

I soon added music posters, lava lamps, black lights and black light posters, body jewelry, skate boards, and grunge clothes, all booming trends among teenagers. I would never wear nor use any of the items I sold, but what I liked had nothing to do with my business. What would sell was what mattered the most. Once I discovered the teen niche, my store became popular almost overnight. This was before Hot Topic or PacSun caught on, so I cornered the market in the tri-county area. In those days, any teenagers visiting the mall wouldn't leave without swinging by my store. They were dying to see what crazy or cool stuff I had that they wouldn't find anywhere else in the state of Mississippi.

I even had a visit from a movie star once. *Ghosts of Mississippi* was being filmed in nearby Canton, and every Friday afternoon, the entire movie crew, including director Joel Shumaker, breezed through the mall.

"God, there's that hairdresser again," my employee Sandy said one day as he strolled by.

"What? Who?" I asked, confused.

"That arrogant hairdresser with the long hair," she said, and I followed her index finger to where he stood, looking in a shop window. I realized she had no idea who he really was.

"How do you know he's a hairdresser?" I asked, sure her answer would amuse me.

"He's from Hollywood," she answered. "He came in one

day and asked where he could park his bicycle, and I knew from his accent he wasn't from around here. So I asked where he was from, and he told me he was a hairdresser on the movie set."

"Well, I guess that's who he is, then. Stop staring at them like they're aliens from another planet and get to work,"

I was more excited, though, when Sandra Bullock visited the store, buying a soccer shirt—another new hot item in those days—and a few scarves. Her personal assistant carried her bags for her, and he had at least six large bags from other stores. I tried not to stare at her the entire time she was in my store. She was flawlessly beautiful even with no trace of makeup, and her thick dark hair fell in a shiny sheet down her back. She wore a plain white T-shirt with blue jean overalls, something I thought only rednecks wore, but somehow she made them look good. I went out and bought a pair for myself after that.

When Sandra Bullock got to the register, she looked at my sign that read, *No cash refunds* and asked, "So I can't bring it back if it doesn't fit?"

Without hesitation, I answered, "You can bring it back."

I hoped she would come back and shop some more so I could brag to my friends all over again. I was nervous ringing her up, but somehow mustered up enough courage to ask for an autograph for my son, and she graciously gave me one. I couldn't believe a movie star was in my store, buying shirts from me. She spent $150 and paid in cash, and as soon as she was out of the store, I picked up the phone and called my friends to tell them the story.

Even without the business of movie stars, however, my business boomed, and, finally, the mall caught wind of my sky-high monthly sales report. PJ called me into his office one afternoon for a meeting, and I knew the news couldn't be good.

He was already sitting with a guy from the corporate office when I arrived. The visitor was in his late thirties, half bald, and spoke with a thick Yankee accent. I disliked him from the get-go.

"I'm Leon," he said, shaking my hand. "I've heard about your success, Ms. Kang—very impressive." I could tell by his condescending tone he was used to dealing with national tenants, and that I was nobody in his eyes, just another local trying to make a buck.

"You're making too much money to be a temporary tenant," he said. "You'll have to become a permanent tenant and sign a long-term lease if you want to stay in our mall."

"How much will my rent be?" I asked, my eyes narrowing.

"Twenty dollars per square foot," he answered, "plus a fee for common area maintenance, a real estate tax, and a six percent break point at the end of the fiscal year."

I quickly did the math in my head and decided all of that together would actually make my rent about $35.00 per square foot, or roughly six times what I had been paying. So much for my near-free ride as a temporary tenant.

"You'll also have to move into the unfinished space down by one of the anchor stores," Leon continued.

I tried to hold back my anger and be gracious, but I knew that space still had a dirt floor. The sewer line wasn't even connected! I knew then I would build my own store. I planned out every detail of the 2,400 square feet, managing its construction as the general contractor and hiring subs to save costs. The work didn't require a license, and my friends came by on nights and weekends to install the wall units and help with construction. I wore my hardhat and barked out orders as loudly as any burly man, making sure they built everything exactly to my specifications.

I kept the inside trendy, using high-powered lights with galvanized metal and a wooden floor with an exposed black ceiling. I installed Bose speakers everywhere to blast music the minute teens walked in. I called it *Underground,* after a popular bar in New York. The store created a teen frenzy and was naturally a shoplifter's heaven. I saw that as the price of good business, so I didn't mind paying security guards to be on hand at all times. Parents and grandparents came into the store to get presents they had never heard of. My store held everything a teenager would think was cool.

I would have been the last person you'd think would own such a store. I had been on the verge of starvation in the rice paddies of Korea while Jimmy Hendrix played guitar as if there were no tomorrow, and I had been busy trying to get to America during the seventies, when American teenagers listened to *Stairway to Heaven* on repeat. I had never watched MTV. I hadn't snorted or smoked drugs, and I had never taken more than a few sips of alcohol. I couldn't even relate to those teenagers, but I knew what sold, and I sold it all. One day, an older lady came to complain about something her son had brought home from my store and asked to see the manager.

"I'm the manager," I said.

"Well, who's the district manager?" she huffed, crossing her arms.

"I am," I said again, keeping the smile on my face.

"Who's the owner?"

"Me."

"No, you are not!" she yelled as she stormed out. Maybe she had expected the real owner to be a dope head with dreadlocks or a grease ball dressed in grunge. Or perhaps she couldn't believe a tiny Korean woman who spoke only broken English could run such a successful business. Either way, I never got to find out what had made her mad as hell about my store.

One way I kept up with what would sell was by hiring teenagers to help me learn about the latest trends. They always knew what was cool, and they continued to tell me what teen-minded items they liked, and what their friends liked, and wanted. Having lived in New York and knowing where to find the wholesale markets helped, as did speaking Korean. That alone gave me an edge since most of the vendors I dealt with were Koreans. After about the fiftieth customer asked about naval piercings, I sent a few of my employees to a piercing place in south Jackson to find out about pricing and piercing techniques.

Once I saw how lucrative doing piercings could be, I wanted to learn how to do it myself. Forget about letting someone else make that money. I would be the best navel piercer in the city. I even pierced one guy's nipple for $100 bucks. He almost passed out after I'd done the first nipple, and his face went white as chalk.

I hit his forehead with my palm a couple of times and held his head so he wouldn't fall backwards, and he came to. He walked out of my store with 18-gauge rings in both nipples that day, but I never did another nipple piercing. I didn't need a lawsuit. After that scary episode, I decided to focus on navel piercings instead, and I charged $50 for each one. I pierced at least six people a day, some days ten.

One day a heavily overweight lady came in to get her navel pierced. I almost said, "Lady, no one is ever going to see that ring," but I bit my tongue. I decided I wanted her money more than I wanted to speak my mind. I acted like an expert doctor looking at a sick patient, trying to figure out how to heal the extra-large woman, who was dying to pay me $50 cash to get her navel ring no one else would see in her triple belly.

"Can you come here?" I said as I walked toward an empty wall.

She said, "Sure."

"Raise your arms, lean against the wall, and stand still," I said with a sigh. I showed her how to raise both arms. She had no idea she had triple layers of belly fat. I was just trying to find her naval, but she thought that was the way everybody got their navel pierced. I cleaned the area with betadine in a circle where her actual navel was, used triple antibiotic cream on a 14 gage needle, and dug around until I found her belly button. Thank God, it was a normal size. Then I stuck the needle through her skin and followed it with a 16 gage ring. I was $50 richer, and she was proud to have her ring there somewhere under her triple fatness.

Some of the funniest things happened when I least expected them. Proud customers whose navels I had pierced were so excited to see me in public, they would come forward and hug me as if I were their best friend, ready to pull out their navels to show me how the rings looked, some showing off diamond rings hanging off them, asking me if they looked good. Men, especially, would say, "What in the hell?" as they talked to each other. "Did you see that, dude? How'd she get them to show their bellies?" I would always think *What in the world is wrong with you?* but I would still plaster a big smile on my face and recommend they buy a new ring. Eventually, all of the belly buttons looked the same to me, even though some were hairy, and some were not. That didn't matter to me; they all cost $50.

The rings cost me fifty cents, the needles twenty-five cents, and the gloves five cents. So for each navel I pierced, I cleared a $49.20 profit. Not too shabby for five minutes of hard work, and piercing navels sure beat selling fake Rolexes on a street corner. That was the easiest money I had ever made, with the biggest profit margin ever, too.

The days weren't long enough, though. I wished the store could be open 24/7 so I could make money around the clock. Why sleep when making money was so much fun? I could bring my fold-up bed and take a nap and then work some more. The only thing that kept me from doing that was that I needed to be at home with my boys.

Even while I was running the store, I kept my kiosk in the same location. That little kiosk was a money-making machine, especially during the Christmas season. I targeted impulse shoppers, housewives who spent their husband's money, and people looking for gifts to exchange with family members. I had gifts in the perfect price range, too: $20. I even went further, telling the customers that if they bought the first item at $20, the second would be half price. I told all my employees from the minute they clocked in, to focus on "Sale!" "Sale!" "Sale!" If they stood around rather than talking to potential customers, I whispered in their ears, "Sale! Sale! Sale!" Pretty soon, they said the same thing back to me anytime I walked up.

I also moved my focus from watches to things I could mark up at least 300 percent. Earrings, necklaces, bracelets, and sunglasses sold like hotcakes. Each Christmas I would select one item I could move at the price range of $20 or less. I kept up with my Korean vendor friends in New York, not to get knock-offs, but to know ahead of time what would be popular. I would order the goods in advance before the holiday rush, so I could sell them at a price no one in Mississippi could beat. One year, purses were popular; another, scarves; the next year, ponchos, gloves, gaucho pants, anything colorful and at the right price point. The year that power beads were so hot even Julia Roberts wore them, I got my Chinese supplier to sell them to me for $1 a bracelet. They were $20 in other stores, but I sold them for $5, still making a profit while ensuring no one else could compete with me. I imagine every woman in the tri-county area had one of those bracelets on her arm that year.

Because my kiosk was always surrounded by a crowd, it drew even more buyers. They wanted what everyone else got. That tiny three-by-ten foot space was in a real frenzy during the Christmas season, when I had two registers and four people working to accommodate customers. My annual kiosk sales, once I factored in the Christmas rush, were $250,000.

What had started as an obsession with independence became fun. I got a thrill from each ding of the register, from counting cash. Even a $2 sale made my heart sing. I wasn't greedy; I didn't put my money away to hoard it. Now that I knew how to make money and that there was always more down the line, I spent generously on things for myself, my boys, and my mama in Korea. I kept the promise I had made to her all those years before and sent her $1,000 a month. On her birthday and my dad's birthday, I gave them an additional $1,000. I showered my mama with fancy reading glasses she didn't need but wanted to have just to make her look distinguished. I also sent her a sapphire necklace, an 800-year-old Spanish coin, coral rings to bring her good luck, and a diamond bracelet to show off to her friends and relatives. I even wiped out my dad's gambling debts and bought my mama a little house with a rose garden, where she could live peacefully and not worry about finances for the rest of her life. Our welfare days were long gone.

I added one store at a time until I had six in all, one each in Ridgeland, MS; Monroe, LA; Meridian, MS; Hattiesburg, MS; Vicksburg, MS; and Jackson, MS. I worked fourteen hours a day, seven days a week, and I was tireless. Making money and counting the cash made my swollen feet and tired body stop hurting by the time I had finished. I was now virtually debt free, except for my open-net terms to my vendors, and $28,000 a month covered my stores' rent, employee payrolls, unemployment taxes, federal and state taxes, and insurance premiums. Whenever I looked at my bank account, always ballooning higher, I felt faint. Was all of that money really mine? I tracked my sales daily, comparing the six stores' profits and brainstorming how to increase my bottom line profits.

With all of the money flowing in, I decided we needed a bigger house, and I bought a newly built five bedroom home at the Castlewoods Country Club. My back deck overlooked hole number 8 on the golf course. I didn't play; it looked like it took a lifetime to finish a game, and I didn't have those hours to spare, but every now and then I would see bad golfers looking for their balls near our deck. Sometimes, I even found the little white balls in my planters and would toss them back onto the green. I never understood what was so fun about hitting that tiny ball up in the air to see how far they could hit it, anyway.

I also bought myself a new Mercedes and continued to buy a new one for myself every year. That car was my personal treat for working so hard and driving from store to store daily. As a work car, it was even tax deductible. I also brought my brother Younghee and his family to live with us, and I eventually gave him one of the stores. I remembered how, so long ago, he had been the only one who had asked, "Will you come get me, sister?" and I was glad to make that dream come true for him. He would not have to struggle to reach these American shores as I had.

When the time came for all of my family to visit my home, I bought round-trip tickets for all of them, including their children—fourteen people total—so we could sit at one table and enjoy a meal as a family for the first time in decades. None of them had ever flown before except for my mama and my dad. They were world travelers by then since I had flown them in almost every year to visit us, sending them home with a pocketful of cash and a suitcase stuffed with presents. My mama never failed to remark about how rich America must be because so much of the land wasn't cultivated. She truly thought it was a magical land of plenty, as it had been for me.

I hadn't met my sisters' husbands or my brothers' wives until that year since I was still a social outcast in Korea and hadn't been invited to their weddings, but I didn't hold a grudge against them. I was so proud and happy I was able to show them America, my new country that had given me a second chance to live my dream. We even spent a weekend in New York. I wanted to show them what America looked like outside of Mississippi.

I wanted to book rooms at the Stanford Hotel on 32ⁿᵈ Street, in the heart of Korea town, but it was booked, so we stayed at a hotel down the street. We took a city tour by limousine, and everyone was awed by the Empire State Building. My mama went all the way up to the top, confused by how dizzy she became up there.

"I must be getting old, Jeanhee Ya," she sighed. "Too much excitement, I am so dizzy."

"Mama, it's the wind," I said with a laugh. "The building sways in the wind."

"This big building?" she asked, shaking her head. "No, buildings don't sway. They would just fall down. I am just old and dizzy."

I took them to Ellis Island, the Statue of Liberty, and Times Square, where they were dazzled by the crowds and the lights. For dinner, we ate Korean barbeque: lettuce wraps dipped in garlic, pepper-shredded scallions with bean paste, soup, fish tang, nakggi bokum, and mandu tang. I ordered just about everything on the menu. My ever-frugal mama asked, "Ulmayyu—how much?" the entire time, trying to get the younger kids to share a large Coke between them. She didn't understand why everyone had to pay for their own drink.

"Mama, just enjoy it," I said, trying to reassure her. "I have plenty of money. I own six stores now. A few Cokes aren't going to break the bank."

She sat back and accepted my generosity, but she didn't stop mumbling about how expensive things must be here in America.

That night after dinner, as I settled in with Meehee and her youngest daughter in our room, a hard knock rattled the door.

"Please help me!" a female voice shouted. "Oh, God, please help me. Someone's trying to kill me!"

I instantly jumped up and pulled open the door. A trembling blonde woman stood in the hall, her hair tangled and her feet bare. She wore blue jean shorts and an *I love New York* T-shirt, and her voice was raspy either from screaming or crying.

"Come in here," I said, reaching for her wrist and tugging her inside. "What's going on?"

I dead bolted the door and put my hands on her shoulders, trying to get her to make eye contact with me.

"Please help me. He's going to kill me," she said, trembling harder.

"We'll call 911," I answered.

"No!" she yelled. "He works the front desk. He'll know, and he'll kill you too!"

"We'll call direct," I said, trying to reason with her. "We don't need to go through the front desk."

She ran into the closet and then the bathroom, even looking in all the drawers to see if anyone else was in the room.

I now regretted letting this woman into the room. I had a bad feeling about her.

"How can I help you if you won't let me call 911?" I asked.

"The police will kill me!" she cried. "I'm not safe anywhere. I need to use the bathroom."

She shut herself up in there, and her heavy, frightened breathing echoed through the door. Slowly, she calmed down, and then she became silent.

When I knocked a few minutes later, she didn't answer. I called 911 right away and explained the situation. Within ten minutes, armed police were at the door.

They banged on the bathroom door and called out, "Ma'am, it's the police. Open up so we can help you!"

When she didn't answer, they broke down the door and tumbled inside, finding only an open window. When they looked out, they saw her lying eight floors below in an alley, her neck broken. She had died instantly.

We were shaken. My poor sister was in shock, and the clock reached midnight before we were both able to fall asleep. But the night wasn't over; we were jarred awake a little while later by yet another knock.

"Not again." I groaned. I put the pillow over my head. I was not answering the door this time.

Then a deep male voice shouted, "New York Police! Open up, please!"

Two criminal investigators stood outside the door and held their badges up to the peephole. They were both well past middle age, their eyes hard and their New York accents sharp. They were all business, asking me all kinds of questions about what I was doing in New York. Meehee, who didn't speak any English, sat looking confused on the bed, nodding without comprehension whenever they asked her a question.

"Why would you open a door for a stranger, especially in New York?" one of the men asked in annoyed disbelief at the end of the interview.

I was offended by his lack of compassion as well as his choice to grill me in the middle of the night; this could have waited until morning.

"I'm from Mississippi," I said with a crisp snap of irritation in my voice. "If someone needs help in the middle of the night, I open that door. I didn't know she would jump out of the window, or I never would have left her alone in that bathroom. Have you found her family? Who was she? Have you found who was trying to kill her? You should be chasing that man she was afraid of, not bothering me."

They didn't have any answers, and I didn't see anything about the woman's death in the paper the next day. When Meehee and I relayed the story at breakfast, my family thought I was joking, but eventually they believed us, the dark circles under our eyes telling them something bad had happened.

The rest of our vacation was uneventful in comparison, and my family went home from their dream trip to brag to all of their friends about the things they'd seen and to share what they'd learned from their stay in that hotel in Korea town: "Don't open the door for a stranger in America, even if they are being chased by a killer."

*****

My success back home didn't go unnoticed by the community. At one point, newscaster Sherri Hilton from WLBT called to ask me if I would be interested in telling my story.

"What story?" I asked, suddenly suspicious. I was proud of my success, but certain parts of my history weren't anyone's business.

"We plan to call it 'Rags to Riches,'" she said. "It'll be part of a business segment about successful business men and women in Mississippi who made it to the top by working hard. You are one of those people."

The title of the feature confused me—*Rags to Riches*. I wondered how in the world they knew I had gone from pushing dirty rags across a mud floor every day at sunset to living the good life in America. Who had this woman talked to?

"Jeanhee, several people mentioned you when they found out I was looking for candidates to interview," she continued.

Her proposition caught me completely off guard. Honestly, I was so busy working to make money, I didn't even know how much I had most of the time. Until my accountant had pointed out the numbers on my tax return the year before, I hadn't even known I was rich.

I reluctantly agreed to be interviewed, remembering that not too many years ago that same TV station had blasted me and smeared my name when they had reported my trouble with counterfeit goods. Now the same people wanted to put me on a pedestal and talk about my success.

"That might be all right," I said, "but I'm not a millionaire. Not even close. And I'm still gun shy about my success."

"But your story is great. And if you're not a millionaire

now, you're well on your way. Just let me do most of the talking on camera, and I'll guide you through the interview."

The next day, she and a burly cameraman were in my store, taping an interview with me to air the next night on the 6 p.m. news. I pretended the camera was a person and tried to talk as warmly to it as I could. This was great publicity for my store. I used my best smile, the one I'd learned from Woojung a hundred years before, and talked so glowingly about my store that I was sure everyone in the Jackson area would soon be in to shop.

Sherri interviewed me about street peddling, my store in Northpark, my hard work, and how heart-wrenching it was to have lost Ahmad. The feature was so successful the news station repeated it the next day, and my phone rang off the hook with customers calling to say they'd seen me on TV. I was their gutsy Jeanhee who had gone after her dream. Though I didn't realize it at the time, I was an inspiration to them.

The story came on right after the six o'clock news and was introduced by longtime WLBT TV newscaster Maggie Wade. "And tonight our business segment features Jeanhee Kang, who has truly gone from rags to riches." Her smooth newscaster's voice told my story. "Jeanhee Kang was born in South Korea and came to America to live her American dream. She's lived in Brandon, Mississippi, starting off as a street peddler on welfare to raise her two sons after her husband left her with $50 in the bank account. She started her business with eight-hundred dollars working at flea markets on weekends, door to door sales during week days in cars borrowed from her girlfriends, and now, only five years later, she's a millionaire, and now she has her own chain of stores. She's no stranger to personal heartache either. She lost her son to an abusive ex-husband when the baby was no more than sixteen months old, stolen away to another country. She got her son back from Amman, Jordan. Her words were interwoven with my interview. When Sherri asked what was the driving force behind my success, I proudly replied, "Have a Dream!" "Everyone should have dream, and—as long as you believe in it, it will come."

That was the end of the segment, my proud smile and my

words echoing in the minds and hearts of Jackson, Mississippi viewers. I liked the sound of the segment's title—*Rags to Riches*—and that was exactly my story. No other millionaire embodied that title quite so literally.

My first store 1994

Epilogue

Sometimes I think back to my childhood—to God's face carved into the rock, the starvation, the shame, and the hurt that sent me fleeing from South Korea—and I'm glad everything in my life happened as it did. I would change nothing, and despite how far I have come, I would not trade even that one rebellious night that changed my path forever.

I'm oddly unchanged. Though Josh's death left a hole in my heart that will never be filled until my own passing, when I see his handsome face again, I'm still the same small Jeanhee from the rice paddy in so many ways.

I've never gotten tired of Hershey bars or fluffy white rice, and I still carry that big smile Woojung taught me so long ago. *What a life have I lived!*

Jeanhee Kang has finally made it. I will never be hungry again.

Appreciation

"Thank you so, very much!"

Anya Groner - Erica Lovett - Dana Lyle - Melanie Atkins

"I couldn't have finished my very first book,
Run Away – One Woman's Story of Resilience without you!"

Message from
Jeanhee Kang to Her Friends in Jackson, Mississippi

Ladies!
Together, we are going to make Mississippians proud with
"Run Away: One Woman's Story of Resilience."

Allene Balgord -Amanda Fountain – Amanda Green – Amanda Carroway – Amy M. Klotz – Amy Litton Davis – Angie Cook – Angie Cotton- Angie Deleon – Angie Keys – Angie Tucker – Anita Modak-Turan – Ann Culpepper – Ann Dautenhahn - Ann Fry – Anna Groner – April Savell – Ashley Moss – Barbara Edwards – Barbara Hapkins – Barbara Regan – Becky Conley – Becky Davidson – Beth Szabo – Beth B. Townsend – Beth Jackson Bryant Gordin – Betsy Primos – Betty Shormick – Brandie Womack Mead – Brenda Muse – Brenda Thames – Britton Wean – Brook G. May – Carley Page – Carol Booker – Carolyn Van Zandt – Cassandra Walter – Cathy Baily – Cathy McIntyre – Celia Coffey – Christie Bennett – Cindy Clegg – Cindy Ford – Cindi Ponds – Cindy Tauchar – Clara Wimberly – Claudia Barnett-Connie Chastain – Dana Lyle – Deana Pendley – Deanine Bullock – Debbie Bryant – Debbie Moser – Debra Boutwell – Debrah Crystal –Dennis Jones – Donna Jones – Donna Smithhart – Dorris Mathew – Elle Halvertson-Elsa Foley – Erica Lovett – Erin Burnham – Eunice Williams – Eve Berry – Fran Adams – Gayle Gordin – Gayla Elliott – Gayle Butler – Gayle Gordin – Glenda Allman – Gloria Beauchamp – Georgia Spencer – Gwen White – Hart Sullivan – Heather Barry – Heather Dyess – Heather Mixon – Helen Thompson – Holly Evans – Jackie Roman - Jacqui Katool – Jamie Woods – Jaehee Kim – Jan Collins – Jan Hughes – Jana Bell – Jane Bell – Jane Becker – Jane Ellen Wolf – Jane Foster – Jeanette Berg – Jeanie Butler – Jeanie Malouf – Jeanie Taylor – Jennifer Anderson –Jenny Woodruff – Jessica Clark – Jessica Schwartz – Jill Connner Browne – Jonna Welch – Judy Hearn – Judy Hightower – Judy Troupe – Judy Mason – June Nixon Kandy Stringer – Karen Eaves – Karen Penna – Kathi Carney – Kathy Kelly – Kathy Nail – Kay Troxler – Kelley Williams – Kelly Collins – Kim Ponds – Krista Brown – Kristie Peed – Lacee Chagnon – LaReeker Rucker – Leanne Leach – Lee Martin – Lesley Mosby – Linda Alford – Linda Paul Byrd – Linda Walker – Linda Watson – Lisa Peacock

– Lynn Dixon – Malinda Batty – Margaret Herndon – Mary Adair –
MaryAnn-Downey Kirby – Mary Ann Schwartz – Mary Beth Reeves
– Mary Catherine Guest – Meg Muse – Melanie Atkins – Mende Alford
– Michelle Irshvin – Missy Kim – Monica Day – Nancy Bain – Nancy
Hicks – Nichole Baker – Nikki White – Olivia Fight – Olivia King – Pam
Goza Cochran – Pam McCartney – Patsy Burks – Rachel Douglas Cullen
– Rene Hinojosa – Revelend Wheat- Rita OverCash Roberta Howell–
Rosemary Morris Woods – Sammie Gambles – Sandra S. Garvin –
Sanfra Forshee – Sara West Manor – Sarika Chandak – Shanel Stuart
Barney – Sharon Albriton – Susan Anderson – Sharon Grubs – Sharon
Jernigan – Shelly Mcleod – Sonia Bedi Chandak – Stacia Muse – Stacy
Maddox – Sue Gray – Sue Kennedy – Sue Yarbrough – Susan Ferris –
Susan Marquez – Susan McGreger Crisler – Susan Runnells – Suevadee
Kennedy- Suzanne Burns Stubbs – Suzanne Cox – Suzie Allen – Tami
Conley – Tami Bouchiillon – Teresa Renkenberger – Teresa Windham
-Terrie Moorhead – Terrie Sartin - Terrie Solomon – Terry Cole – Thelma
Fisher – Theresa Brumbley –Toni Willingham – Tracy Jones – Tracy
May – Tracy Reynolds – Tye Burnham – Unchalee Verspun – Vanessa
Williams-Vicki McDowell – Virgie Breazeale – Virginia Anderson –
Virginia Hodge – Wendy King

Glossary

Algo	Sigh...similar meaning to 'Oh god"
Banchan	Various side dishes for Korean meal
Bulggogi	Korean style beef
Choggi	Striped bass fish
Chopche	Clear noodles with mix vegetables
Kimchi	Fermented Korean cabbage
Makuly	Made from fermented wheat or rice or milkly colored wine.
Mudang	Shaman Priest
Mychutsyu	Crazy
Myungtae	Pollack fish
Na do dyuteggo ga	Take me with you
Na Mottssalyu	I don't want to live
Napalzza	My unfair life
Nega mynjuyookyua Hanunde	Should have died before you
Ozingyu	Squid
Sangbok	Off white funeral clothes made of poplin
Sangchae	Relish salad
Unummi	Mother
Wonbukyo	Syncretic Buddhism in Korea best known as Sot'esan

Jeanhee Kang was born in Iksan, South Korea. She first came to the United States in 1975 and made it her goal to attend an American high school. At age thirty, a single mom on welfare, broke and almost homeless, she reinvented herself in order to realize her childhood dream. Within five years, she went from being a street peddler in Jackson, Mississippi, to a self-made millionaire. Until now, Jeanhee has told no one of her past, the secret of what she had to endure in order to have a second chance in America. Ms. Kang dedicates her inspirational story of survival to the 50 million American women who face similar hardships every day.

"RUN AWAY: One Woman's Story of Resilience
is her first novel.
Visit Author's Website
www.jeanheekang.com